# Going Out
## in
# Style

# Going Out
## in
# Style

## A Guide to Planetary Departure

Marcia Beachy, M.S., L.P.C.

BALBOA.
PRESS
A DIVISION OF HAY HOUSE

Balboa Press books may be ordered through booksellers or by contacting:

Balboa Press
A Division of Hay House
1663 Liberty Drive
Bloomington, IN 47403
www.balboapress.com
1-(877) 407-4847

Author photo by Scott Smith
Cover Design by Ann Boyden, la.boyden@gmail.com
Front Cover image: iStockphoto

ISBN: 978-1-4525-3478-7 (e)
ISBN: 978-1-4525-3474-9 (sc)
ISBN: 978-1-4525-3479-4 (hc)

Library of Congress Control Number: 2011907614

Printed in the United States of America

Balboa Press rev. date: 6/7/2011

# Contents

# On the Same Page

I BELIEVE WE ARE ALL ON A JOURNEY, a soul journey. It's the wildest adventure imaginable. We seldom realize that at the beginning and often spend a great deal of time groping our way in the dark. There may be a plan we set up ahead of time, but once we are here on Earth, all that information often slips into the background and we set sail, ready or not, on the mysterious seas of life.

Someone gave me a magnet for my fridge that says, "This life is a test—it is only a test. If it had been an actual life, you would have received further instructions on where to go and what to do!" That's how we feel at times—taking on a life without instructions. In the true nature of any adventure, however, how can we know how to do it unless we dive in? We don't know how to be a parent until we have to be one. As children, it takes a while to learn how to get our mother's attention, or how to tie our shoes. We spend our entire lives learning how to love. The truth is we are in continuous on-the-job training. I believe that life is training for something else important—our departure.

That's right. Though no one tells us that this journey includes learning to die well, and that a choice to let go of being cranky now creates more space to smile in heaven, it's true. Getting through our final transition with more finesse is a primary goal behind the bustle of life. I have learned that there are actually many "right" options to choose from, and some that are less than ideal. I grew up being told that it was all in God's hands, and if we lived our lives the way we were supposed to, there was no death itinerary per se. It was all taken care of.

Now I know there is more to it than that. However, at various times in my life, I've wished someone could have offered me a guidebook on what really happens when we die, and what we can do to make a difference. Not a book of platitudes or scary outcomes—but authentic, substantive counsel that would make sense to my heart. Better yet, I wish someone could have guided me, could have suggested something like, "Why don't you walk down to Grandma Eva's cottage? It's quiet there and you can chat about living and dying. Go rock with her on her front porch. If you listen to her you may understand more."

Perhaps life itself becomes our own wise grandmother. The quest to understand brings us down the road to that cottage any number of times. There seem to be universal themes on this dying issue. They show up in ancient teachings, consciousness research and daily life. There are truths peeking over our shoulders more frequently as the great heart of humanity grows restless and pushes to evolve. Faced with huge tidings of death, both personally and globally, we want new tools and perspectives. Not only do our minds need updated information, our hearts long to be comforted. Our consciousness wants to break through the barriers from the past. Death is the big bugaboo waiting to dissolve into a grander truth.

Have you tried to guess what it is like to cross over? Do you ask why we have to die the way we do? Or why we have to die at all? Perhaps you're curious about what might be on the other side and want to make it a good trip for yourself. Maybe you'd like to be an ambassador of goodwill for someone else who is dying. If so, welcome!

In this forum, all questions are welcomed. For example, you might find yourself questioning the advice you've been given about what happens at death and in the afterlife. I'm not talking about the lofty notions you've been taught *should* happen or you *should* believe, but the really profound stuff that gets down to the business of the afterlife. In our death-avoidant culture, are you brave enough to wonder? Whether we've thought much about dying or not, the questions are still there inside us. They may have bubbled up in grade school or are now whispering in our present life. Either way, it's the nature of death to pop in to say "hi" now and then.

So let's give ourselves permission to lay it all on the table. We are opening a discussion to not only ask any questions, but to admit any fears. Here we can share our traumas. We can reveal our deepest hopes. We can talk about near-death experiences or anything else without holding back. Humor and irreverence are welcome. We can also admit to cynicism—and claim faith. We could even argue that speaking of loss and death is central to being alive and real. Most of us would probably be greatly relieved to see what our death prejudices and beliefs are. We might even be excited about pushing our own edges and opening up the dialogue.

As we sit together, various topics will be presented in hopes that you will add your own. Perhaps you will open a conversation with another and wander where the secrets of your heart take you. As you dare to speak of your fears, perhaps you will find a smile on the other side. Seldom have we felt free to reveal our private conversations with death to ourselves, let alone another. Instead we have pushed away the topic like annoying mosquitoes on a summer night. Now we welcome it all.

Although we have more material on death and dying than we did when I was young, in some way I want to create a guidebook for you. I want to represent that grandmother of life who offers comfort and counsel; the wise one who rests in both this world and the next, who knows that death is both a problem and a teacher, a terror and a friend. I invite you to join me in being a part of the cadre of souls who are building bridges and easing fears as we take ourselves into a new era of human possibility.

So that we can be on the same page, several key concepts are important in our conversation on planetary departure.

1. *Conscious Living.* Becoming more conscious is the opposite of living our lives unaware of who we really are. Getting conscious has to do with being alive to what is actually going on inside us. And around us. Not only what we wish were true or what we want to portray to others, but what we are really feeling/believing and why; then deciding if that works for us. Conscious living is about being more and more authentic, more soul-driven, and less persona- and glamour-driven. It's the practice of becoming our true, essential selves.

   For example, are you aware when you become insecure or judgmental? When you revert to addictive behaviors? Are you learning to listen to yourself and firmly and gently defuse the patterns with compassion? Or do you find yourself doing what most people do when they are unconscious—blame someone else or run and hide emotionally?

   Conscious living is an exceptionally good way to wake up—and grow up. With this way of being, we take responsibility for our choices, however uninformed we may have been at the time we made them. In like manner, we let others take responsibility for their choices. It can be quite empowering to realize that we always have a choice. In any given situation, we can choose to be a victim or learner, a reactor or responder, critical or compassionate, angry or grateful, robotic or authentic. The more we choose the learner-responder-compassionate-grateful-authentic way, the more conscious we become.

All this is bigger living. We look up and out, around and within. We don't just look down at our feet as we walk through life. We don't want to miss it. We see ourselves more and more fearlessly and clearly. We see our fears and flaws. We see our amazing spirit and gifts. We see our strengths and name them. It's as if we've taken off foggy glasses and can better see what is.

Conscious living also allows us to be more attuned to our bodies. Listening to our bodies deepens and grounds us. It is often said that the body doesn't lie, so listening to the truth of the body keeps us honest. If someone asks how you are and you say, Oh-h-h, I'm just fine, but meanwhile your heart is pounding, your blood pressure is rising and your back is killing you, we could safely say that your body is the truth-teller, not your social self. It may or may not be appropriate to share with that person how you are actually feeling. The important thing is that deep inside you are seeking to be aware of what is going on. Conscious living requires taking tender care of our amazingly wise bodies. It invites us to bring our spirits into our bodies and become more soul-filled and body-wise.

Conscious living helps us step out of rote behaviors and open to our spiritual nature, by whatever name we want to call it. I'm not referring to religion. I'm talking about that part of us that is unlimited, creative and wise. If you are reading this book, you are opening to this part and stepping into more conscious living. You are probably able to say this part of you feels ongoing—even eternal.

2. *Conscious Dying.* Conscious dying intertwines with conscious living in every way. We come to understand that just as we are able to shepherd a wholesome and conscious approach to living, so are we able to consciously influence our dying—from this side, *and* when we pass to the other. As we choose to face our stumbling blocks and live fully now, we have much less to deal with on the other side. By learning to listen to the body, we will know when it's time to let it go and step over the threshold. We get tools for traveling the inner worlds, because in life—and death—that's where our real joy originates.

If you are comfortable with your inside world, your inner landscape, you can better understand about letting go of the body and the personal identity you have developed. It's not as foreign or fearful. Conscious dying involves dropping into that bigger self that we are, the infinite mind, and using that as the most accurate navigation device there is. This is our true nature that we glimpse while in deep meditation and prayer, or while relaxing in nature's grandeur. This soul-self is alive in that magic stillness you felt when a snowflake sparkled on your mitten in the winter storm—and the whole world held its breath in wonder.

Conscious dying flows onward from the consciousness we have built during our lives, whether from a lifetime of eyes-open or whether suddenly truly "getting it" with our last breath. What happens next when the body melts away, takes wing according to how we've grown the garden of our soul.

3. *Reincarnation.* Seeing the soul as eternal comes full circle when we embrace rebirth or reincarnation. Reincarnation is simply the understanding that some part of us—soul or consciousness—is on a journey of infinite learning and returns to Earth over and over, gradually achieving mastery and contributing to the greater good. In order to obtain a well-rounded education in Earth School, we choose lives of both genders and all races, religions and conditions. Simply put, we are here to grow, to learn, and to love via the unique contrasts and challenges present on Earth. We are here to evolve ourselves and the human race and to be stewards of this beautiful planet. Many souls have come to Earth at this time to help with and experience the dramatic changes swirling through every strata of social awareness.

How all this works and why has been the background passion in my psychotherapy practice—and my life. It is what has compelled me to add past-life regression (PLR) therapy to my work. I have come to appreciate the deep subconscious mind, which holds the memory of all our experiences both here and beyond.

Through PLR work, we discover more about what happens when we die. When the client enters a past life, he or she also goes through the death of that life and into the afterlife realms. Much is gained from these past-life regressions that not only assist clients in their own healing, but provide wisdom helpful to others, as you will see.

If you are unfamiliar with reincarnation, have fun considering it as an option in this vast cosmos of infinite possibilities. It is, interestingly enough, a concept woven beautifully within all spiritual traditions, sometimes overtly—as with Hinduism and Buddhism—and sometimes subtly, as with some teachings in Christianity, Islam, Judaism and others. It is a concept we will find interwoven with conscious living and dying.

4. *Spiritual/Religious Terms.* This material is gathered from many spiritual traditions, from science and from personal/professional sources and experience. Given that, how does one speak of the luminous, the transcendent? Shall we use God? Allah? Buddha? Divine? Source? The Lord? The Unknowable? Light? Quantum Mind? Ultimate Being? In order to honor the many ways we speak of the transcendent quality of consciousness, I intersperse terms. If you prefer one over the other, please substitute your favorite term. The truth of the matter is that the Great Oneness that breathes through all creation and throughout all that is, is *All That Is.* It cannot be contained in any words we know. So we won't get too bothered about terminology. Let yourself grasp the concept, rewording as is necessary for your particular beliefs.

5. *Confidentiality.* All names have been changed to protect the privacy of clients and other individuals whose stories are used in this material—except for those few who specifically wanted to be open with their identity and for those resource people whose work is in the public domain. With a few exceptions, real names are used for those who have passed on, in honor of their amazing lives.

I am convinced that our departure, our death, deserves a direct and lighter attitude or style. However, in no way do I mean to discount or dismiss the very real agonies that death brings to our doorstep. This material is not necessarily intended to be a guide through the enormity of grief and painful losses that many are suffering. But I do offer it as a secondary source of comfort. Perhaps the perspectives given here can bring balm to wrenching loss and sorrow. There may be suggestions that satisfy the longing for connection to the departed loved one. Perhaps the sense of a grander grace will calm some of those troubled waters. That is my hope.

I have chosen to categorize the many attitudes and beliefs we have about life, death and heaven or no-heaven into *styles*, or ways of framing reality. Our way of looking at life creates a certain field of energy around us. We might say we "cloak" ourselves in openness or close-mindedness, love or fear. Certainly, any style or way of being in the world is not only our personal choice, but our sacred space. There is no judgment. Just as we find our tastes in clothing styles change over time, so may we discover that we try on a number of departure styles before we are done. If you are looking for another style that fits you better, I hope you will find some interesting options. Therefore, in Part I, we will look at various styles of thinking we may have taken on with regard to death—and therefore life. These first four chapters give an overview of everything from our basic avoidance styles to the transcendent teachings of wisdom traditions.

In Part II, we look more closely at why this exploration is vital to our well-being as a human family. In Parts III and IV, we gather tools for the journey and end with some lovely stories to light the fires of our hearts.

Stepping outside the box of orthodox departure teachings requires only a small courageous first step. Then another. As you follow your heart and educate yourself, I know that you will make a difference in your own and another's planetary departure. You will feel affirmed that you, and they, may depart on the wings of grace. I want you to be so inspired by your death that you make a quantum leap into life. Then you will have discovered that you can, in fact, go out in style!

# PART I

# *What's Your Style?*

# PART I

## *What's Your Style?*

### *Introduction*

HOT, LAZY FLIES BUZZ in the high church windows. A smattering of bees drifts in from the alfalfa fields, curious about a country church with fresh flowers on the pine altar below the pulpit. In the hot southeastern Colorado summers of the 1950s, the AC consists of fans but not the electric kind; the hand-held ones with Jesus praying in the Garden of Gethsemane on the front side. They belong in the rack with the hymnbooks. Mostly women and children use them. Some ladies carry their own fold-up fans in their purses. The farmers seem inured to the heat with their sun-bronzed arms resting on the back of the pew, around their wives. My mother has accomplished a minor miracle simply getting a gaggle of children off to church. What time is left for remembering fans?

Everyone is there—bachelor farmers, spinster aunts, grandmothers and grandfathers, neighbors, and complete mother-father-children families. My cousins arrive, as do the kids from the other side of the valley who we don't know so well, especially the Wietzers. They are a bigger family than my own, with even more imperfection to hide. Child abuse we'd call it now. To my parents, it is simply understood that Mr. Wietzer is "hard on his kids." No one knows what to do with his darkness.

Old Brother Kauffman always sits toward the front on the right so he can hear. He seems unspeakably ancient to me. I gaze at his bald head and his red-pink skin from several pews back while the sermon drones on. In my child-world, he is a fixture, an enigma of oldness with no beginning or end. A steadfast, dependable presence, like long, deep summers and breathtakingly delicious Sunday dinners—fried chicken or roast beef with all the trimmings. I love the full-throated four-part harmony as we sing hymns, though I'm

3

confused as to what all my sins are that Jesus needs to save me from. So I make lists. Yet, I embrace my church teachings with all my heart, for I have a deep, kid-style love for God, whose wonder I see on vast starry nights and in the wild places we explore with abandon.

My country church folks labored diligently to please God, to become a pious gathering of devout Christians. And by the standards of the day they were. They were also a juicy and colorful cross-section of 1950s rural America, Mennonite-style, filled with twists and turns, unspeakable shames and long-sought triumphs. By some mysterious choice of soul, I dropped into this wealth of land, culture and family, guaranteed to challenge every tender child-fiber of my being. In those windy childhood years, births, marriages, illnesses, abuses, healings and deaths were announced from the pulpit or whispered in the cloakroom. Within the gossipy, tightknit container of rural community, life birthed itself into our midst and departed on unknown wings. There were no words for grief, or room to question the dogma of the day. In the struggle to understand life and death, we were counseled to leave it up to Jesus. In going by the book, we were promised a somehow-way back home to God.

It was a system that worked sufficiently well then. Gradually it lost its appeal for some of us. Nonetheless, the church has evolved, smaller but alive. So has the community—smaller but alive. Old traditions and new thought have been rewoven with the human propensity to create order out of chaos. But in the religion of my childhood, there wasn't much room for change or novel thinking. The "heathen" religions from Asia hadn't yet reached the shores of our community. Most of the fussing was between the Methodists, the Mennonites and the Catholics. When it mattered, everyone pulled together, like when the high school gym burned down or the farm family next door needed help with harvesting alfalfa. Nonetheless, even now when the topic of dying and heaven comes up with some church or family members, it could still be the 1950s.

My 89-year-old father is a touching example of the challenges of navigating a rapidly changing culture while holding onto traditional religious teachings. As the dearly loved patriarch of his huge and vibrant clan, he worries that some of us will miss the boat to heaven. It's understandable, given the mix of Christian beliefs and nonbeliefs, Buddhist, New Age and pagan undercurrents he senses with us. Rising from the comfort of that protective, homogeneous nest of mid-20th century Christianity, he finds himself wondering how the Lord is going to work this thing out.

At a recent family reunion, my father gathered all 30-some of us around him and spoke from his heart. In his wise, German simplicity, he laid out his concerns for us. Seldom, he reflected, had such an eclectic group of people and belief systems been gathered under the banner of family. He wondered if he had done well by us. Were we going in the right direction? Did we carry the Lord in our hearts? Bottom line greatest fear: Would he, in fact, see us in heaven?

As he finished his "sermon," he sat quietly in his kitchen chair. We sat also—squirming, agreeing, disagreeing—but respecting him, loving him dearly, uncertain what to say and how to reassure him. Suddenly my eldest daughter, Gwendolyn, rose, stepping over babies and cousins on the living room floor in order to reach Grandpa. She swept him up in her arms, a silent embrace of love with no division. He didn't see her tears. He seemed unable to comprehend the incredible family encircling him, so great was his concern. Later she whispered to me, "Oh, Mom, if only Grandpa could know that we will *all* be there in heaven. He will be able to meet us *all* when we die." She was as convinced we would all reach heaven as he was that some of us wouldn't make the grade. Different strokes. Contrasting awareness. There in that living room of divergent views, love triumphed, evoked by the very one who feared we weren't going to get it. My father knew only one flag to wave on the way out the door of life, and that singular focus gave him no ease.

Yet, as we saw it, he was performing his patriarchal role perfectly by living out his faith in the daily coming and going of his principled life. The rest was up to us. His family, after all, had gathered at his beckoning from nearby and all over the world, bringing their own experiences of many cultures, languages and beliefs. We brought youthful rebellion, a wild array of talents and the super-stretchability needed to hang out together for a weekend in some sort of grace. In the end, the gift for us all was learning to more carefully tend our love for each other. Though my father's belief system couldn't accommodate the broad belief spectrum of his family, all our love together could. Unbeknownst to ourselves, we had bumbled into a sort of tentative family heaven. We were all there. We had all arrived—after all.

My family's conflicting beliefs about how to live and die well aren't breaking news. Families invariably provide us with the highest degree of try-to-love-'em-anyway challenges. From diehard fundamentalism to eye-rolling liberal sighs, from religious sincerity to intellectual disdain, families like mine can often claim the whole lot under one roof. Whether with family, coworkers or neighbors, we bump up against each other's beliefs. It can become particularly bumpy when the topic of dying shows up.

Obviously, we are a culture in transition—and in confusion—when it comes to understanding planetary departure. The variety of styles or attitudes toward death, dying and beyond is a fascinating mix. The next four Style Chapters take us from avoidance into the enriching wisdom available for the journey of consciousness we are traveling together.

# CHAPTER 1

# *Basic Styles*

*Just tell me the rules and I won't ask questions...*

THE SEMESTER IS ALMOST OVER and I am in the midst of grading psychology exams. "I don't want to deal with this. I do not want to talk about death!" This answer to the essay question in the last *Human Growth and Development* exam grabs my attention. The question—"What do you want for your funeral, memorial service or last goodbye?"—is simple enough, but obviously isn't going over well with this young nursing student. I smile at her candor, admiring her courage to speak her truth, and possibly lose some credit in the process. She's young, just out of high school. I've noticed that younger students tend to avoid the question or parrot what they have grown up with. Death, after all, seems far, far down the road. Mature students give it a go. They are more candid with their traditional and nontraditional beliefs and afterlife hopes. They may want their ashes strewn over the mountains or their loved ones to dance at their memorial. It's a wild mix of creative last hurrahs and tenderness.

Occasionally, near the end of the semester, we have a class discussion in which students share their thoughts and experiences on death and dying. I tread these waters cautiously, not particularly wanting to kick up religious fervor or secret grief. I want to know where my fellow travelers are with this topic, so I plum my small corner of the culture—community college students. Sometimes nothing happens. No one is in the mood and the discussion dies on the vine. Other times, the clouds open. Pain, fear and dogma arise. Some admit to sweat-laced terror. "I have faith. I'm a Christian, but I'm terrified," admits one woman in her early 40s, showing her trembling hands for all to see.

We are winding down the fast-paced summer session. The classroom is finally cooling in the early evening. She sits with three other women friends at the back of the room. Two nod their heads in agreement, too uncomfortable to speak. The fourth one declares, "No, not me. I'm calm. I'm not afraid. I have things I want to accomplish first, like raising my children, but I'm good to go."

The room is hushed as each, in his or her own way, peers into the face of death with someone else's hand to hold. "Since my grandfather died, I'm not afraid anymore," says a young mother, holding her two-year-old on her lap. "I just feel a lot of peace now." Then things get rolling. Another 20-something courageously mentions reincarnation. She is comforted knowing that not only will she reconnect with her deceased father when she passes over, but they will get to have another life together. The sharing becomes more genuine. Eyes open, ears perk up.

Suddenly a dose of religion is thrown in as a youthful college athlete declares that if everyone knew Jesus as their savior, all that fear would be gone because they would have reassurance of eternal life. A Bible passage is quoted for good measure. People begin to squirm again, this time in reaction to the "preaching," not the subject matter. I listen, guiding our ship through these potentially choppy waters as the class winds to a close. The students have dropped the bored-student look. Some are genuinely invigorated. It's been a good hour of thought-provoking interchange, as far as I'm concerned. Personally, I can empathize with that gut-gripping fear. I've known it intimately. And in my youth, I must confess to quoting a few Bible verses. I also know the ease of the student who found comfort in a deeper sense of the afterlife and rebirth.

My psychology class reminds me of my family. Old school meets new thought. Once again, a wide spectrum of fears, calm, absolutes and indifference presents itself. To be honest, many of my students seem more identified with my father's conservative Christianity than my ever-changing system of thought. But they are searching. Recently I asked them to participate in a small death/dying survey. One question asked, "What do you feel would be helpful in assisting us as a culture to become more informed (less avoidant) on the subject of death and afterlife possibilities?" I was pleasantly surprised when a number of them listed education as a key component. They wanted exposure to new ideas and research. They were cautiously ready to expand their minds, their consciousness.

If, in my corner of the world, people want to get more educated and see the dying-well topic as viable outside the perimeter of church and synagogue, then let's proceed. For it's likely that people in all corners are discovering a need for more understanding.

To do this, we may need to re-examine our mental closets a bit and update our departure wardrobe. Let's start with the basic attitude styles we might find.

## Basic Blinders Style

Horses sometimes wear bridles with small leather shields or blinders on the outer sides of their eyes to limit their peripheral vision. This makes them less likely to shy at sudden movements around them, thereby enabling the carriage driver or rider to remain in control of his or her steed. When we say someone "has blinders on," we mean he or she can't see what is going on—and probably doesn't really want to. This is similar to "putting your head in the sand," a myth of ostrich behavior. Ostriches were rumored to play this trick on themselves when suddenly frightened, providing a brief reprieve from fear.

My daughter, Gwendolyn, told me the story of a golden retriever she knew with similar propensities. Hobbs would be let out into his fenced backyard to play, which he dearly loved to do. Then, alas, it would be time to come in. His owners would stand on the back porch and call for him to return to the house. Hobbs, not being at all ready to go inside, would run to a certain tree and hide his head behind the trunk, holding very still. The calls continued while Hobbs held motionless. Although the rest of his body was plainly visible from the back porch, to Hobbs' way of thinking, if he couldn't see them—voila!—they couldn't see him and he wouldn't have to surrender to the inevitable. When we chuckle at Hobbs' magical thinking, we can also smile at our own.

Simple, funny, illogical avoidance. The core belief in this way of thinking is, "If I don't see it then it will go away and I don't have to deal with it!" It's the great illusion of escape from that which makes us frightened, uncomfortable or just isn't any fun. We have this attitude for all types of feelings and difficulties. At some time in our lives we have all put on blinders when it comes to death.

When we are in Basic Blinders Style thinking, we might say things like:
- Don't know. Don't care!
- I'm not dying. I'm fine. So why talk about it?
- In fact, I'm not going to die—ever!
- Yuck, who wants to think about dying? How morbid!

- That scares the bejeebers out of me! No way am I talking about dying!
- Not now. Maybe when I'm old...
- I don't want to talk about it, okay?

You get the drift. You don't need to be a young nursing student taking a *Human Growth and Development* exam to realize how firmly anchored death-denial blinders can be. Medical doctors, for example, are so thoroughly trained to extend life that compassionate dying-support skills often come later after banging into death's inevitability a number of times. How many soldiers die on the battlefield still holding the adolescent invincibility belief? It won't happen to me. I can't die yet.

Denial of death isn't limited to the young, of course. My 81-year-old mother, a firm member of the strong-and-never-give-up club, lay in her hospital bed one evening, all 90-plus pounds of her. She looked beyond frail, hooked up to her tubes and asking the same questions again and again as her mind, struggling with a deteriorating brain, tried to make sense of her situation. Seeing she was aware in her own way, I quietly approached her. I asked if she might want to talk about dying. "No, I'm not dying!" she declared. "Whatever gave you that idea?" To admit that she was dying seemed a confession of weakness of some sort—an abhorrence in her personal psychology. Sometimes, death is seen as a defeat or failure, creating a desperate effort to hang in there, to be more powerful than death. So even when you are at death's door, it's still just not cool to die.

The subject of death is illegal in the Basic Blinders system of thinking. Thank you, but we just don't talk about it.

## Basic Religious Style

This might be a touchy one for some. It was touchy for the student athlete in my psychology class. She was resolutely convinced that her system of belief was paramount to the others being expressed. Many religious systems have their sacred cows, their array of absolutes in the we-know-more-than-you-do-about-getting-to-heaven game. The absolutes may provide comfort, but they may also be used to stave off the fear underneath.

So when death is staring us in the eye and we haven't really gotten ourselves educated, it's easy to fall back into whatever we picked up in Sunday school. That's not all bad, certainly. Sometimes it works. Other times it's not very comforting if what we recall is something like "You are going to hell if you haven't done it our way." Now that makes death really fun to contemplate! When fear gets stirred up, it's difficult to intuit your way through—especially if you are of the nature to want to hear the sweet voice of your angel calling you to heaven for a fireside chat.

Basic Religious Style needs simplistic solutions and rules. It helps make sense of a confusing world. Just tell me the rules and I won't ask questions. Basic Religious Style also shows up when we carry ambiguity toward religion and haven't found an authentic replacement; or when we've spent our time in Blinders Style and decide to reach for religion, just in case. It's a little like grabbing any food that's in your fridge before you take off on a sudden trip. No planning really, but some supplies are better than none, right?

When we are in Basic Religious Style thinking, we might say things like:
- So maybe I'd better find the Lord, pray to Allah or talk to the rabbi after all these years, just in case.
- If you do this, this and this, you will get to heaven, no question about it. That's how it is!
- I've never really felt anything spiritual in going to the church, mosque or synagogue. I don't even know if I believe all that, but just in case....
- Jesus, if you are for real, I hope you will forgive me and take me home.
- I've been a basically good person and attended some religious services so I should be all right. Right?
- Jehovah will raise me up with the trumpet's sound because I've been true. (Though to be honest, I'm scared of going to hell!)
- My parents believed in all that religious stuff, so maybe it's not too late for me to use it.
- I'm ready to meet God—or whatever happens after death.
- What if I'm not good enough?

Undercurrents of doubt seep through these comments. Basic Religious Style seldom engenders a sense of true confidence to affect the nature of our death and our experience beyond. Instead all power seems to reside outside of us, and our own authentic nature is given little validity.

When religion comforts and empowers, it serves our departure. As I reflect on all the PLR crossing-over experiences I have conducted with clients, religiosity was not the crucial issue for the dying soul. Their ability to grow, learn and love were instead the markers of a successful life—and a successful crossing.

An example comes to mind from my client Maria, who regressed to a life 1,000 years ago where she was the woman shaman of a small nomadic tribe. This close-knit group lived an intense and peaceful life in the harsh Mongolian desert. The spiritual teachings, such as they were, consisted mostly of a simple, synergistic understanding of the oneness of all things. Upon her passing, the shaman described a very easy transition, rising into "heaven," where she met her grandmother, and walked with her horse that was slain in order to accompany her in the next world. She recognized her heaven as familiar and proceeded to evaluate her life. Without any guilt teachings or fear of the afterlife, and a very simple system of spiritual understanding, her crossing seemed as natural as stepping over a mountain stream. Basic *trust* would describe Maria's style.

## Basic Zealot Style

The Zealots of the first century AD were a radical, warlike group of Jews who advocated the overthrow of the Roman government. When someone shows excessive fervor for a cause and is seen as overly "zealous" by others, we would call him or her a zealot. In our context, zealotry for a cause and the death that might result are wrapped up together. Black-and-white thinking appeals to those who like simple explanations and are frightened of change. A great high can result from thinking that our system of thought is unquestionable and absolute. What a great way to die—in complete rightness. What greater prize could we bring to God? Problem is, this way of framing life leaves out a lot of other folks. The righteousness train to heaven doesn't allow for many passengers.

Karen Armstrong, author and former nun, says it eloquently when she writes, "There are some people, I suspect, who would feel obscurely cheated if, when they finally arrived in heaven, they found everyone else there as well. Heaven would not be heaven unless those who reached it could peer over the celestial parapets and watch other unfortunates roasting below." (*AARP Magazine*, March-April, 2005)

In this time of upheaval, fundamentalist systems of thought have gained popularity. Zealous pronouncements are shouted in the din. Rigid religious and political laws are enacted in an attempt to control the citizenry and reign through the winds of chaos. Intolerance becomes cloaked in virtue. If we can, instead, embrace the winds of change as an opportunity for recovering our true vision, we open to immense creativity and hope.

Decades ago we were horrified by rare news of a suicide bomber or the destruction of an abortion clinic. Now we are less reactive and somewhat numbed by increased fanaticism. These are the visible extremes. But we must address the zealot psychology toward life and death that may still be found in our own quiet corners. To know what is right for ourselves at any given point in our journey is admirable; to claim we know what is right for everyone else is arrogant and dangerous.

When we are in Basic Zealot Style thinking, we might say things like:
- God, Allah, or Jehovah is on our side. We die for the right!
- With this death, I go to glory!
- Allah be praised! God gives us the victory! God blesses us because we're the good guys. He will help us slay the bad guys.
- Let Jesus save you or you will go to hell!
- My way is the only way.
- My religion is the only religion.
- My God is the one true God. Any other belief is abhorrent to me.
- I defend my God!
- We are right. You are wrong!
- I know more than you do!

Intolerance feels degrading. It bespeaks a need to control others. As a temporary blip, righteous intolerance can be excused as part of the path of learning. We have all been adamantly passionate about some belief system at some point in our lives. But as a way of life, it makes for some difficult departure experiences—and in the meantime isn't much fun to be around. Often left on its own to starve, Zealot Style loses its grip on the psyche and matures into a less abrasive stance.

## Basic Stuck Style

Stuck Style is in operation on both sides of the veil. It starts with, well, being stuck. Here is where our ignorance and poor choices really run amok. We can be stuck in constricting religious beliefs, rigid thinking or heavy emotions during our lives. Various addictions can hold us in unrelenting prisons of darkness. We even get into controlling behaviors where we bring others down, spreading hatred and negativity. Talk about stuck. So if you find you get easily trapped in resentment or anger, now is the time to spin yourself off that road to nowhere.

Have you ever been jolted out of sleep? Remember how it takes a while to regain your bearings and remember where you are? It may take a few moments to feel like you are back in your body and your life. The same thing happens with a sudden or traumatic death. There you are, driving along in your car, when you see a truck heading straight toward you. Crash! The next thing you know, you are walking around the accident scene and no one is paying attention to you. You notice a body lying on the ground that you hardly identify with. You are dead but you don't know it. Obviously, you are still you, but no one acknowledges you because they can't see you anymore. The difference between dying suddenly and waking up suddenly is that when you are jolted out of sleep, you are able to return to your familiar reality. When you get jolted out of your body at death, you try to return to your familiar reality but you usually can't. Your body has lost its ability to receive you back, and because you don't know what is going on, it's difficult to realize you have guides or spiritual escorts standing nearby, waiting to take you on home. You are stuck in limbo until such time as you can realize the truth of your situation.

If you are very angry or scared about something when you are permanently jolted out of your body, that anger or fear may also keep you locked in with the angry situation or person. You may try to still interact with them, not realizing you are now without a visible body. You have become a "ghostly" presence, an interference in Earth life. And you don't get on with it. Sadly, you are wasting your eternity. Now if you had had some conscious dying first-aid under your belt, you would know what to do. More on that later.

When we are in Basic Stuck Style thinking, we might say things like:
- I'm angry and I'm going to stay angry!
- How could you do that to me? I will never forgive you!
- You haven't heard the last of me!
- If I can't have you, no one will have you. Not now, not ever!
- I'll say the right words, but I'm still angry at you!
- I'm so sinful. I will never be forgiven. God can never love someone like me.
- I am without hope. So sad, so sad.….

- I'm not leaving because I'll surely go to hell. Nope, I'm staying right here where it's familiar.
- Hey what happened? Why aren't you listening to me? Wait! I'm too young, too unready, too good/bad to die!
- What happened? Why can't I get out of here? Help me!
- I will have a drink. I have to have that high now! Body or no body, I'm going to the bar to be with my friends!
- I will never leave you.

So our quest is to get smart and kick up our death IQ. We have been uninformed on this process, which breeds more problems. We haven't known there were choices. More understanding helps us engage with the powerful transcendent energy of death and not abort the process. I want you to know better, so that you and your loved ones have guideposts and pointers for traveling from this planet and into your next steps—with pizzazz.

Although it seems many in our human family are still caught in Basic Styles of thinking, in fact, Basic Styles are crumbling. We are becoming more aware and more informed in our thinking. Indeed, we are amping up our awareness—and updating our styles.

## CHAPTER 2

# Traditional Styles

*That's the gift of my tradition for me, the seed of applied spirituality*
*and a longing for God, woven always with sagebrush,*
*sunsets and the long, endless horizon.*

ZWIEBACK, BORSCHT, "FOR LAND SAKES!" and faith rest in the heart of my tradition. In the blood of my people is the rich farm soil of Germany, Holland, the Ukraine and the New World plains of Kansas and Saskatchewan. Deep roots. Precious blood flows through generations of the tribe known as Mennonite, offspring of that wayward Friesian priest, Menno Simons, in the 1500s. Choosing neither Catholicism nor the new Lutheran rebels, the followers of Brother Simons got ganged up on by both sides. Some lived to tell about it. I come from that tribal persecution memory. I also come from good people, honest, trustworthy and willing to work hard. We are in the world—but not of it. No need to swear on the Bible; our word is our trust. Let us live in peace. Let us have our quiet ways. Let us live free of violence and military service. Let us obey the covenant we have made to care for all of humanity, including those deemed an enemy. Our allegiance is to a higher governance—and our traditions. You can almost hear Tevye from "Fiddler on the Roof" raising his voice in the background: Tradition!

Being a Mennonite girl was a mixed review for me. It was certainly sufficient excuse for teasing by those small-town kids who weren't in the fold, mostly older boys on the school bus. Luckily, there were plenty of us, a power in numbers kind of protection. I hated being different, not because I disagreed particularly but because I was shy and embarrassed by being singled out. As an adolescent, I disliked wearing "the covering," that little white net compromise-hat the church fathers came up with so that a woman

16

could keep her head covered. Gotta love the Apostle Paul and his view that women needed to cover up. Why do I have to wear this? I protested. Because it pleases God. My father could have been another Tevye. Tradition and God were pretty tight partners.

That's the way it was—a tradition of community and a vast, prescribed way of being in the world, tied to land and family and God. It was a haven of belonging, though not without price. Nonconformity to the outer world— difficult; conformity within the clan—at times even more difficult. Much has changed, of course. Now little outside appearance sets off the tribe of Mennonite from homogenized American culture.

I question how these roots have served me, and what has fed the flame of my life. What embers remain from that solidity of multi-generational faith that engender the fire necessary to take on projects like a study of planetary departure? Simplicity and quiet still sing in my soul. Certainly, going against the cultural flow was part of the training course—and that continues. I support a review of all that holds us back from blossoming. Pushing the edges allows for a sense of adventure.

Discussions on values and meaning ran deep in that white country church. Application of scripture was the work of life. In my child-world, God was real and tangible. I expected Him to hear me. I didn't question the value of love, of nonviolence, of integrity, of devotion. Nor do I today. Religious guidelines weren't theoretical to me, but were the tangible way in which human and divine walked intimately upon the path of time. The forms and dogma have been dropped, sometimes disdainfully, but the connection to Divine Source has weathered the storms of my life, tethered in my core. I have stepped back certainly, struggled mightily, and grown muscle along the way. All the while an innate eternality has thrust me forward, gently, relentlessly. That's the gift of my tradition for me, the seed of applied spirituality and a longing for God, woven always with sagebrush, sunsets and the long, endless horizon. Even though I came to refuse the sin and shame and guilt beliefs, in the long term, the God-piece worked.

## Traditional Faith Style

The Basic Styles in the preceding chapter have undercurrents of disquiet. Blinders, Religious, Zealot and Stuck Styles aren't particularly comfortable for soul-wear. They often feel restrictive, like a pair of granny's shoes that never were that easy on the feet. As we explore the Traditional Faith Style approach to living and dying, we sense more ease and acceptance. More wiggle room.

Faith is often tied to some religious belief system in which the person has found comfort and meaning. A simple Faith Style may also emerge on its own from an observation of nature, cycles and seasons, suffering and gratitude. You may find nourishment in watching the ebb and flow of life. Observation might reflect to you the innate wisdom of trees, flowers and souls coming and going within their own appointed time. If you identify with Faith Style, you likely have done some sorting, adding and subtracting until a set of guidelines for the journey emerges. Complicated theologies and dogmas may or may not be a part of your final belief system. Often the sorting evolves into a simple hope. You feel you have done the best with your life you knew to do, followed the precepts of your religion or philosophy as best you could, and now you leave your fate in the hands of a Higher Power. You may have unanswered questions, like wondering about the fate of those outside your faith, or if what you've been taught happens after death, in fact, does. But the general goodness in your heart calms your mind and you let it go. Faith, trust and surrender grant you some ease.

My Aunt Esther was not an easy woman. She was strong, adamant, painfully blunt—and deeply trusting of her Lord. During her long life, I witnessed the decreasing of her sharper qualities and the increasing of her surrender. Judgment of those different from herself receded and with a growing kindness she reached out to others, even while strolling with her walker down the hall of her assisted living center. Her simple trust and faith were a treasure for all of us to partake of in her later years. Her prayers seemed to have a direct link to heaven few could summon—probably because she insisted. I feel, even now, the tenderness of her trust in God. When I contemplate the Traditional Faith Style, she, along with many of my forebears, comes to mind. And I thank them for that gift.

If we are in Traditional Faith Style, our thoughts may include:
- I deeply believe in the power of Love, Jesus, Allah, God or the gods of my ancestors. I live according to those teachings to the best of my abilities.
- I have found these teachings meaningful. I believe that I will be guided in death according to these teachings.
- There is a rhythm and wisdom to nature and the cosmos. I trust that wisdom now and when I surrender this body.
- Perfect love casts out fear. I have sought to live in love. I believe that hope and love will take me home.

- I have served the Lord to the best of my abilities. I trust He will meet me and guide me to heaven. Though it is all a mystery and we can't see the truth from this side of the veil, we live our lives in faith.
- Though my body dies, my spirit lives on. I am going to a better place.

The difference is palpable now as we have moved into more spacious attitudes. A longer life contributes to this depth of faith and its more coherent system of belief. You are blessed indeed, to be, or have known one whose faith is true and grounded.

## Traditional Intellectual Style

Perhaps you know someone who simply isn't drawn to traditional religions or delving into spirituality. Perhaps you find that neither are you. Yet you feel open to considering all possibilities regarding life and death questions. The Intellectual Style approach tends to utilize rational thought and deductive reasoning to gather understanding. Under this umbrella we might find more philosophical types, traditional scientists, agnostics, some thoughtful atheists and a few Buddhists. These thinkers might be sitting next to you in the church pew because they delight in the beauty of High Mass or the classical organ concert on Easter Sunday. They may appreciate the ritual and ceremony of Jewish festivals, with little involvement otherwise. Others may never set foot in a church, synagogue or mosque but be your favorite neighbor. If you are more of a Faith Style person, your Intellectual Style neighbor may be quite an enigma to you. He thrills at scientific breakthroughs or the study of the cosmos, but seems to find your religious leanings quaint and irrational. If your religious training says that the good guys go to heaven, you can't imagine that your non-religious but really-good-guy neighbor won't be there as well.

If we are in Intellectual Style, our thoughts may include:
- After studying science, philosophy, religion and/or nature, it seems probable that there is/isn't a continuation of consciousness after death.
- I'm open to new information.
- Show me the proof.
- Religion doesn't satisfy my mind. It seems to ask me to leave my mind at the door, which I find illogical and demeaning.

- If there is a divine being, it would be accessible to all and uninvolved in the trivia of human life.
- I'm interested but skeptical in the near-death experiences or past-life regression work I've read about. Can this be substantiated? Has there been validating research?
- Religion seems like mind control. I don't buy it.

Intellectual Style folks tend to view the world through logical lenses. Socrates and many other great thinkers have pushed the ability of the mind to interpret reality objectively and bring more coherence to the questions of meaning, life and death. If you are of this nature, objective proofs and clear systems of explaining reality feed you. Mathematics, music theory, cosmology or the classic poets may lift your spirit, for you are enlivened by the discovery of an innate higher order.

Of course, you may be a practical sort and just want to play in the prove-it-to-me end of the Intellectual Style spectrum. Or you may simply want to be left alone on the religion and death front. You are not in Blinders. You know your death is your everyday companion in some sense, but you have no need to champion your rationale. You may be burned out from an overly religious childhood or clergy abuse of power. Perhaps you have come to a place of cynicism because of the pain religion has caused in your life, or the planet as a whole. You may be skeptical of all religious forms on general principles. Whether temporary or permanent, you are taking a major religion break.

If you are a full-blown Faith Style person, all of this may leave you confused or cold. Don't despair. Despite what you have heard, many paths lead to higher understanding now and in the afterlife. There's room for everyone. We may or may not be able to satisfy our intellectual friend's need for proof, but perhaps we can bring some balm to religious wounding and shed light on some of those nagging questions.

# CHAPTER 3

## *Conscious Choice Styles*

*I am the master of my fate*
*I am the captain of my soul…*
–"Invictus" by William Ernest Henley

"HAVE YOU READ THIS?" I find myself striding into the family room—both delighted and incredulous. My husband's back is to me as he empties boxes of books onto bookshelves. Several days earlier, an astonishing book had surfaced, staring at me from the dining table. I devoured it and now have questions. How long, I wonder, has this book been packed away, awaiting revelation? Is my husband familiar with it? If so, did he find it even half as compelling as I do? Why has it taken so long to find its way to me?

The early summer of 1976 has dawned warm and luscious and we are putting our lives back to some semblance of normal. Our two young daughters have survived our stays in Quebec and Colorado none the worse for wear. Returning home to Illinois after my husband's nine-month sabbatical leave from the university is proving remarkable indeed. How long have I known him? Eight years? Nine? In that time, he never mentioned interest in the stuff in this book. How could that be, given the tidal wave now crashing on my small ocean of spiritual awareness? I wait, eager for his response. "Yeah, I read it," he says offhandedly. Silence. No further interest.

I hold the little tsunami paperback in my hand, certain that God Himself has swept it into my life: *There is a River: the Story of Edgar Cayce* by Thomas Sugrue. In my mind—no, in my soul—a door crashed open and I leaped through. At last someone has turned on the porch light! I don't have to grope my way in the dark. A new journey has announced itself with open arms and

I'm feeling welcomed as though for the first time on planet Earth. A gentle wave of comfort has crested onto my shore.

Our summer passes uneventfully on the outside. However, I am snatching moments to read anything I can find on Edgar Cayce, drinking in the feeling of a grander view of Earth life and this thing called the journey of the soul.

Then in the fall, my mother arrives from Colorado for a grandma visit. We are chatting in the kitchen as the late afternoon light shimmers through the southern windows with that magical slant that only autumn lends the sun. Vegetable soup simmers and for the moment, the kitchen is childfree and quiet.

Attempting nonchalance, I broach my new favorite topic. "Hey Mom, see this book I found? So cool! It explains why things are the way they are, suffering, living, dying and (gulp) past lives." She begins to bristle at the past-lives reference. Hurriedly, I blunder on. "Edgar Cayce was a Southern Baptist who prayed to be able to do more to help humanity. He was given the gift of seeing the reasons for people's suffering. He saw remedies that would help their illnesses and reasons from other lives that were causing their present difficulties. It helps me understand how we reap what we sow." Yadda, yadda and a deep sinking feeling.

My mother's traditional Christian hackles are rising. She seems to be readying for a counterattack. Wait, I'm your daughter. You love me, remember? Her eyes are beginning to flash—not a good sign. She's giving nonverbal warnings not to cross over into this forbidden land that seems somehow opposed to—what? I'm not able to verbalize it. But I do know that I probably just blew my chances of dancing in our family heaven and it doesn't feel so great. I am sad and dismayed.

What did you expect, Marcia? Supper will be tense. Your mother will put up her emotional Great Wall of China. Please not now. Not just before two adoring granddaughters rush in to embrace her on her grandma throne. As thrones go, my daughter throne has just been unceremoniously toppled in a brief three minutes of well-intentioned but fruitless monologue. My mother is certain I've gone off into a cult of some kind. Occult. All my grandmothers are surely turning over in their graves, earth torn asunder.

Why is this so upsetting? My mind is swirling. A piece of the puzzle fell in my lap. I'm thinking great-discovery-to-share. It seems, however, that the great questions of suffering and how the "reaping what we sow" teaching might work, is entering territory where no young mother ought to go. Period. I'm not comprehending this place in which I find myself. My mother, a writer for a church periodical, asks these questions with great aplomb. But only God knows the answers. I've evidently gone where all the faithful only let God go. I'm unnerved. I have no ability to prove anything. Yet, I continue to feel the comfort and solace this discovery is bringing to me in the crazy journey of life.

Okay. To be honest, I probably showed little finesse in this endeavor. I also knew I was likely pushing the edge. Nonetheless, I was compelled to give it a try, for I carried a secret desire that my mother and I might share an insightful moment.

It's confusing. There seems to be a religious and cultural banner that says, "Don't ask, but if you do ask, and if you do find answers, don't tell anyone." I'd forgotten about that other god called "normal." Don't rock the boat. Normal children. Normal Christians. It's better to be unhappy than too different. Do not question this wonderful life and all the opportunities to learn. But learn about history and travel and science and cooking and music and art. Do not learn about metaphysics and spirituality. And, watch out for that inner journey.

Experiencing those belief-worlds crashing was more than an oops moment for me. It was a kind of second tsunami initiation. Can you ride these waves? How much do you want to discover about your true nature, your soul? How much are you willing to risk if this new exploration seriously rocks the boat of your family? The Traditional Style was fading fast. I knew it didn't fit but couldn't explain why. It still seemed to be working for my mother, my husband, and my extended family—sort of.

In the mid-1970s the self-help and spirituality movement hadn't hit Middle America, let alone Madison Avenue. It took a while to find others of like mind. With only this inner compulsion, my life, ready or not, geared up for Conscious Choice Style. Despite outer disapproval, I loved the feeling of this new fabric against my soul skin, the brilliant colors shimmering on my inner landscape. I loved feeling like I was remembering, coming home to myself.

Perhaps equal to this breakthrough, was a deep and necessary lesson on the nature of this path. Succinctly put, my required homework was to realize that I need embrace only my own journey. It's a silly waste of energy to hold anger, hurt, confusion or superiority regarding another's path. It has been essential for me to appreciate my own breakthroughs, but to also appreciate that each soul, each precious child of the Universe, has their own timing, own choices and own awakening. Because I am having an epiphany doesn't mean it's suddenly time for everyone to have a similar experience.

In my heart, my parents and my spouse hold a place of honor for the roles they played with me so perfectly. As I pushed against the traditional, which is the energy they held for me, I could use that resistance to birth myself into my next step. In like manner, my next step provided them exposure to a nontraditional viewpoint. We all chose, consciously or unconsciously, how we would grow as a result. It was a service we provided for each other.

For me, Conscious Choice Style has been like turning around and gazing into the mirror with greater perception. It's still me in that mirror, but I'm not limited to my ego's self-interpretation. I can see a self that has become more resolute, kind and real. As I grow, the reflection continues to shift accordingly. The glorious nature of getting more conscious is that consciousness is unlimited.

The three Conscious Choice Styles that follow reflect a clearer image of this more expansive approach. Many clients and friends have shared their unique journeys of awakening that have inspired this chapter. I extend my deep appreciation to each of them. Whether through large waves or gentle ripples, their awakenings have some lovely common threads. We will explore these commonalities as we investigate the Big Picture, Inner Knowing and Conscious Departure Styles.

## Big Picture Style

Big Picture people ask a lot of questions. In fact, they may prefer life outside most cultural boxes of the mind. They may drive you crazy with the feeling that any absurdities in your philosophical system are blatantly apparent to them. But they also chuckle at and struggle with their own ever-changing sense of reality. They may sit quietly beside you, not saying much, but you know they hold a different sense of things. If you are traditional in your thinking, you may not be certain you want to know about their bigger picture because it feels threatening—not bad—just uncomfortable. They may have been where you are, and seem to understand you, but you can't figure them out.

Some Big Picture people seem to have been born that way—with their eyes of consciousness open. Some seem to suddenly wake up and know things they never learned from family or religious schooling. All Big Picture people carry some sense of a grander plan unfolding in their lives and on our planet. They feel a deep connection to the Divine or Greater Reality. They don't have much interest in endless small talk, social pro forma or religious dogma. Most say they know that their soul is rich, multilayered and existed before this life and will continue on after. Often I find them passionate in their desire to bring greater awareness, health and harmony into the world. The bigger picture bequeaths them a quiet comfort.

People may migrate from Basic or Traditional Styles to Conscious Choice Styles. However, many struggle within the grip of powerful belief systems—whether religious, scientific or skeptical—unable to push further. Years ago when I visited the small church in which I grew up, Clara, one of the older women, turned to me in anguish. "What will happen to all those who never knew Jesus, who never had a chance to find the Lord?" Her heart was deeply troubled by the teaching that only through believing in Jesus can souls reach heaven. She wanted to hold this teaching as unquestionable truth. But the inability to reconcile a loving God with one who sends most of humanity to hell because they weren't in the right place at the right time weighed heavily on her heart. However, finding the bigger picture was not an option to her way of thinking. In the end she tucked away her question, shut the door on her anguish and returned to Faith Style, embracing the words of the hymn, "We'll understand it all by and by."

Many people within that particular belief system have asked her same question. Holes in the ideology and discrepancies in the translations, at the very least, have contributed to this anguish. To be a loving example to the world and yet part of an apparently ruthless justice system is a crisis of belief few care to face.

In the Big Picture framework of thinking, if you have the ability to ask the questions, you also have the ability to find meaningful answers. Obviously, the part of your consciousness that asks the question hasn't found answers within its present understanding. As a Big Picture person you give yourself full permission to dive in and explore. Embracing the Big Picture Style means stepping into the adventure of self-discovery. It means becoming courageous enough to face your own dark side, and embrace your innate divinity. It becomes a compelling, painful and joyful process—opening to a landscape of infinite possibilities.

If we are in Big Picture Style thinking, we might say things like:
- Strict heaven-and-hell philosophies feel limiting. I sense the Universe is wise and benevolent. Exploring new questions opens my world. I want to understand how it all works.

- Black-and-white interpretations don't serve me here or after death. I'm learning about opposites and how they serve us. Instead of needing to judge, I can start by being kind toward myself. I can learn to care for my body AND my soul.
- Having only one life makes no sense. The ancient concept of reincarnation is held as valid in so many traditions. It helps me understand the origins of our suffering and our talents. I have died many times before. Though my body dies, my spirit is eternal and continues to grow.
- I am opening my mind to discover my greater purpose and to explore what happens after death. I am part of a bigger plan.
- I feel like I'm waking up! I'm remembering things that I've always known—about who I am, about spirit, about life. Death is no longer so unknown or frightening.
- I see the synchronicity within the events of my life. I feel a sacredness and magic within it all.
- What is really going on here? What is the true history of our planet? Who is behind the forces of light and dark?
- I'm learning about the multidimensional worlds here and beyond.
- It's not what it seems to be about. It's much more than it looks like!

Choosing the Big Picture helps judgment fall away. The freedom to ask any and all questions liberates the mind. Big Picture people smile as the answer to one question opens up 10 more intriguing questions. The search for new answers enlivens us. The Big Picture helps release the pain about there being only one way to God, or one political view, or one way to any outcome.

Most Big Picture people find the only-one-right-way thinking wearisome. It simply holds little if any water. However, if others need to believe that way, Big Picture people are likely to understand that each soul chooses its own path. Therefore they generally respect others' decisions while supporting the highest learning possible within those choices.

When working with clients who have wrestled with great suffering, I find that as they arrive at some learning from their adversities, their healing is well underway. They expand into a greater sense of themselves, a larger grace. The Bigger Picture process grants them courage to embrace challenge as an opportunity to learn. It brings calm so that their lives are held in a bit more compassion, instead of so much judgment.

## Inner Knowing Style

"Know Thyself" was the dictate written above the entrance to the Delphi Oracle Temple in ancient Greece. To truly know yourself, to gain understanding of your deep inner nature, was the highest calling. This deep self has been given many names—kingdom of heaven, inner knowing, true self, soul, higher self, superconscious, inner voice and higher power, to name a few. By whatever name we choose, Inner Knowing Style is a dedication to walking more closely with that inner self. It is the work of becoming more adept at traveling into our inner landscape.

These realms of the heart and mind are more fascinating and complex than the outer universe we gaze into on a summer night. Ralph Waldo Emerson's words, "What lies behind us and what lies before us are small matters compared to what lies *within* us," eloquently portray this truth. Dr. Carl Jung, after many years of exploring the vastness of human consciousness, said the wonders of the outer universe cannot compare to the marvelous inner worlds waiting to be explored.

This trek into the inner world is *key* to Conscious Choice Stylers and reigns supreme as a consistent teaching down through time. You've got to climb inside of yourself. If you are choosing the Conscious Style road, you've got to fall in love with your body-mind wisdom. Inner Knowing folks are compelled to listen to their intuition and gut, sometimes called the still, small voice. They begin to hone themselves into radar detectors, discerning both heavenly support and negative interference. They understand that the body is an energetic marvel, full of vital information waiting to be downloaded into consciousness. You will often find them exercising, studying martial arts, improving their diets, listening to Mozart or meditating. They may keep dream journals, use self-hypnosis or go into psychotherapy. Why? Because these various techniques clear the clutter and help them access their Inner Knowing.

You probably won't find Inner Knowing types much interested in nonessential pharmaceutical drugs, junk food, pesticides or rigid systems of thought. They say no to whatever aspects of the consumer/political/fear culture that distract them from their path. They are very cautious about recreational drug usage. Why? Because all those things can carry disharmonious energies which interfere with clear reception of those wonderful intuitive downloads. Plus Inner Knowing folks seem to have a deep sense about protecting the planet as a whole.

As Inner Knowing Style deepens, people tend to give their bodies more wholesome attention. This may include exercise, diet and positive affirmations. For example, natural, alive, lovingly prepared food really can taste better. You can sense the vitality or depleted nature of what you put in your mouth. You realize that saying a blessing over your food is actually ancient magic. It's an energetic blessing you bestow upon your dinner and your health.

If we are in Inner Knowing Style thinking, we might say things like:
- If something resonates with me, I know it is my truth. The feeling of truth may happen immediately, or over time. It's as if my heart says yes, or my gut says no.
- I feel excited about studying quantum physics/alternative medicine/ sustainable business/organic farming, etc. When I feel compelled, joyful and creative I know I am on the right track.
- This not the right time for that. I will know when it is.
- What she said is true, but what he said is not. I can feel it.
- My body is truly hungry for that salad. That is what I want.
- I notice the energetic difference between worry and compassion. Worry feels irritating. Compassion washes my heart clean.
- Choosing to be in charge of my focus—the thoughts and feelings I want to cultivate—helps me now and in my departure.
- It's time to acknowledge this fear I have. Bring it into love. Fear hampers my inner knowing reception. When fear kicks in, my inner knowing level drops.
- I feel the loving presence of my guide/angel/grandmother assisting me today.
- I'm coming home to myself.
- I am here to make a difference.

What does Inner Knowing Style have to do with dying? As a general rule, we find that cultivation of our inner guidance has a dynamic carry-over effect. Did you know that right now you are fueling your transition experience? What is alive in you? What are you fired up about? What gives you deep peace? What wreaks havoc with your peace? What are you growing with your day-to-day focus? What we focus on grows and flourishes, creating an energetic bridge we travel upon into the afterlife.

Our inner knowing becomes more authentic as we do our shadow work, i.e. getting to know those parts of ourselves that we don't know and don't like. We habitually cast these parts into the shadows of our inner landscape. If we are avoiding seeing our fears, arrogance, victimhood, addictions, guilt, shame, beauty or power—whatever we aren't comfortable with—then life will throw us a few curves to trigger it all. Plop our avoided parts into our laps, so to speak. Our avoided parts often show up as someone or something we really find aggravating or don't like. Then we can see where we still don't know how to dance. This awareness work is actually serious business. Inner knowing counts big in the human homework grade book. We've got to go for the inside job. Part III, "Tools for the Journey," will help with this "homework."

## Conscious Departure Style

There is a knack to dying. That's what we are exploring here. We don't have to shuffle blindly through death and beyond. Nor need we feed ourselves religious fables we hope are true. Conscious departure is waiting for our discovery.

Some years ago, when I began working as a clinician in a nursing care center, I anticipated being near those who would soon be passing on. I wanted to sit quietly with them and listen to their fears and the wisdom they had garnered over their life span. Perhaps they held insight into the soul's journey that I could add to my repertoire. Those of you who have worked in similar settings might be smiling at my naiveté. I was disappointed. I was in the right place at the right time, but the learning I would be given came in a different form altogether.

Instead of hidden wisdom and insights, I more frequently heard religious platitudes. I saw great fear of dying and also great fear of living further in deteriorating bodies. I saw minds that tried to understand but often seemed too drugged or demented to fathom a greater reality. That is not to say that deep soul healing wasn't going on beneath my radar, for I believe various things were working themselves out within each person's challenge. Amazingly sweet and humorous wisdom also slipped through on occasion. But the profound lack of skills to speak openly of death and the worlds beyond was painful for patients and staff alike.

A precious few of these elders seemed to have collected the courage and faith to nourish themselves in their last days. Mostly, I found people lonely, confused and seemingly unprepared to die. *I discovered that the end of life is not the time to begin getting conscious about dying.* The mind has often become too crystallized, too set in a prescribed groove to be able to absorb new concepts or practice simple conscious dying techniques. There are exceptions to this observation, of course. But by and large, we seem to die as we have lived, and if we have not developed inner-world awareness during life, it becomes a foreign country to travel in our final days.

Conscious living promotes conscious dying. Both have been a relative luxury on our planet, given all the trauma and ignorance in which we live and die. In the past, conscious living and dying assumed homage amid ashrams and gurus, monasteries and saints. It was available to those with sufficient food, shelter and a sense of internal peace to live and die well. Today we are blessed, because more people have the option to make the conscious living-dying choice.

### Frequencies

Let's take a moment to explore a concept essential to our discussion; frequencies. We can understand conscious living and dying more readily if we have a foundational framework on frequencies and energy. This will help us improve our consciousness aptitude. Very simply put, everything is energy. If we put anything under the proper microscope, we see a dancing array of atoms. Everything is a dance of atomic energy in a way that is unique to itself, whether that thing is a tree, a baby or a rock. Energy moves at different frequencies or levels of vibration, allowing for the uniqueness of all things, down to each grain of sand.

Thoughts and feelings are also energy and vibrate at different frequencies. This is of particular interest to us. Our layered thoughts and feelings are part of our unique blueprint or consciousness. Essentially, lower-frequency thoughts and feelings are slower and draining to our life force. Higher frequencies enliven, bring joy, and engender acceptance and compassion. Our predominant frequencies influence our experiences—now and when we cross over.

As you might suppose, low-frequency emotions include rage, hatred, manipulation, shaming, deep depression, terror, powerlessness and resentment. Check off the ones you have experienced or given out. Don't be shy. We've all been there. We just don't want to *stay* there.

Trauma causes painful emotions to become stuck and stored in our nervous systems. These difficult emotions are easily retriggered by similar events or people long after the initial event—until there is effective intervention. Trauma memory resides not only in our bodies but also in buildings and land. Disturbed land, places of trauma, and anger-filled homes need healing from trauma and sadness. Have you ever noticed how some natural settings bring you joy while others make you sad? Your inner knowing goes off as you pick up the frequencies. It's the same with people. Around some folks you feel uplifted, around others, you feel drained. Your nervous system is giving you a readout.

Another group of negative frequencies that impact our health and well-being are electromagnetic fields related to technology. These are measurable radiations from power plants, cell phones, microwaves, computers, televisions, electrical devices, etc. A guideline I read years ago suggested that for every hour we spend in front of the computer, we need to spend an hour out of doors. Now that's a challenge! Nonetheless, we have the power to minimize exposure to "bad vibes" and become conscious creators of wholeness within and around ourselves.

High frequencies, or good vibes, generally increase our sense of well-being. They also stir up the dust of our insecurities and outmoded beliefs because these are what we want to release. So high frequencies can free us up, if we are willing to be jolted forward on the conscious choice path. Bruised egos are survivable. Challenges to our pride can be an uncomfortable but timely aspect of high-frequency jolts.

High frequencies include:
1. Heart—caring, compassion, love, courage, empathy
2. Passion—joy, creativity, curiosity, delight
3. Depth—grace, wisdom, deep knowing
4. True power—firmness, groundedness, clear action, self-discipline
5. Integrity—inner self and outer self in harmony
6. Clear thought and speech
7. Positive self regard, good boundaries and self-confidence
8. Clear and joyful sexuality
9. Trust and connection with Divine Source
10. Sense of oneness with All That Is

Our thoughts, words and actions carry certain frequencies. These frequencies build in the body and its surrounding energy field. The frequencies of our thoughts radiate from us and are felt by others, just as we feel their radiation. The energies of our thoughts, feelings and actions feed or deplete our consciousness. Because we obviously don't take our bodies with us when we pass over, our consciousness is what remains. It's the bank account we are left with. Death is the continuation of consciousness—without a body to cart it around. We understand better why St. Francis-types espoused simplicity and kindness, and the ancient yogis were so keen on pure diet, meditation and other yogic practices. All of these disciplines energetically assist souls into the realms of light after death.

Conscious departure then, requires conscious living—a choice to learn, become empowered, love deeply and think outside of boxes. It begs adeptness in meditation, contemplation and other internal modes of travel. Conscious living takes courage. It is an amazingly funny, difficult, joyful trip. It requires seeing ourselves through the lens of infinity, while doing the fundamental work of being human. We are powerful, grand beings who decided to take on the human experience because, well, it's such a wild ride. And in our heart of hearts, don't we fancy ourselves as something akin to cosmic adventurers?

If we are in Conscious Departure Style thinking, we might say things like:

- Meditation, prayer, diet, yoga, exercise, etc., all count in creating a conscious vehicle for this life and beyond.
- My attitudes, thoughts and feelings tell me how I am doing today. I want to listen so I can express my grief, defuse my fears and enliven my joy.
- I choose compassion, self-discipline and wisdom as a high-frequency path, learning as I go.
- I understand that the frequency I hold as I leave my body influences where I am able to go. Higher frequencies draw me into the higher planes; lower frequencies draw me to the lower planes.
- I see that conscious dying involves conscious living. Everything that helps me see myself and others honestly and compassionately serves conscious living. Staying in anger, avoidance, denial or bitterness keeps me trapped.
- This unpredictable time in planetary history offers me unprecedented opportunities to discover my true self—and to be of service to the whole.
- When my inner knowing is clear, I can know when my exit time has arrived. I can then surrender in peace.
- Deep stillness and meditation/prayerfulness/contemplation aid the quiet inward focus so conducive to conscious departure.

I want to close with a story that illustrates the option and the simplicity of conscious choice-making at the end of life. We have in large measure forgotten how to die when we are ready. My friend, Don, shared the story of his mother's passing. Lillie's story is one of remembering this innate art.

## *Lillie's Story*

Lillie Watts lived a long, and some would say, difficult life. Born in 1901 into the Cherokee lands of Arkansas, she developed an early appreciation for the value of family, for at age 10, Lillie's mother died. She became the young matriarch of her family while her father struggled to make a living. She mothered her younger siblings and managed to attend school through the eighth grade. After she reached adulthood and married, her husband contracted tuberculosis and Lillie again became the mainstay of her family. Throughout her life, Don remembers his mother as striving to keep family together and encouraging supportive relationships.

At age 89, Lillie received word from her doctor that a small metastasis had been found on her liver, but he assured her she still had months of quality life left. Lillie decided differently. Within 10 days she was dead. Here is what she did. She began going "downhill," i.e. withdrawing her energy from this world. Don could see in her eyes that "she was somewhere else." On the eve of her departure, she said to Don, "Let's sit down and talk. Are my bills all paid? If not, I want you to pay them." Don wrote out the few remaining checks and she signed them. Then she became even more specific. "Would you go down and put them in the post office box before 9 p.m.?" This evidently would ensure the timely payment or postmark that she wanted.

When he returned from mailing the bills, Don found Lillie in bed. She asked again, "Are you sure all my bills are paid?" Don assured her all was taken care of. She then reminded him of her verbal will and how she wanted her simple estate handled. She lay quietly in her bed as he sat beside her. Suddenly she raised her arms upward and said, "Jesus, Jesus take me now!" Don protested, but his mother turned to him and said curtly, "Now you go to bed!"

The following morning Lillie was only partially present in this world as she waited for her adopted granddaughter to arrive for final goodbyes. When this was done, her to-do list was complete. It was November 18th, her birthday—and also Don's. Her eyes remained transfixed on a small glass hummingbird sparkling in the light that he had given her for her birthday several hours prior. She quietly apologized for dying on his birthday, hoping it wouldn't spoil future celebrations. Shortly thereafter she surrendered her body and stepped over the threshold.

In reflecting on his mother's dying process Don said she asked no questions and had no fear. She focused her intention on getting it done. She decided that she didn't want to die of cancer. She had been self-sufficient all her life, having learned all those mountain skills from her Arkansas childhood, and was self-sufficient in her dying style. Lillie had intermittent church affiliations but was most grounded in the Earth and in her family.

I find it interesting that November 18th held such significance for this family as a planetary entrance and exit. Lillie was tuned in to the timing of things, and very conscious of making this choice under her own steam. It was never in her character to be a victim or cause suffering to others. The diagnosis of cancer was her personal signal for imminent departure. Her train was pulling into the station and she decided it would be very imminent! She kept it calm and simple, aided by Don, who played the support role of *departure midwife*. Lillie didn't have many conscious dying tools, but she had her free will and a sense of personal power gleaned over a long, rich life, which fed her to the end—and even now, blesses our understanding.

We appreciate that Conscious Choice people often walk incognito among us, hidden in the company of our restless human family. They may step on our sacred cows or disturb our safe little worlds, but we feel expanded in their presence. As we catch the updraft of consciousness, we join them and continue the work of quietly raising the awareness of our planet.

From our review of Conscious Choice Styles, we better comprehend that conscious departure is a full-fledged, 24-7, conscious living march to the finish line. It's about every day being filled with opportunity to choose frequencies—to choose self-discipline, healing, stillness and wholesomeness. It's not about some rescue mission from the Messiah, or ETs or the lottery or any other "divine intervention" or escape.

Instead, it's about formulating authentic questions and opening to the answers that make us grow beyond where we were yesterday. It's about being comfortable with our eyes closed and surveying our inner landscape. It's about being so at home with compassion that compassion slips us on through the portal. It's about being free of entrapping belief systems about what must happen after death. That way, we can glimpse the bigger picture of who we are because that helps us to see the bigger picture when heaven opens.

Then, when we actually depart—whether we are nine years old or 99—we consciously depart with skills in place that guide us to our true home. We keep our deeper mind on the process of dying well. We ask loved ones ahead of time to be gentle and peaceful at our bedside, so that we may focus on the conscious continuation of our soul's passage. We hold ourselves tenderly in the arms of all that strength and compassion we have woven from the challenges of our amazing lives. And we birth ourselves with our inner eyes open, on through, step by step into the light. Beautiful—and in style.

# CHAPTER 4

## High Style

*The triumph of the human soul over the human dilemma…*
—anonymous

PAPERS AND NOTES LIE SCATTERED over my desk. These include three *High Style* versions in various states of unreadiness. In front of me are stories of this teacher and that master who have transcended the limitations of body, of matter, of mind, of time. However, I am restless with a feeling of writing a research paper instead of prose. Writing from a soulful place, though more appealing, is elusive. I'd like to feel that Wise Grandmother energy, rocking on the front porch of my mind, smiling to me saying, "Okay, now you are onto something. Now you are going where you need to go with this."

Study of the High Style way has been my teacher over the past several years, so I'd like to offer what I understand so far. High Style takes us further than we thought we could go with our mind-over-matter work. It steps into Now and claims the unavailable miracles from past masters and teachers that are waiting to birth through us. It means that our bodies are becoming light-filled, or as the quantum physicists would say—are vibrating at a higher frequency.

High style means that we are living from a growing sense of unlimited consciousness right here while getting the groceries and writing a check for the mortgage on a cold December evening. High Style takes all we learned in Conscious Choice Style and ratchets it up. It's a feeling of the personal self being swept up in an expanding wave of transpersonal grace. This energy puts us so at ease that we drop in and surrender to a kind of eternal flow. In moments of flow, it feels like nothing was ever wrong or out of balance. Like our higher self says, "Hi! Welcome back. I've been here all along."

Death is a powerful vehicle for experiencing miracles. Death, after all, is the new hot topic. Death is *in* because we now have the motivation of sufficient global consciousness and global pain to want to move the old carcass out of the way. Forget the grim reaper, the vampires and the monsters. Forget the trauma of wars and misinformation. Forget all the ways in which death is paraded through our days as a terror to be avoided at all costs.

Obviously, the death topic is complex. There is no way to wrap it up and tie it with a bow that says, "We have all the answers and this is how it goes." Nor is it completely unknowable, including those miracle death stories that come down through time. Death is, instead, a mystery luring us into greater comprehension. It asks to be known, for in knowing more of death, we know more about who we are. So death asks us to play courageously with the phenomenon that it is. Our conversation is not about finally arriving at all the answers, but about pulling departure out of the Dark Ages and into the clear light of day.

It seems an invitation has been extended to push ourselves on through this baffling death-birth canal, into a new way of perceiving. So it's no accident that some days we feel squeezed and despairing and that we may not survive the stress and get to the other side of whatever this is we are waiting for. It is also no accident that the following day we may feel exuberant. We are in the midst of grand High Style work and it's not without some choppy waters. Clear sailing may still be downwind on the river, but we are paddling in the right direction.

Can you imagine being fearless with your death? Can you imagine, even through the difficulty of goodbyes, welcoming your transition just as fully as you welcome tomorrow's sunrise? Many of us might nod with Woody Allen when he said, "I'm not afraid of dying. I just don't want to be there when it happens." But can we grasp the idea of meeting our death head-on instead? In High Style, a deeper oneness supports us until we realize our death will crown our lives, for we have overcome all fears associated with it.

In the wisdom traditions of India and Tibet, gurus and lamas hone the inner discipline of meditation, eventually controlling body-mind forces. Many miracles occur as bodies become subject to the expanded mind. Heat, cold or hunger has little consequence. Restless, angry minds dissolve into deep peace. Higher states of consciousness become the way of transcending the limitations of 3-D reality and liberating the soul from endless incarnations. The wise ones of *all* traditions espouse the transcendental, timeless state that transforms the lower mind. High Style suggests that not only can death be changed in this process, but that death intertwines itself with our vast, unlimited nature.

In 1992, I attended the International Transpersonal Conference in Prague, in what was then called Czechoslovakia. It was during the time when the Czech and Slovak people were emerging from Soviet rule. We conference attendees arrived from all over the world, joining the Czech citizenry in a collective deep sigh of hope. One of our speakers was American teacher and author Ram Dass. His convocation speech kept the 1,200 or so of us in joyous laughter and grateful tears.

Ram Dass spoke of the changes to come, of the challenges facing our planet and its people. His point was clear: Facing death is a key in releasing our fears of all kinds. Facing death expands us as well as saves us. Facing our death enables us to face all the other things we avoid—and be amazed at the vista before us. Expanding our minds enables us to ride immense waves of change, rather than drown. He offered a way through these overwhelming changes. It exemplifies how the transcendental state of consciousness transforms the fearful lower states. He suggested that we can think of ourselves as having several levels of perception, rather like TV channels or radio stations. These channels are described something like this:

> ***Channel 1: Physical self.*** This is the part that identifies with our physical appearance, our bodies and how we present ourselves. It holds awareness at the basic physical level. By illustration, he jokingly said that this was the handsome, elderly gentleman we saw before us.

> ***Channel 2: Psychosocial self.*** This is the personality self and our intelligence. It's the identity associated with the many roles we play each day, our costume changes, our persona—such as daughter, dad, boss or sports fan. This was his "Ram Dass-ness." These first two channels are what we are all trained to pay attention to. We are trained to ignore all the following channels, which then become background static to us—we hear some of the incoming information some of the time, but mostly we tune it out.

> ***Channel 3: Archetypal or mythical.*** Here we are "The Seeker" or "The Hero" or "The Wise Grandmother" or "The Warrior," etc. This

bigger self has a sense of mission and purpose and rises from the higher astral planes. We can access it through prayerful meditation, dreaming and deep observation.

***Channel 4: Soul.*** Here we realize that we are a soul incarnated into a body with a personality and a mythical identity. We can perceive another person as a soul in personal form and say, "Hi, how are you? How was it getting here to Earth this time? Nice to see you again in new form." We know that this is another being just like us only in different trappings. Here is where we feel that intuitive heart connection. Soul meeting soul.

***Channel 5: Self looking at the Self looking at the Self.*** At this channel, there is only One. When we extricate our identity from channels 1-4, all that is left is "is." Awareness. Being—the active verb of God. You could call it Love. Our true nature is beyond all categories. No time. No space. No form. Yet more real than all the others. We truly are all one.

At Channels 3-5 we experience our greater selves. These are the levels from which miracles arise and we feel limitations fall away. We also begin to realize that there aren't really miracles. From this greater perspective, "miracles" are simply the natural way of things. Channels 1-2, our physical and personality selves, are the identities meant to ground us in this human experience but often they hold us in fearful limitations. Our death and dying fears take up lodging here. We grow karmic debts and linger in guilt-filled sorrows. Furthermore, we can't imagine not having this body. We see our personality as our true self and wonder what will happen when our body falls away. Who will I be then?

Ram Dass's higher channels are the part of our nature that holds no fear of death. Imagine that. We already have this part that exists beyond all pain and death concerns. This higher awareness provides us with alternatives. We can re-do death, similar to what happens with near-death-experiencers who say they no longer fear their death. We can grasp departure from a more transcendent mindset. That's what we want—we want to hear those higher channels. And that's where we are headed.

However we comprehend High Style, it's definitely about many levels of mastery—mastery of matter, of mind, of emotions, of energy, of dimensions, of time. We master the complexities of being a spiritual being while inhabiting a biological body with all the demands of both. We blend an ego that wants to shine, with a soul that feels lonely and demands meaning—until the higher self more gracefully runs the show. Mastery becomes a joyful commitment. Souls of power and service go for the gold, the High Style mastery of mind over matter, living from their higher nature. For some, this includes all manner of unusual occurrences at or around death, invariably turning death on its head.

Various High Style mastery talents may include:
- Manifesting objects from the unmanifest realms, or "out of thin air."
- Bi-location. Consciously being in several places at once—a sort of "Beam me up, Scotty" with internal technology.
- Giving instantaneous healing to others.
- Resurrecting the body after death and returning to visit loved ones— in body.
- Imbuing the body with such high frequencies that after death, the body does not decay.
- Moving into the highest light after death, free from karma. No need to return to Earth. However, some may choose to return to help in uplifting humanity, again and again. This is the path of the bodhisattva in Buddhism, saviors and ascended teachers in other traditions.
- Expressing eternal compassion and wisdom, transcending the first two channels, while living fully in this life.
- Exerting benevolent influence over the forces of nature.
- Ascending at death with a unified physical-soul-spirit body, transcending the physical death process altogether.

## Ascension, Resurrection & the Quantum Human

In case we have any hesitancy about ascension and resurrection because those terms seem inapplicable to us, we might consider the likelihood that they are part of our wiring. So let's give ourselves a break from any perfectionism from Sunday school and catechism class that might be causing us to doubt our options. While we are at it, let's heave out hidden guilt about being merely human and horribly flawed. These just smoke up our vision. Let's open up the shades. I want us to see through our window of consciousness with as much clarity as we can muster.

These concepts are rich and complex. Our discussion is meant to open the doors of various possibilities that are rising for us. We may not know quite where our High Style evolutionary journey is taking us, but it behooves us to check out some options that are showing themselves. At this juncture, we don't have to understand—and probably can't comprehend the full nature of these concepts. But we can get better acquainted.

If what you know about resurrection and ascension comes out of the Christian New Testament or the Hindu Bhagavad Gita or the Jewish Torah or Egyptian mythology, you have a start. But doesn't that seem faraway and unreachable? Old scriptures and stories alert us to something deeper, stir up the soul. But then we have a life to lead and we go back to washing the dishes and walking the dog. Is this important? What do resurrection, ascension and the quantum human have to do with the practicalities of daily living?

## Resurrection

Let's have another look because this classier, High Style wardrobe requires it. *Resurrection* means bringing back to life—like spring after the cold darkness of winter. We can resurrect a project or a marriage or a better attitude. We resurrect ourselves from a dead-to-the-world sleep and come fully back into waking consciousness, wondering where we were while we were "out." Sometimes past-life regression clients go so deeply into hypnotic trance that they struggle to return to this reality. It takes a while to come back to the present life. They are stunned with how much time has passed, two hours seeming like 20 minutes. But they "resurrect" themselves back to this life and let the other one go.

The resurrection we are examining activates this talent of switching realities and is brimming with possibilities. Traditionally, resurrection connotes coming back to life after having died—literally a lifeless form re-enlivened or re-materialized and fully functioning in our world. That feat of mastery packs a wallop. The Egyptian god Osiris (ancient mythology), Jesus (2,000 years ago) and kriya yoga master Sri Yukteswar (1936) are some resurrectees that come to mind.

Metaphorically, resurrection is the raising of the mind and body out of endless traumas and into higher awareness or quantum functioning. This happens at an expanded mind level AND at a cellular level. The molecular structure of the cells are re-enlivened, en-light-ened. There is a quickening in the body and a sense of higher presence. As we increase our resurrection ability, our whole person—body, mind, soul and spirit—aligns with absolute mind and we are lifted up or resurrected into our natural state of union and wholeness. This experience may occur in split-second breakthroughs where we catch glimpses, or last for days or years. It may happen through meditation, a near-death experience or some other event. Some part of our being has resurrected itself from limitation and we are no longer the same.

## Ascension

*Ascension* shares similar qualities to resurrection. Traditionally it refers to the miraculous departure of masters and saints reported to rise upward at life's end, taking their light-filled bodies with them as they melt into the ethers. Stories of Maha Vishnu (Hindu god) and Jesus are examples of this classic ascension style.

Metaphorically, ascension is the process of rising to a higher level of functioning, like climbing up the mountain of consciousness. It is about raising our consciousness and transforming our bodies as we go so they hold greater light. You could call it being enraptured, joy-filled and merged with the Christ self, higher self, beloved self or our true nature.

You might practice ascending by choosing to be in the energy of ascension. As you sit down to dinner, for example, let the energy of your dining room be transcendent, even if you aren't sure exactly what that is. As you gaze at the beautifully prepared food before you, intend that it be filled with the highest gratitude, grace and aliveness, nurturing you on all levels. Take a breath and allow that aliveness to soak into your body, then exhale out as a blessing to the world. Take the higher view, no, better yet, *feel* the higher view. *Feel* bigger. Drop the tension in your shoulders. *Feel* the blessing your higher nature gives the world.

This higher energy feels exquisite, both a part of and in contrast to our daily life. It feels like the joyful self we are and have always been. Over time, that true self may have become invisible. Ascension energy lifts us out of the density and heaviness of 3-D reality. The contrast can be painful—but delight, creativity and rich possibilities wait in the wings. Ascension energy lifts difficult situations so they can be seen as an opportunity to hone our compassion. Humor, love, constriction, sorrow for the world, all become the many flavors of our love affair with ascension.

As higher energies are sorted out in the body, emotions and mental processes, there are readjustments. The challenges of ascension affect us in different ways, including strange aches and pains, moodiness and fatigue. Other symptoms some people experience are high blood pressure, heart palpitations and digestive sensitivity. One person described her experience of higher frequencies as a feeling of vibrating faster than the world around her, leaving her feeling tired and frustrated. Her mind might be striding on ahead but her body seemed to have a hard time keeping up. Plenty of rest, fresh foods, water and exercise on the Earth are of great assistance to us. Stillness is essential.

The ingredients of ascension are exactly what lie on our plate of life. They are ours to take in and transform into the magic that makes us cry, then smile, then soar in quiet mastery. We choose to see what is before us as sacred. Our vast reservoir of pain is the jet fuel for our launch. What sits facing us is part of our mastery. Self-compassion is finding the heart to embrace it all. If we manage to accomplish some of that, haven't we ascended from where we were yesterday?

Succinctly put, ascension is the process of becoming the embodiment of our higher self, our higher consciousness. Resurrection is redirecting consciousness to a higher state or expression—resurging, coming alive again. As this unfolds quietly within us, we transcend more and more of the limitations of 3-D density.

## Quantum Human

If you prefer scientific rather than theological and mythological terms, try this one: *the quantum human*. Ascension and resurrection look like quantum physics in action. Quantum physicists tell us the mind influences the reality it perceives. The observer, by observing, changes and reinterprets reality. Conscious and unconscious beliefs color what we are able to see. In this understanding, we become what we believe we are—for better or worse—because it's the truth we hold about ourselves. Mind *is* over matter—an innate truth. Quantum humans grasp this and use it to expand themselves.

The natural state of the mind is unlimited, spacious and multidimensional. It has many channels. We can interpret the world through limited mind or expand into the vast stillness rising on the breath of higher thought. The teachers that have gone before us don't just believe we are unlimited, quantum beings—they KNOW it from experience.

Our "quantum-ness" happens right in the body. Quantum physicists are observing that we can change our DNA and that compassion, for example, can positively activate DNA. Author Gregg Braden (*Walking Between the Worlds: The Science of Compassion*) says that compassion is what we become, not something that rises occasionally. As we feed the energy of compassion, allowing and forgiveness, our DNA changes. New neural/genetic shifts occur.

Some visionary thinkers are seeing the "junk" DNA and the unused portion of the brain as actually the housing for consciousness. We might think of these minute DNA structures as the places where body and mind meet and greet. This part of our physiology has the capacity to be activated and attuned to higher grids of energy/information.

As we choose to evolve, the human energy field, DNA and nervous system kick into higher gear. We are more psychic, intuitive and aware. We realize that the longing for sensation is our longing for Spirit. These physiological and energetic structures house our High Style gifts waiting to be worn. Consciousness waits to be activated. It's not that we have nothing to go on. We have innate wiring for all this ascension and resurrection activity. We are hard-wired for being quantum humans. It's a process. It takes focus and group effort. In the past, great beings came to the planet and activated consciousness periodically to keep it from snuffing out and to help it flourish. Now we are asked to step into our own greatness together. With the massive consciousness changes occurring, we, the quantum human tribe, are rousing from our slumber and able to imagine ourselves as high-stylers in-the-making.

The following are some examples of High Style traditions, affirming that the quantum human is more than theory.

**High Style Traditions**

## Kriya Yoga

We begin with a fascinating lineage that traces its present beginnings back to 203 AD, though its origins are lost in time. (This account is given by M. Govindan in *Babaji and the 18 Siddha Kriya Yoga Tradition*.) We commence with the birth of the child, Nagaraj, on November 30, 203 AD, in a small village in the state of Tamil Nadu, India. Early on, this child seemed drawn to spiritual pursuits. After many trials and a great longing to know God, the young Nagaraj found a guru who would be his teacher and initiator into the Kriyas or deep spiritual practices that included yoga asanas, meditation, breath work and mantras. After meditating for up to 48 days at a stretch, and with the help of his teacher, Boganathar, Nagaraj's mind broke open and his consciousness was freed from the imprisonment of the rational mind. His personal awareness merged with limitless Reality. Some folks have had this transcendental experience; Nagaraj dived even deeper.

The Kriya lineage sought to perfect the body-spirit union, seeing the body as the sacred vessel of the Divine. While many old traditions took to denigrating the body and even competed in all manner of bodily abuse to prove spiritual superiority, the Kriya yoga folks traveled in the opposite direction—for which we are grateful. They believed the body was designed for Divine penetration and much happier for the experience. They understood the Divine found grounding and joyful expression by descending into form. They taught that, when invited from our deep heart, the higher frequencies move from the spiritual planes into lower states of consciousness: intellectual, mental, vital and physical bodies. In this process, they saw each layer transformed into harmonious expressions of God.

What I find particularly fascinating is the sophisticated grasp the Kriya yoga practitioners had on the struggle between biology and spirit. They came to see that the body's natural tendency to break down cells faster than it replaced them made the enlightenment process a struggle against time itself. How could you attract Divine cell-transforming energies faster than the natural catabolic breakdown of cells inherent in the aging process? Could you stop the aging process by enlightening the body-mind so completely that death was transcended? This is especially challenging when we realize that aging begins taking over the show in our 20s and 30s. How can you jump-start anabolic cell growth so that enlightenment literally supersedes biologic decline? This could allow the soul to live an extremely long life in the same healthy body, and if desired, take the body with it at death. Besides the various meditation practices and initiations, the yogis experimented with supplements such as herbs and mineral salts. All these practices assisted the creation of happier cells to hold all that spiritual light they were imbibing.

Our young Nagaraj dived into these rich, uncompromising spiritual waters, completely surrendering his ego, body, mind and soul to the highest God-transformation possible. Through vigorous practices and unflinching commitment, he eventually transcended all limitations of 3-D reality—including the death process itself. No need for death at all if you have your spiritual technology in high gear and your biological systems in joyful agreement—a major High Style event. Thus, Nagaraj became known as the beloved Mahavatar Babaji, the Deathless Guru.

That was hundreds of years ago. Babaji is still with us. The beautiful gift that Babaji has given humanity is the translation of his body into a lighter frequency, so much so that he comes and goes from 3-D Earth at will—materializing, dematerializing and then materializing his body once again. Throughout the centuries since, Babaji has continued to watch over the spiritual progress of his students and the evolving consciousness of humanity. And no Starship Enterprise technology needed.

Various acclaimed yogis of the Kriya tradition are recorded as having achieved the ability to ascend in their transformed bodies, never experiencing death. The unique gift that Babaji brings to us is that his presence endures. Though born several centuries after the birth of Jesus, he continues to associate himself with Earth. His ashram is in the remote Himalayas, where he works with a few of his students in person. But many others around the world report feeling him near and a few see him manifesting himself in body at different times. The Deathless Guru's commitment to humanity is staggering and filled with effortless, transcendent love.

You may be happy to know that the Kriya yoga lineage is alive and well today. Many have come to know Kriya yoga through the bestselling book, *Autobiography of a Yogi* by author and teacher Paramahansa Yogananda (1893-1952). Because of his tireless efforts, Yogananda's work has touched the hearts of thousands of Westerners, exposing them to the timelessness of Indian philosophies and the Kriya yoga path of inner transformation and mastery.

In his autobiography, Yogananda tells the particularly gripping story of the resurrection of his guru, Sri Yukteswar, that I want to share with you.

About six months after the death of his guru, Yogananda was meditating in his hotel room in Bombay. He described what happened. *"I was roused from my meditation by a beatific light. Before my open and astonished eyes, the whole room was transformed into a strange world, the sunlight transmuted into supernal splendor. Waves of rapture engulfed me as I beheld the flesh and blood form of Sri Yukteswar!"* Yogananda told in great detail the reunion with his beloved teacher, whom he grasped so tightly that Sri Yukteswar requested he relax his grip. They spoke of many things, including the astral planet that was now Sri Yukteswar's home and where he continued to teach. Much information was given to be shared including the dimensions beyond Earth and the nature of resurrecting a body. Yukteswar saw Earth reality as a dream, an illusion. He assured Yogananda that it truly was he who stood before him.

*"Yes my child, I am the same. This is a flesh and blood body. Though I see it as ethereal, to your sight it is physical. From cosmic atoms, I created an entirely new body, exactly like that cosmic dream physical body you laid beneath the dream sands at Puri in your dream-world. I am in truth resurrected—not on earth but on an astral planet. Its inhabitants are better able than earthly humanity to meet my lofty standards. There you and your exalted loved ones shall come someday to be with me."*

Yogananda and Sri Yukteswar spoke for some time regarding the dimensions and realities beyond our planet and the journey of the soul into these realms. As their startling visit was nearing conclusion, Sri Yukteswar added more insight for our particular discussion. Yogananda was pondering the miracle of his guru's body returned. *"Angelic guru,"* I said, *"your body looks exactly like it did when I last wept over it in the Puri ashram."*

*"Oh yes, my body is a perfect copy of the old one. I materialize or dematerialize this form anytime at will, much more frequently than I did while on earth. By quick dematerialization, I now travel instantly by light express from planet to planet, or indeed from astral to causal to physical cosmos."* My divine guru smiled. *"Though you move about so fast these days, I had no trouble finding you in Bombay!"*(p. 398-415, *Autobiography of a Yogi*, Crystal Clarity Publishers)

The recent history of this documented resurrection event makes it poignant and provocative for us. It does not come from misty centuries past but from within our own past 100 years, making it worthy of our consideration.

After Yogananda's death in Los Angeles, California, on March 7, 1952, the Los Angeles Mortuary director who handled his body issued an amazing report. He stated that the body of Paramahansa Yogananda was as fresh on March 27th as it was on the day he died, 21 days earlier. It was unlike anything he had witnessed before. The events around Sri Yukteswar and Yogananda's High Style departures add undeniable proof to the possibilities that lay before us. The Kriya yoga lineage shows us the exceptional potential for our own journeys of living and dying consciously.

## Tibetan Buddhism

In the remote lands of Tibet, Buddhism arrived from India in the eighth century AD, coming to flourish and deepen in a way unique to other branches of Buddhism. Here in the high and isolated Himalayans, a world of practical spiritual research evolved and flourished. The methods of this research were tools for plumbing the laboratory of the mind—including meditation, reason, Buddhist teachings, debate, yoga and tracking consciousness—with and without a body. The Tibetans developed a particularly detailed understanding of the different layers of awareness. They were/are sticklers for specifics. For example, they have assigned eight stages to death. Each stage has specific characteristics which provide information and guidelines when passing through the *bardo* or afterlife.

Much energy is spent on what occurs after consciousness leaves the body because being conscious at this point is believed to engender an auspicious return. From the Tibetan Buddhist point of view, what benefit is your life to others if you keep choosing chaotic, unconscious lifetimes? By getting up to speed and knowing the post-body road map, you become a contributing human when you return rather than a headache for others.

Buddhism holds the whole of life with great compassion. In Buddhism there is nothing that does not deserve its fair share of compassionate consideration. (Remember our earlier discussion of compassion being an activator for DNA and consciousness?) Every experience benefits from a dose of compassion. All things can serve in gaining wisdom. The Buddhist approach seeks to anchor compassion into the physical world, and extend it into every aspect of the journey. This greatly assists in embracing the conundrums of life and releasing attachment. Buddhism is happy to lend itself to whatever philosophical bent you prefer. It suggests a more conscious, disciplined and spacious nature benefits everyone.

Because of difficulties between the Chinese government and the Tibetan people, great changes have occurred with the traditional Tibetan way of life. These difficulties forced many Tibetan Buddhist teachers to flee Tibet and find their way to India and the West. We are the wealthier for our exposure over the last half-century to this tradition born from solitude, discipline, real grief and the long view. The Dalai Lama, Tibetan spiritual leader in exile, has touched the heart of the world. He, along with many others of this tradition, is bringing the Tibetan Buddhist understanding of life and death to our attention. Let's briefly discuss some of the Tibetan Buddhist teachings that point to the High Style consciousness we are exploring.

*Impermanence.* To really settle into the living-dying truth of things is to realize that nothing in this world lasts. When we come to see that so much of our suffering is about regretting something that is over, worrying about something to come, or fearful of what is passing, we see the immense value in accepting impermanence. We see that we are resisting the basic reality of Earth life; everything changes and nothing is permanent except that really spacious place that opens when we surrender.

Tibetan Buddhists say that the true nature of the mind is pure and open, spacious and joyful. To experience this is to experience the liberated state, free from *samsara,* or suffering. Then we can achieve some semblance of true sanity, for we are not fighting with the structure of the phenomenal world. Seasons change, people change, joy changes to sorrow and sorrow changes back to joy. Happiness comes and then it goes. To Tibetan Buddhists, compassion is the gift that helps us to cease grasping and to embrace impermanence as reality. We watch the clouds of life float by rather than trying to stop them or push them away. We enjoy clouds without needing them to be anything other than what they are. When life is viewed as an illusory and fleeting journey, so is death. The quest becomes that which is our true nature.

Nonetheless, grief is real in the time of grief. Heartache is real in the time of heartache. The crucible of death burns away nonessential elements. Compassion for our suffering deepens us. Even grief shows itself as impermanent when our sorrow eventually transforms into wisdom.

**The Bardo.** Knowing the bardo realms and how to journey through them is considered essential. The bardos are the levels and stages of the afterlife realms described in great detail in the teachings. Bardo experiences have been portrayed by the *delogs,* those who have died and returned to tell their stories after days spent traveling in the afterlife. In Tibetan Buddhism, death becomes the most important aspect of life. Why? In this tradition, the training goes something like this:

- A devout life is imperative and positively influences your death experience.
- Devout living then, is about being able to die well.
- Dying well is about being able to stay awake and focus in the afterlife realms.
- Being awake in the afterlife realms is about being able to choose an auspicious rebirth.
- An auspicious rebirth enables you to deepen your spiritual practice and be a compassionate influence in the world.
- A compassionate influence lifts up many souls, which releases you and others from the wheel of unending suffering.
- Liberation from unending suffering comes as enlightened souls reach the higher realms of light.

At the end of his life, Plato was asked to summarize his life's learning and writing. He said simply, "Practice dying." He would have made a good Tibetan Buddhist. Navigating the dying and after-death journey with the highest and clearest consciousness gives us options we don't have access to otherwise. The road into the heavenly states is learned and earned.

***Assistance.*** The Tibetans have exacting guidance for the dying. Compassion abounds as bedside assistants pray, chant and quietly exhort the dying one to arrive in the Pure Lands of the Buddha of Infinite Light. Scripts are available for guiding the departing soul. These include a simplified version for the neophyte assistant as well as more thorough scripts for the adept meditator and initiate. Assistance assumes that the departing person has familiarity with Buddhism and understands the terms and concepts. If you want to utilize the specifics of this tradition, you would want to have all parties involved be somewhat familiar with the teachings.

***Mind creations.*** Tibetan Buddhism often sounds like ancient quantum physics given its take on the power and influence of the mind. For example, the experience in the bardo (transition into the afterlife) is said to be of our own creation. It arrives out of what we have built over the span of our life, our predominant attitudes, underlying feelings, and the positive or negative nature of our actions in the world. A negative, hellish life would draw us to one of the three lower realms: hungry ghost realm, animal realm or one of several pretty impressive hell realms. Of greater preference are the realms of demigods, gods and human. Of highest preference is rebirth into the Blissful Pure Land.

Consciousness creates. It is the nature of having a mind. We create our lives and we create our deaths. The Tibetan delogs, or near-death experiencers, sought to remember that the fearful things they saw were reflections of their own consciousness. Difficult reflections needed to be faced, penance paid, and perhaps embraced as gifts.

The nature of having a mind is that we get to become conscious users of this gift. The Buddhist system is set up to plumb the depths of the mind, and to liberate consciousness from ignorance and suffering, both in life and death.

# Christianity

Prior to the sixth century AD, early Christians were a rebellious, mystical, disorganized lot. They had access to the early writings of devotees and disciples as well as oral traditions on the teachings of the enlightened Master Yeshua, or Jesus as we have come to know him. Many of these groups ascribed to the innate love of God within all beings and the teachings of reincarnation. They embraced inclusivity and love, understood the necessity of inner stillness, and practiced enlightened community living. They embraced a direct channel to God and practiced drawing that energy into their bodies. Sometimes they met in secret, depending on the nature of their ascribed threat to those in power.

We have records of various early groups, including the Essenes and the Gnostics. The Dead Sea Scrolls, the Gnostic Gospels and the Gospel of Thomas provide a wealth of mystical teachings that offer a fuller picture of the enlightenment process espoused by Jesus. Why are these historical footnotes important to our discussion? These materials show early Christians had an understanding of the deep inner life necessary for transformation. Theirs was more of an evolving system of thought than the strict interpretations of many present teachings. There was a sense of masters and teachers gently walking the earth, teaching and healing in the shadow of mystical earlier traditions.

The title of "Christ" means perfected one or divine perfection. It is a title like "King" or "Queen." When added to a person's name we have the human identity associated with perfect, divine expression, thus, Jesus Christ. We all have this Christ self, the perfect spirit that we are becoming. In expanding our consciousness, our Light, we step more fully into our own expression of divinity. In its essence, Christian teachings resemble the other wisdom traditions we've discussed. Ascension or resurrection or enlightenment is not out there or far away but right here in our bodies and our quantum minds. This energy is as intimate as the breath, as powerful as an earthquake, as tender as the heart.

The Christianity that came after the sixth century took form as the institutionalized church, which, in effect, often separated the people from direct experience of the divine. Believers were expected to go through the priest or the church fathers with little access to books and writings. Claiming your own Christ self would have been seen as heresy and worthy of death. Those who continued to delve into the mysteries and bypass the control of the church, such as the Cathars and Earth-based spiritual traditions, were severely punished.

Standard teachings, as presented today, leave many I've spoken with feeling undernourished. What we can remember is that at the core of the wisdom traditions, there is coherence and wonder. Whereas Buddha brought the powerful wisdom path, Yeshua brought to us the personal divine, devotional love and a major uplift of human consciousness during a very bleak era. That uplift and deep compassion is awakening again in the hearts of humanity. Awakening our compassion may or may not be identified with Yeshua or Buddha, or Babaji, etc., but it is the unifying factor in these High Style traditions.

As the centuries passed within Christendom, mystics rose on the wings of their devotion, though not without suffering—sometimes caused by the church itself. St. John of the Cross (1542-1591, Spain), St. Teresa of Avila (1515-1582, Spain) and Padre Pio or St. Pio (1887-1968, Italy) are some who found the High Style way of the soul. Through the darkness of the Piscean Age, enlightenment often came at a price. Nonetheless, through great devotion and prayer they've shown us the path of ecstasy, healing, bi-location and miracles. The great light that the body can hold even years after death is given in the account of Padre Pio's body exhumed in 2008 with little deterioration. With these examples, we discover the breakthroughs into higher channels these souls and others like them brought to the human experience under the banner of Christianity.

## Ascended Masters

Ascended masters are those souls who have achieved mastery of this dimension and are free of the birth and death cycle. They have finished with their rounds in Earth life. The ones we come to know are those who have made it their mission to assist us when we are ready to accelerate our growth in consciousness. They are highly involved in all levels of planetary concern, assisting in stabilizing, guiding and quietly intervening as it serves the greater good. They readily and exactly utilize inter-dimensional travel, materialization of objects, high creativity and inspiration, and teachings on mastery of heart, mind and body.

Ascended masters are in the proverbial esoteric news, especially in the past several decades. Nineteenth and 20th century writers such as Madame H.P. Blavatsky and Alice Bailey opened the minds of many as they reintroduced ascended masters and their roles in assisting humanity. The Theosophical Society published theirs and other metaphysical books of depth, bringing a sense of fresh air into the somewhat stale world of mid-1900s western religion.

I first visited the Theosophical Society campus and Quest Bookstore in Wheaton, Illinois, in the early 1980s. I remember the calming music and the intriguing books on topics I'd only dreamed about. Here I learned about the worlds beyond this one and the variety of higher teachers available to assist us on our journey as souls. I wanted to know more about them and how it all worked. I learned about guides and masters, angels and devas. I went to workshops on healing and listened to folks who talked with and saw these beings regularly. Very shortly after, I was incorporating this knowledge into my growing spiritual lexicon.

Then I met a teacher, Caray Uri, who became my guide into these worlds, sometimes known as the Great White Brotherhood (so-named for the white light seen around them), the Brotherhoods of Light and the Spiritual Hierarchy. I studied the Rays of Light and came to appreciate more fully each soul as a unique expression of Divine Source. The vast efforts of the multidimensional worlds on behalf of our struggling planet stunned and inspired me. I better grasped the magnificent vision that various Creator Spirits hold for our Earth.

More recently I studied the writings on the ascended master St. Germain, reading and re-reading Godfre Ray King's *Unveiled Mysteries* and *The Magic Presence*. In these stories, St. Germain ushers the reader into the remarkable world of the ascended masters. His particular focus is on America and he holds a radiant view of what a land of true freedom and enlightenment can be.

St. Germain's teachings include the transcendence/ascension process as every human's destiny. He says that our physical embodiment is for the purpose of preparing, perfecting and illuminating a body so that it can merge with the higher self—or as he calls it—the "Mighty I AM Presence." When fully embodied, the I AM Presence becomes the body of light or the seamless garment that Jesus spoke of on occasion.

In the traditions we have reviewed so far, we can easily include Sri Yukteswar, Jesus, Babaji the deathless guru, and a number of Tibetans in our collection of ascended masters. Other names associated with this august list are Lord Kuthumi, Djwhal Khul, Lady Nada, Mother Mary, Sanat Kumara, Serapis Bey, Maitreya and Quan Yin. The ascended masters rise from every continent, every religious tradition and every age. They richly embody the Ageless Wisdom and Infinite Light.

High Style is a reminder. And an option. We are reminded of where we are headed and what we can be. This is actually not fantastical. It's about complexities of energies and levels of mastery. High Style is bodily quantum physics under the auspices of compassion and higher mind. It includes miracles and synchronicities that become the norm because we've clicked on to those higher channels. Comprehension of High Style does not rise from the day-to-day mind that doubts and dismisses these options. Instead, it arises from within the evolutionary processes of the body and the intention of the soul.

# PART II

# *Why Bother?*

# PART II

# *Why Bother?*

## *Introduction*

HERE ARE THREE EXAMPLES of why we want to become educated about departure:

**1. Loretta.**

Several years ago, I met Loretta. I will not forget her. The hospice director of the county where I lived asked me to work with a patient who had completely withdrawn. She was exhibiting all the symptoms of depression and unresolved pain. She refused to talk with her husband or children, choosing instead to lie on her bed facing away from life, while attempting to avoid death. Loretta was a challenge and an important teacher. I came to understand she had lived a standard "good life," very much following the social, religious and gender expectations of her generation. She had guarded her feelings and seldom caused waves or drew attention to herself. Having lived a life of external validation, the concept of an inner life was strange to Loretta. So even though she was traveling more deeply within herself, she had few tools with which to travel, much less to speak openly about what she felt and needed.

For the few weeks we had together, I sat quietly with Loretta. During a more courageous moment—and after some encouragement—Loretta whispered that she feared her death would be shameful and undignified and that God would disapprove of her. Here I witnessed the self-doubt and unworthiness this lovely soul had taken on as part of her identity. She revealed the restrictions she had woven in her mind and the unnamed fears she tried to hide. She showed me the way religious dogma can orphan the soul. The despair caused by unsettled life issues became more apparent. Though we may sometimes wonder if our lives will warrant approval on the other side,

57

Loretta's experience mirrored the greater difficulty of unconscious living, and its contribution to her insecurity as she faced departure.

### 2. Stella.

One of my first past-life regression (PLR) clients introduced me to the troubles associated with a difficult passage. A PLR session typically follows the past-life character through their life and then into the afterlife for life review and further learning. They often describe their departure experience as feeling relieved, lighter and aware of great love. However, this particular client, Stella, found herself stuck in a very unpleasant reality for a time.

"Wait a moment…" I said to her. She had already found her way through the unpleasant murky place that she called "purgatory." She was grateful to have landed in a heavenly realm of some sort. "Please go back. Turn and look at the murky place you have just been through." I wanted to examine this place and hoped she would be receptive. Stella gave a brief synopsis of the purgatory experience and then returned to describing her place in the heavens filled with groups of souls and an indescribable love, "a multilayered, beautiful heaven."

Stella explained that this stuck place seemed like a brown, murky area surrounding the Earth. It was filled with souls in confusion. Some felt tortured and were crying out for help. All were having trouble finding light or love and moving on. She saw hands reaching to assist those who suffered, "angels" she called them. The angels offered support and encouragement, but the souls were often so distraught that they missed seeing the very comfort for which they were crying. She noticed that the prayers of loved ones still on Earth were helpful to those who had passed on. These prayers enabled some to turn and see the angels ready to assist them.

The reason that Stella experienced such a difficult passage was because in that past life she had been angry, despairing and demoralized at the time of her death. Her consciousness was not evolved enough, light enough to easily transition. That was 4,000 years ago. Since then, she has had many lives in which to gather the consciousness level for a higher style of departure.

That session ignited my own flame. It resonated. It held truth. I felt I needed to learn more, and share what I was learning about becoming conscious in our dying—and living. I wanted to be more astute in assisting and educating others. It was apparent that fear and misunderstanding foster the "purgatory" layers, which contribute to the congestion of the Earth.

## 3.   One out of 10.

Loretta and Stella's stories are representative of many and portray why it is important to bother ourselves with living and dying well. Shamanic teacher and author Alberto Villoldo, Ph.D., adds further perspective. He estimates that one out of 10 people have a difficult passage, a challenge finding their way to the other side. That's 10 out of a 100, 100 out of a 1,000, 1,000 out of 10,000—you get the picture.

In this section, we are going to explore in more depth the whys and wherefores of this adventure. We might blast through some old beliefs while we are at it. We are going to give ourselves permission to address it all: the questions, the fears, the ambivalence, the triumphs in living and dying. We will pause for an overview of dimensions and realities.

Then for good measure, we will explore what can happen when we get lost on the other side, all the while learning more about how consciousness, or the way we think and feel, affects our experience.

# CHAPTER 5

# *Whys and Wherefores*

*And did you get what you wanted from this life, even so?*
*I did.*
*And what did you want?*
*To call myself beloved, to feel myself beloved on Earth.*
—"Late Fragment" by Raymond Carver

THIS AMAZING SOUL ADVENTURE, with departure as the outcome, begs us to question and probe. Guidelines make themselves known through investigation and experience. Let's grapple with some of the questions that tend to rise in this search.

## 1.  Why must we talk about this? I mean really—why bother?

I believe that talking about death is part of setting ourselves free. Have you ever finally talked with someone about something that bothered you or you had kept secret? And then felt so much relief afterward? We are doing that with dying. And it's feeling better and better. There is more openness about this primary mystery. And since we are all going on this journey, why not get educated and prepare? We can chat with folks in our neighborhood of life about the journey, like we would if we were traveling to Italy. Others are interested. "Ah, so you are going to Italy this summer? Are you looking forward to it? Are you practicing your Italian? Will you go on a guided tour or on your own? We will miss you but have a grand time. We will keep an eye on things while you are gone."

In our neighborhood of life, some people *are* interested in the afterlife, and how to get there with class. There might even be someone down the block who gets what's percolating on your adventure radar. "Ah so you are learning about departure? How's it going? Are you practicing your conscious dying skills? Sounds like you plan to go out in style. Tell us what you know so far."

I imagine that you don't want to get to the end of your life only to realize you never asked the really intriguing questions. So you might want to give yourself permission to ask, and to be delighted as you find out more than you knew before.

**2. I know about preparing for a journey, but preparing for the "death journey" still seems so unnatural.**

I understand. In our culture that's how we are programmed to think. But the basic naturalness of death wants remembering. Death and life are integral partners on this planet. I don't have to tell you that without death, life could not continue as we know it.

So everybody's got to move over. That's how it's set up. You've got to take your turn, then go. We are all part of the death-regeneration-rebirth cycle. In the old paradigm, life and death were separate; death stopped life, death was life's enemy. In the new paradigm, life and death are part of the same continuum called consciousness. And consciousness continues on after the body dies. So it's all very natural. Actually this discussion is not only natural, it's empowering.

**3. Avoidance suits me right now. Can't I focus on other things for a while?**

Certainly. You can have a good life. But might you be missing out on a fascinating conversation? It's a dialogue everyone is having in his or her own head, in some fashion or other. And what about the children in your life? Are you prepared to help them understand? Even five-year-olds pose amazing questions regarding death—how it works and why. "Where did Kitty go? Will I see her in heaven? Is she with Grandpa, then?"

There's no denying that talking about departure brings up some basic philosophical questions. If I'm just going to die, what is the point of being here? It forces the issue. It forces the quest for meaning. It helps break through the narcissistic morass of ego identification. You don't take much of that ego to the other side, so what do you take? Why not focus on that? This search invites us into what's real.

Let's approach death like we have done with conscious birthing. To bring babies into our world we are learning to be aware and kind, providing a more welcoming entry onto planet Earth. Conscious birthing has involved becoming educated, gathering tools, and making lifestyle changes to enhance everyone's well-being. It may involve water birth, quiet music, low lights, regularly talking to the baby in the womb, and other ways of recognizing that a beautiful soul is entering our midst from the refined realms beyond this one. We mitigate the shock of entry. We pay attention.

Let's approach planetary departure in a similar way. Let's train and gather tools that are hidden inside us. Let's have a change of attitude. Let's approach death as part of the Mystery we live in every moment, here, now. Let's also mitigate the potential for shock. Let's pay attention.

So I know you might prefer denial but I have a question for you: What if you are suddenly taken from us tonight to start your death adventure? Are you okay with that? Might one of these ideas be just the right tool that assists you across that bridge and beyond?

4.  **Perhaps the other side is worth contemplating. I'm willing to consider that I probably need tools, but the actual dying—why do we have to die like we do, often so unpleasant or even gruesome?**

I'm with you. Death is often unpleasant and difficult. To see life force seeping from a body or witness the degenerative process goes against our own sense of aliveness. It can be traumatic to the living and can look and smell bad. We sometimes treat death as if it's catching—a "disease" that may spread to our day-to-day reality.

It's also really harrowing to experience someone dying suddenly. They were alive and vibrant, then it happened and they are gone. Everyone is in shock, speechless or sobbing. There is nowhere to put the experience. Emotions run rampant, hearts are wrenched. Sometimes, in their despair, the living wonder if they shouldn't just join the dead. Whether the death was lingering or sudden, it's often indescribably difficult for the living to find a new resolve.

There is a certain truth in the dread we feel around the dying process, especially if medical interventions create more fear and depersonalization. It's often not pretty or elegant. It may seem like one big disappointing lie. We aren't sure if death—or life—is a lie.

In some older cultures than ours, Tibetan and Hindu, for example, it's considered important to wander among the bones of the dead until fears subside and the seeker grasps the truth: The body is temporal; focus therefore on that which is eternal.

I postulate that we have some kind of racial/soul/primal memory about departing the body in grace. There is that in us that wants to reclaim a lost inheritance here. There is a sense of a memory or skill or spiritual ability available to us for dropping the body in a timely manner with little or no suffering. Even little or no decay. We sense that we house a kind of secret inner technology for ascending with or without the body as we know it.

As we learned in Chapter 4, certain highly evolved teachers have continued to use death as miracle and grace, reminding us that we can transmute the old death stereotype and fly free. It's appropriate that we seek access to the other side, the eternal, right now, while on this side. It's appropriate that we rediscover this inner technology, even though we aren't sure how.

If enough of us are determined, we can break the bonds of the old ways of suffering with dying. We can also invoke miracles and grace. I believe this is quietly occurring around and within us.

## 5. What do you mean if enough of us are determined we can change the way we suffer and die?

It's the yeast in the bread or the hundredth monkey principle. Perhaps you've heard that story about monkeys living on the Japanese island of Koshima who had yams to eat. Some began washing the dirt off their yams, rather than eating them as is. Sometime later, a few more tried it. This process went on from 1952-58. Then in the autumn of 1958 almost all the monkeys on the island were observed wholeheartedly washing their yams. Amazingly, at the same time, the idea spread across the waters, and monkeys on adjacent islands all began washing their yams. It seemed the idea just suddenly caught on.

The hundredth monkey principle means that when a small, but significant number of people, let's say 99 folks, open to a new idea, and then the 100th one climbs on board, the whole larger related group, of hundreds or thousands, can suddenly get it. A very small amount of yeast can cause a large batch of bread dough to rise. We could call it exponential growth in consciousness. So even if you simply take a small step toward getting better educated, you are helping the whole family of humanity. You become the yeast.

# 6. So are there stages to departure, just like there are stages to birth?

Yes. This is a lengthy answer. For the sake of more clarity and a workable road map, we are simplifying a process that has many variations. Let's gather understanding from several camps. Our Tibetan Buddhist brethren are exceptionally insightful on this one, as are the ancient rishis or sages of India, so we will build on their centuries of wisdom and experience, adding our knowledge from past-life regression and near-death-experience work.

This generalized review offers what I hope will provide you with a sense of the process. Keep in mind that within each phase is the option of either restricted or expanded awareness. Depending on the circumstances, each person will also have his or her own speed; some drifting through the stages with a focused quietude, some catapulting rapidly onward, barely aware of the different phases. Consciously or unconsciously, we are the directors of our own experiences.

a) Our soul or life force begins releasing from the body or *physical layer*. This may be accompanied by sensations, sounds and colors. For some, the sound becomes a buzzing, ringing or roaring noise. It may seem unsettling or fascinating. Some hear bells or angelic choirs. The life force or vital energy gathers itself into the spinal column and proceeds to leave the body, sometimes via the heart area, sometimes the third-eye center on the forehead or sometimes out the top of the head, the crown center. The more conscious you can be of this, the better. Aim for the crown center.

b) Sensory awareness shifts. You might hear voices on both sides of the veil, for example. Life force releases from the denser *emotional layers* of the energy field. You are pretty much done with the physical body but not the energy bodies that you also inhabit and that are woven around the physical form. Various emotions may rise in this phase: fear, elation, apprehension, uncertainty, relief. Images related to the emotions are noticeable. Unfinished emotional issues will influence our experience. For example, anger and fear may trigger angry, fearful visages. A calm, peaceful spirit can evoke a lovely vista or a deepening sense of Presence and Love.

I find myself appreciating the words of the 23rd Psalm, "Yea, though I walk through the valley of the shadow of death, I will fear no evil for thou art with me. Thy rod and thy staff, they comfort me." The psalmist calls forth higher protection during the time of transition, seeking divine guidance rather than succumbing to "evil"—either his lower emotional nature or the lower negative realms. His "valley of death" is like the valley, tunnel, tube, cave or corridor often experienced at departure.

At times during b, c or d, we may find ourselves floating over the land or visiting family members.

c) Life force releases from lower *mental layers* of the energy field. Here the departing soul begins to remember its bigger nature, realizing the constrictions of the human identity it had taken on. If the soul is aware, it can simply melt more fully into this bigger mind with which it is already familiar. This is entering the true nature of the mind—clear and spacious.

d) Our soul completely releases itself from the body and the lower layers. This can take minutes, hours—or days if given the option. Tibetan Buddhists recommend the body lie undisturbed for several days and that this release from 3-D be thoroughly completed before removal. In the cool climes of Tibet, this works quite well. For other warmer climates and other cultural traditions, this may not be acceptable. However, the idea to grant the dying person additional undisturbed time can be honored.

The soul rises completely out of the body in a process often described as floating. There is also a sense of expanded identity and lightness. We may see light or lights that are compelling or familiar.

e) Our soul consciousness drifts away from the Earth and focuses on becoming oriented to its new surroundings. We are alternately uncertain, curious and in wonder. We may feel as if we are arriving or approaching something in the distance. Often familiar souls come to welcome the new arrival. Many things influence our experience: our beliefs and expectations of the afterlife, our stockpile of love and service while on Earth, our karma, the content of our emotional world, and any guilt, addictions and vows still in place. Here is where we notice the relationship between how we've framed our lives and what kind of heaven is reflected back to us.

Sometimes PLR clients arrive in the afterlife, finding it quite familiar, "I've been here before!" Their orientation then takes place quickly. Sometimes they find themselves in a familiar room or land, yet realize that it is not quite the same as on Earth. They expend some energy making sense of their surroundings. Other times, due to sudden death, they are in shock and their orientation takes a while.

f) Once oriented, we receive counsel and evaluate our life. The evaluation time may include:

- Sitting with our soul group to discuss our recent experiences on Earth.
- Being shepherded by one or two higher guides who have been overseeing our progress.
- Going to a high Council of Elders for loving counsel, infinite wisdom and indescribable compassion.

Clients describe many settings for these occasions, from pastoral scenes, to looking out into the cosmos from a star-like vantage point, to a replica of their home village only brighter. Their Council of Elders can be waiting for them within shimmering marble chambers in another dimension of the heavens.

The Tibetan system is very specific here, coaching the departing soul on how to wrangle with the Lords of Karma, how to avoid the hell realms and advance to the heaven realms. In this system, you are proactive. You work and negotiate your landing into the most auspicious place of consciousness for your highest good. It's worth taking note. How might we argue before the courts of heaven on our own behalf?

g) Exceptions to the above. So far we have given the preferred afterlife route. There are other routes. For example, someone who has lead an excessively chaotic life, or a series of chaotic lives will, in the afterlife, still have little awareness of the more orderly nature of growth and planning options, much less the reincarnation process. Such a soul may be caught in entrenched chaotic behaviors, or be a soul rather new to the journey. Just getting experience on how to be human is important for new souls. What we find with either of these folks is little, if any time has been spent in the afterlife evaluating, learning and setting goals for mastery when they return to Earth. Instead they may choose to move quickly into another life, where they may continue on as before, chaotic and unaware.

### Joe's Story

Joe, one of my early PLR clients, found himself, after a medieval European life, floating briefly in a quiet pastel sky. Then he saw a pregnant woman below and dived back to Earth. Despite my best efforts at slowing him down to evaluate the life just lived, he was off and running. His evolutionary path evidently required rapid build-up of experience with infrequent down time.

I had to surrender and trust that a higher guidance was propelling him on his journey.

In his present life, Joe is thoughtful and measured, learning to monitor his impulsiveness and grow his mindfulness. He has come a long way in the growth he is bringing to his soul. I know his next afterlife experience will reflect this maturity and he will take advantage of evaluation and planning opportunities.

Our concern here is the lack of awareness that clutters up the ethers of our world when souls don't evaluate and plan. Avoidance isn't just a psychological issue on Earth. A propensity for avoidance may remain in someone's energetic matrix when they cross over, continuing to clutter the lower levels of the afterlife. The patterns then return with them into another incarnation. We can have souls that are hooked in addictive behaviors, for example, jumping back in where they left off. We can have old karmic patterns continuing, simply because the soul didn't take the preferred route. They didn't make the most of the afterlife opportunities to really get a handle on a plan.

*Reminder: Each of our journeys is rich with many layers of service and learning that occur in ways the human mind does not comprehend. So we release judgment of another for their apparent shortfalls. We do not know what vast learning is unfolding or what service is being provided under the guise of "handicaps" and "mistakes."*

h) Learning opportunities flourish on the other side, just like they do here. It's all about learning. A few tradionalists might have a yen to play a harp or sit on God's lap for eternity. If that's you, you may be granted some version of your wish if it's important to your journey. But opportunities abound to refocus, hone your talents and set up a plan to master your impulses for your next incarnation. You are encouraged to see yourself clearly. No hiding. You likely will be reminded that you are deeply loved no matter what, but you are responsible to make amends and use your gifts wisely.

Once the councils have heard your story and given you their wisdom, you can choose where you want to go for joyful afterlife development. There are many options for your advancement. You might want to have more scientific or musical understanding. You might be drawn to the healing arts or other halls or temples of learning. You might want to explore universal truths—whatever aids your growth and contribution. Most likely you will be planning to return to Earth, bringing greater resolve and more gifts of service.

Some of you, however, will not return. You will be done with your "tour of duty" on Mother Earth. You may even be graduating from the physical universe, incarnating on astral planets or even going to the causal planes, which are more rarefied dimensions. Some of you could call it quits, but will choose to continue your service, returning to Earth to aid in the uplifting of our human family and the rebuilding of our planet. Some of you will choose to return to your home base, whatever that may be for you. You may notice how things have developed while you've been away. A few of you will be ready to go home to Divine Source, knowing all your longings are fulfilled, your service complete, and that Joy and Light are your eternal identity.

7.  **There seems to be confusion about heaven. Many groups claim theirs is the true way. It becomes so muddled. Is there a better explanation for the many interpretations of "heaven" and "hell"?**

We have some honored pioneers who have pushed through heavenly barriers and paved the way to help us understand. Swedish scientist and mystic Emmanuel Swedenborg (1688-1772) brilliantly solved scientific and engineering problems of his day. In the second half of his life, he became fascinated with the problems and questions of the inner world and the afterlife. He penned eloquent volumes on his travels to the dimensions of heaven and his understanding of hell. He spoke with those he called angels and provided a diagram of the structure and variety of otherworldly spheres. Swedenborg affirmed, in his volume titled *Heaven and Hell*, that "Our nature (and experience) after death depends on the kind of life we lead in the world."

Another pioneer is American out-of-body (OBE) researcher Robert Monroe (1915-1995), whose work and methods continue to inform thousands. Monroe began experiencing OBEs in the late 1950s, made more troubling by the lack of someone knowledgeable with whom he could converse. He courageously began documenting his experiences over the years, eventually publishing his first book, *Journeys Out of Body* in 1971. As Monroe gained skill in out-of-body travel, he performed many experiments, and visited many astral "heavens" which he named and categorized. His students have gone on to further the work, including author Bruce Moen, who has written of his compelling experiences in *Exploring the Afterlife*, a four-volume series.

As mentioned earlier, we are also blessed in our understanding by the growing body of work with near-death experiencers and past-life regression subjects. A PLR researcher who has contributed so much to our understanding of the afterlife experience is Michael Newton, Ph.D., who documented thousands of cases and shared his findings through his books *Journey of Souls* and *Destiny of Souls*. Another pioneer in consciousness is hypnotist and author Dolores Cannon. Her series, *Convoluted Universe,* blows a hole in the ozone layers of the mind as she chronicles the vast wealth of information rising from the human subconscious. Studying with each of these innovators has markedly influenced my own work and further whetted my appetite for exploring the worlds within and beyond this one.

From all this work, we can safely say that many "heavens" exist. Many heavens have been created over the eons by human predilections in any given direction. From Monroe's work we learn that if you are Roman Catholic, for example, then you have likely been trained to think in terms of a certain type of heaven available to you. If your beliefs are firm in this regard, a heaven similar to the one you believe in may be yours for a time—a "Roman Catholic heaven," if you will. If your focus has been on sensual pleasure addiction you will be drawn to a 'heaven" which you share with others who are lost in the same addiction. Others who don't have much in mind but "a better place" might end up in the white picket fence type of heaven. And so it goes.

The stages of death listed above are suggestive of the general process within which we each have our own unique experience. It is a process influenced by the type of death we have opted for, our karmic and religious influence, and the level of love and service rendered. All of this creates our heaven. So if we aren't too concerned with meeting Jesus or Muhammad, or the harps, the trumpets and the crowns, we will likely be met by some loved ones and find our way to our soul group. This experience closely follows Newton's work and is often a wonderful homecoming complete with loving support and good humor. At some point we will likely be met by our more advanced guides who shepherd our earthly sojourns and know us well, as we mentioned in the previous answer.

However, if your strongly held view of heaven does not include your guide and your soul group, you will be less likely to recognize them and instead find yourself waiting for your *real* heaven to manifest. Can you understand a bit better how confusion rises? So many interpretations of "heaven" are created from this assortment of human beliefs.

### Letha's Story

Several years ago my friend Christine Peters emailed me. Christine is a gifted intuitive who can easily travel the dimensions psychically. In her email she wrote, "Marcia, a soul came to me today. She said her name was something like Leata, Latha or Letha. I couldn't quite get it, but she wanted me to communicate with you. She said she is your mother." Christine did not know the name of my mother, which is *Letha*, but was very aware that my mother had died a year or so prior. She continued, "Your mother said that she thought she knew more about dying than she actually did. Her death wasn't like she thought it would be." Christine went on to describe what my mother was now doing—learning more about appreciation of family, evaluating her life and her relationship to my father. My father, she realized, was the love of her life after all—something she hadn't been able to see while alive.

Later, Chris and I did a follow-up session together, inviting Mama Letha to chat with us again, and she did. She lent me personal support that she had been unable to give in person and mentioned some items she wanted me to have from her sewing room. When I asked specifically if she would share more about her dying experiences, she declined. Perhaps it simply wasn't appropriate or she didn't have the words. Perhaps it was uncomfortable to talk about. I couldn't know, but I respected her choice.

I share this story because entrenched religious training on dying and getting to heaven may not necessarily mean that that will be our experience. My mother's story, as best I can receive it, simply reveals that her expectations were different than what she actually encountered. I sense that she felt something akin to confusion that was unsettling. She seemed to have gotten through that period well enough, however, and was in a position to be reflective and more expansive in her perceptions. Her heaven seemed to include continued exploration on the issues she was seeking to master. She was growing and learning. I find that comforting.

## 8.  So is there a road map of sorts? It still seems confusing.

The road map we need for learning the art of departure is written in the fabric of our neural pathways and the longing in our souls. In other words, your own particular road map lies within *you* waiting for *you* to ignite the fire. The deeper our meditation practice and our healing, the more fuel we have for our fire. If we are drawn to study the enlightened ones, we might follow that lead. These marvelous souls used time-honored techniques for activating the DNA, the chakras and the nervous system. We can be reassured that our spinal columns and our brains are already set up for this. It is a step-by-step business that asks us to deepen into gratitude and spaciousness of mind. We will talk more of these things in "Tools for the Journey," Part III.

The road map that might have been appropriate for you 10 years ago is not likely the one you need now, unless you have not grown over the past decade. Your road map for dying well changes as you change. Let's say you've cleared some major limiting beliefs. The after-death options you have after clearing yourself of the limiting beliefs are much more enlivened and beautiful than before you plowed through all that hard inner work. Instead of that bumpy dirt road, the on-ramp to the smoother heavenly highway is before you.

Roshi Joan Halifax, a Buddhist teacher and founder of the Project on Being with Dying, says that she once asked the Dalai Lama if what near-death-experiencers report about the afterlife is the full death experience. He said no, implying that there was much more to understand. Their brief exposure to the other side was just that, a limited peek, a quick hello and goodbye.

Our work here is not about examining those vast realms of the Infinite so much as it is about getting you as far into them as you are capable of going. The road map includes bridge building through accessing those realms here and now via meditation or unexpected "mind-blowing" events. Sometimes, we open so deeply to the Divine that the personal self melts into the background and the soul moves into the driver's seat. The spiritual path has been activated, made more tangible. The heart lights up and we *feel* the road map.

**9. I'm not sure I really understand how reincarnation and karma work, especially with conscious dying.**

Generally speaking, reincarnation and karma are about balance, recompense and mastery. We could leave it at that—balance, recompense and mastery—but a brief overview may help.

*a) Balance.* If, for example, you have had many feminine lifetimes because your soul is most comfortable with that energy, you will also be guided to choose some masculine ones for the balanced perspective it gives you, and vice versa. It's the same with political, economic and racial options. You will be rich and poor, powerful and powerless. You will likely be of every race, religion and many lands before you are done. You are honed and loved and expanded via an endless array of learning experiences in Earth School. If you've been selfish, you get to learn generosity. If you've been too narrow, you will learn to be more broad-minded. The point is to learn, and learning comes via experience. It's more difficult to be critical when you have seen life from all sides. When we have reincarnated into every kind of person and grown in understanding, then it is hard to hold negative judgments. And we come into balance.

*b) Recompense.* Recompense or karma plays the parenting role behind the scenes of life. There are consequences, results and rewards for all our thoughts and actions. It's just the nature of getting oriented and getting real, like a child learning the ropes. Eventually you learn that it's quite rewarding to behave yourself—and easier on everyone. However, these behaviors and attitudes may or may not be the ones we are taught as children. The higher truths may or may not be embraced by our family and cohorts, so sometimes we have to leave the fold as part of growing ourselves in the way our heavenly parent, our own divinity, is recommending that we do.

*c) Mastery.* Mastery is practice, practice, learn, learn and then AHA! That grand sense that finally there is a breakthrough, a skill set, a heart knowing. That AHA! may come on this side while we are on Earth. It may not come until we are on the other side reviewing our life story and we suddenly realize the gift in some major life riddle. Mastery includes inner discipline, wisdom, ability to forgive, surrender, fortitude, compassion, self-care, generosity, focus and deeper insight.

Unfinished business from past lives can create energetic clutter. All that unresolved clutter waits for our karmic broom in the next go-round. Then we have the "privilege" of dealing with it again, sweeping the slate clean. So dealing with life as directly and effectively as we know how, and invoking grace are great "brooms" for the mastery we are seeking.

The more we know how it all works, the smarter we can be in the game of life. We take shortcuts by inviting in higher frequencies. Much may be asked of us, but we do it. In the process, we may come to know that our death and our life are companions, and that these two companions are available to raise us up and set us free. It's our choice to dive in or not, but by choosing to become more conscious, we are better able to stay the course of compassionate living and transition in higher style. It's the gift given back to ourselves, to all those we love—and to the Universe whose love for us is immeasurable.

# CHAPTER 6

## *Permission Granted*

*Ah-h-h…fellow traveler, welcome here!*
*Take off your shoes, your dusty boots.*
*Lay your hat on the grass nearby.*
*Come…Sit 'neath this shady cottonwood tree*
*And pause a while…*
*Let us share a glass of wine or cup of tea.*
*Let us drink the afternoon's light and speak of life and death*
*And all points held between.*

WHEN I WORKED AS A CLINICIAN in the nursing care center, my clients would ask me privately, "What happened to Mr. Noble? He hasn't been to the dining room for three days. Did he die?" The nursing care residents were aware on some level of the changes. The staff, having been through so many deaths of those they held fondly, was also grieving and stressed—or emotionally shut down. So, no one talked about it. However, there were those residents who needed to know what had happened. Behind their inquiries were questions about how their own death would arrive and what the journey would be like. And would anyone notice their absence from the dining room?

Robert, one of my clients, gave me his theory. "I think death must be painful. It's just got to hurt when your heart stops beating or you can't breathe." "And what about after that, Robert?" I would ask. "What about after this pain that you sense?" He absolutely wouldn't budge except to say he didn't have much use for religion as he had known it. Being of the Traditional Intellectual bent, Robert pursued an answer with his rational thought processes. Then he reached a dead end and stopped, not willing to entertain further possibilities.

Death information is often withheld or unknown. Yet death begs to be addressed, though not in the old ways that re-traumatize or create fear. We, like Robert, are still unshackling ourselves from some of that hellfire and brimstone, only "one right way" background noise. We are trying to create an updated version of death and dying—often while holding onto the familiar. That's hard.

Feeling inhibited to speak openly, and having no real dying tools, is to me, a topsy-turvy madness. It's as if we are afraid we will jinx life if we talk of death. Or that we will be socially kicked out onto the street for "being so morbid."

As a culture, we are often protected from death, and its unfamiliarity makes it frightening. Many people die in hospitals, not quietly at home as they may have wished. Few have the fortitude to buck the medical system once it becomes involved, and so death is removed from its natural setting within the midst of community and family life.

There are beautiful exceptions. My friend, Walt Cranson, died as he wished. In his late 80s, he felt his life was blessed and complete. As he was obviously failing, he chose to refuse tests, doctors and procedures. He dropped into acceptance. He remained active at his eccentric, used bookstore, only working when it suited him. His large family acquiesced to his wishes, treating him with soothing essential oils and natural therapies. The goal was simply comfort and completion of the journey under his own steam. He died in peace, with little discomfort, surrounded by his family. There was no focus on the actual physical cause of death. That great curiosity was simply laid to rest. It served no purpose in the dying style he had chosen. He died as he had lived—independently—and free of the institutions and restrictions he disliked. Simply put, Walt died of completion.

Making our own choices is empowering. It's part of facing our own death. It's part of giving ourselves and others permission to be direct. My colleague, Priscilla, and I taught an "End-of-Life Care" class for the staff at the nursing care center. Priscilla, an R.N., skillfully explained the physical components of the dying process and I taught the psychological/spiritual aspects. One C.N.A. was having trouble understanding the behavior of Mr. Rodriguez, who would often complain bitterly to anyone passing by, "I don't think I can make it. I don't feel good, etc." She would try to cheer him up, telling him he could do "it," that he was doing well. Since we were encouraging staff to be more open about the subject of dying, I suggested she may want to empathize with him and say that it sounded like he was having a hard time wanting to live and that maybe he was wondering about his own death. The next week she tried it. It worked. Mr. Rodriguez sat quietly in his wheelchair as the grateful tears began falling. Someone had compassionately granted permission for the topic of dying to be put on the table. And he reached out and accepted.

Not everyone, even in their last months, wants to talk about death. However, this resistance is often more about cultural programming than lack of curiosity. Wouldn't we all like a video camera on the other side that could give us the inside scoop? Then we could review the film and say, "Ah-h, so that's how it goes!" Because cultural programming is still powerfully in place for many, to speak of death may seem like giving up or betraying your family. A few hold an apologetic shame about not being in power any longer. For the more narcissistically inclined, death can be turned into grand drama. Unfinished personal and family issues may overshadow the true event at hand. None of this supports the calm cradling of the soul, so revered in conscious dying.

## What scares you?

Let's talk about what scares us. You may never have put your dying fears into words. Try it for a moment. Put the book down and jot down what comes to mind. What do you come up with? What concerns might you have? Notice what you feel in your body as you contemplate your own death. The fears we have about *life* are often similar to our fears about death. For example:

| | Life Fears | Death Fears |
|---|---|---|
| 1. | I'm not good enough. | I haven't earned a positive afterlife. |
| 2. | I'm not safe. I'm scared about everything! | I'm scared I'll be unsafe, lost and unloved. |
| 3. | I've made a mess of my life. I'm ashamed | I'm so guilty that I don't know if I can face eternity. |
| 4. | I must appear invincible. | But what if I will no longer exist? |
| 5. | My body feels unsafe, afraid of pain. | I'm terrified of a painful death. |
| 6. | Change is hard. Endings are hard. | I can't bear the profound ending of death. |
| 7. | No one really understands or loves me. | I don't even believe that God really loves me. |
| 8. | I feel lost. | I might get lost when I die. |
| 9. | What will happen to my children? | I'll have no ability to protect my children. |
| 10. | What if I fail? | What if I've failed my life? |

### *Biological Fears*

My counseling colleague, Michael, died of a brain tumor in his 40s. He was a well-loved and powerful presence in our community. The long course of a terminal illness gave him sufficient time to get his affairs in order and to spend precious time with his family. It also gave him time to contemplate the manner of his dying. He confessed to his sister-in-law that he feared his strong, healthy heart would keep his body alive long after any quality of life had passed. His concern was about his biology, his body. Otherwise, he felt at peace. In the end, Michael died consciously and well.

Biological fears are real. Survival instincts are real. Michael's concern was a valid one. He wondered if his body would fight to survive even though mentally and spiritually he had surrendered. The body is programmed to attempt heroic survival against all threats. Death is perceived as the greatest threat, until we relax into a larger, stronger identity that provides ease to the nervous system.

Neither does the body want to suffer—an understandable avoidance. That can translate into a profound fear of physical pain. We have experienced physical agonies or know someone who has, so the body says, "If death includes pain, why would I want to die!?" We carry these stories and fears in our nervous system memory bank. We even carry fears of pain and death from past lives, and mistake these nervous system responses for our present reality. These fears may loom large or be so fleeting as to be missed by the conscious mind.

If biological fears could be verbalized, they might include these comments:

- "I'll be annihilated!"
- "I can't die!"
- "I have to protect myself..."
- "It's terrifying!"
- "If they don't hurt me, I'll be okay..."
- "Step back. Just step back. Give me a moment to breathe and relax."
- "No pain. If there's too much pain, I'm out of here. I'm voting for sudden death!"

Thankfully, as the life force energy ebbs, the biological instinct typically surrenders. It has served its time and now relinquishes its power to higher consciousness. Ebbing of life force is a gift to our biology. The body can lay down its armor; the assignment has been completed.

## Ego Fears

Ego fears can have great impact on our attitude toward death as well. However, the ego plays a necessary role for healthy navigation through life.

> "The ego's...function is related to personal development and survival in complex family and cultural systems. When healthy, it forms a strong identity with our biological, psychological and social needs. It seeks to help us get those needs met and to protect us from harm...
>
> The ego has limited visionary...abilities as its memory and feelings have to do with self-protection and gaining personal power. However, our ego-based ability to identify with our body and personality is necessary for healthy functioning...." (from *This Divine Classroom*, M. Beachy, p. 140-141)

In my mid-20s, I decided to look my death squarely in the eye. "You are going to die someday, Marcia. You will no longer exist in this form," I announced to myself one afternoon. Thereupon I had immediate, overwhelming anxiety. I carried no real tools for that endeavor and precious little maturity. My ego and biology dived into a brief tailspin.

The ego is somewhat like the body, in that its days are numbered in its present form. So in true instinctive survival mode, the ego reacts with fear to the possibility of its death—that is until it is integrated into a larger, more mature identity. This larger identity feels more deeply satisfying and therefore begins to hold its ground as a stabilizing force within the psyche. This enables some of the instinctive fears to release their grip. It's as if we've developed a parent inside to calm a terrified, reactive, two-year-old self. We can honor the biological and ego survival instincts but needn't stop there. These fears can be surrendered into our greater being—the soul, God, higher consciousness—however you want to name it. This creates more likelihood of true transition magic.

In *The Phaselock Code*, author Roger Hart described his ego's surrender in a dramatic near-death experience in which he lost his footing while climbing Mount Everest. "I remember the horror of my body scraping over steep, sharp ice. I thought at the end the pain would be unbearable. I screamed and screamed." The terror of the pain he would feel if he hit the rocks below suddenly snapped Roger free of his body. As he separated from his body, he felt instead the wonder of it all—no cold, no pain, no fear and connected to the magic of creation. Even seeing his body falling through the night was an amazing sight.

Days later, Roger was given the opportunity to talk about his experience with one of the Nepalese Sherpas or mountain climbing guides from Katmandu. This elder Sherpa, Chombi, chuckled upon hearing the story. Chombi's interpretation of Roger's experience fits well with our discussion. He saw the part that screamed as related to the lower self or the part of us that masks our true nature. When Roger realized he was going to die, the lower self or ego identity let go and what remained was Roger's higher self—floating peacefully and without any fear. Chombi had further insight into some of our Western behaviors. From his perspective, the reason so many Westerners crave the dramas of war, high adventure and other death-defying odds is the longing to meet that higher self.

We notice Roger's encounter with his true self happened after the ego and body dramatically surrendered their hold. Once he dropped to a safe place after his fall, and regained some sense of equilibrium, his ego and biological instincts resumed their task of survival.

### Religious and Cultural Fears

Religious and cultural fears are more about programming than instinctive survival. Religious institutions have broadcast certain "absolutes" about death. Heaven and hell get quite a rap. In some Christian groups, for example, if everyone who isn't a "true Christian" goes to hell that includes all Muslims, Jews, Hindus, Zoroastrians and the rest of the non-believers, right? But if you are from another part of the world with another strict system of belief, everyone else besides your group could be doomed. So, by the time we are done counting, every soul on the planet is bound for hell.

If we stand back and look at the ridiculous nature of these massive judgments on humanity, we comprehend the heaviness and confusion around death. Add to that the debilitating nature of the shame, guilt and blame that often goes with numerous teachings, and we are left holding the deep anguish that comes from millions of souls doubting their own innate goodness and their right to a loving afterlife.

Many rich, comforting teachings on dying are found in world religions. For this we are very grateful. Our concern here is misinformation. The natural continuity of consciousness is relatively recent in Western thought. At a really core level, we've learned to be afraid to die because we're afraid that Love won't be there when we do. We are afraid of being lost and alone in the Cosmos without a hand to hold. On this side we form opinions; we think we know something. The fear is that on the other side we may have been wrong, we may know nothing.

## I'm not afraid

Perhaps you are one of those folks who can honestly say you aren't afraid to die. Your concerns lie more with your family's welfare or that you are able to finish a pet project before passing. You may have been in a situation in which you have had to face death many times. You may have had a near-death or out-of-body experience where you traveled to the other side and found yourself very much alive, though outside your body. You may have done some past-life work where you had the feeling of familiarity or "home" within the higher realms. Whatever your experience, death now seems less troubling and more of a simple step through the portal.

Knowing that someone has made it to the other side and returned with fearlessness and calm provides reassurance for others. This reassurance is what we seek, particularly when we have lost a loved one unexpectedly, before their life span is complete. How impossible it is to accept the death of a child, for example, as being the end. The heart cannot fathom this. Nowhere else in our experience is there an ending without a beginning to follow. How could it not also be so with the death of someone dear?

My client, Nora, and her family were vacationing near a lake in the Minnesota woods. While there, Nora's four-year-old daughter slipped unseen into the water and drowned. This tragedy sent shock waves through the family and community. Part of Nora's long grief recovery included a passionate search for proof that the spirit of her daughter lived on. She demanded to know, not only that Emily was alive in spirit, but how she was doing and what, if anything, Nora needed to do to help her. This journey of sorrow, learning and healing proved to be profound for Nora. She grieved, prayed, contacted psychics, read anything she could find on life after death, and talked with Emily on a regular basis. She utilized NDE and PLR information to understand Emily's likely after-death experience. Having not been religious or much interested in spirituality, Nora activated this part of herself. She came to feel that Emily lived on and eventually experienced equanimity around her loss. Through the enigma of her daughter's death, Nora awakened to the option of conscious living. She chose the difficult and rewarding path of wisdom-through-adversity and birthed herself anew.

Though it doesn't take away the grief, with time, we hold beginnings and endings with more grace. Though we may have cried when leaving our mother's side that first day of kindergarten, that ending was the marvelous beginning of a new world of ideas, books and the challenge of making friends. The identity of being a preschooler was left behind and the new identity of a kindergartener replaced it.

Beginnings follow endings. Sorrow rises. So does delight. Our reluctance to face death lessens with the ability to perceive the seamless flow of consciousness within the innumerable cycles of experience. There *is* a continuity of being, a thread, a river that undergirds our existence. When this continuity is felt, a larger sense enters the picture. It is the way in which we experience our fear of death falling away, like falling through space screaming and then letting go, becoming a part of it all.

## What do you call it?

We have adopted many clever, funny, classic and tender words for our departure. Since working in this field, I've been collecting terms we use for our final exit. Invariably, when the subject is put before a group, the jargon becomes increasingly humorous. Here are some I've found:

- Sleep with the fishes
- Move to upper management
- Kick the bucket
- Cross the threshold
- Cash in your chips
- Depart this mortal coil
- Give up the ghost
- Buy the farm
- Go to the happy hunting grounds
- Answer the last call
- Cross the Jordan River
- Fall off the twig
- Hour of mystic summoning
- Taken out of production
- Join the last roundup
- Meet your maker
- Cross the Great Divide
- Sprout wings
- Croak
- Heads-up club member
- Check-out
- Sing with the angels

As we have mentioned, death wants release from all the weight that surrounds it. Humor becomes our great ally in all facets of living and dying. Once on the other side, PLR clients often report that while heaven is profound and touching, there is also a great deal of humor. In fact, Maria, a PLR client, described the release of her body at the end of each of her lives by saying it was as simple as laying aside a set of clothes. Clients often find their soul groups and guides bring a teasing and humorous approach to the review of the life just completed. We want to bring that lighter spirit, that humor into this side as well, knowing that the departing soul, though "falling off the twig" on this side, is soon to arrive with wings spread on the other.

To assist in laying it all out on the table and to give full permission for you to jump in, try finishing these sentences with as many responses as you can. Better yet, ask a friend to share the conversation with you. See where you are comfortable and where you want to become more astute in your departure know-how.

1.  I'm afraid to die because _____.
2.  I'm *not* afraid to die because _____.
3.  If I were to die tomorrow, the part of letting go that would be most difficult for me would be _____.
4.  The easiest part of letting go would be _____.
5.  What I wonder about dying is _____.
6.  What I really want to accomplish before I die is _____.
7.  If I were to die tomorrow, the relationships or situations where I still have unfinished business are _____.
8.  For me, the completion of my unfinished business would be to _____.
9.  The kind of death I really *don't* want is _____ because _____.
10.  The kind of death I really *do* want is _____ because _____.
11.  My greatest hope for my own conscious living is _____.
12.  My greatest hope for my own conscious departure is _____.
13.  What I really want to experience on the other side is _____.
14.  The skills or tools that I feel would help me most in accomplishing these goals are _____.

# CHAPTER 7

## *Which Reality Do You Want?*

*Peace will guide the planets*
*And love will steer the stars...*
*Harmony and understanding*
*Sympathy and trust abounding*
*No more falsehoods or derisions*
*Golden living dreams and visions*
*Mystic crystal revelations*
*And the mind's true liberation*
*Aquarius! Aquarius!*
*Let the sunshine in!*
—The Fifth Dimension

MORNING TASKS ARE ACCOMPLISHED. My three daughters are off to school. The separation from my husband is beyond the trauma and raw heartache, at least for now. It is the early 1990s and I stand for a moment in my spacious apartment. My gaze drifts over the colorful pillows, houseplants and mix of wicker and overstuffed furniture. I am pleased. This scene is restful yet full of vitality at the same time. It's my new home.

Misty clouds have softened the spring sun as it drifts in light and shadow across the living room. The corner lamp is on. Perhaps there will be one of those lovely afternoon showers that sustain the luxuriant Midwest. In an uncharacteristic move, I sit for a moment in a wicker chair that faces the patio doors, relishing the peace and simple beauty. I never sit in this chair.

Suddenly, I am aware that I am aware. There is an exquisite stillness. Scarcely breathing, I do not move. What is this? My attention is drawn again to the lamp. There is a perfection in this light and shadow—an ineffable light that I feel. Has the light really changed? Whatever is happening rivets my attention. I feel a bestowal of the most tender love. I am very aware of the gentleness of this light. I realize I am perceiving with a bigger mind. My linear time world seems to have opened up to receive this drop of otherworldly, exquisite perfection. My life isn't perfect, neither is my world. Yet, through these eyes, it appears to be exactly that—perfect as is. Everything exudes grace just as it is, warts and all. This unconditional love, this unconditional acceptance of me and my world sparkles in the stillness. Not only my personal reality is altered, but this whole troubled planetary reality feels cocooned in love.

This moment sits big within its fragment of time—so intimate, so expansive and gracious. My mind experiences a liberation, a freeing up. Yet, I continue to sit unmoving. So grateful, so grateful, so grateful. It feels as if this bigger mind is always there, whether perceived or not. For some unexplained reason, it was my turn to experience it.

It melts away. The phone rings. The to-do list calls for my attention. I must get ready to meet with clients. Several seconds in eternity presented themselves like a lifetime gift card. Here, take it. It's yours! A lifetime gift card to spend in the vast storehouse of Eternal Being, while also walking upon the path of time. And no chance whatsoever of overspending or going bankrupt. It's free! What a concept. What a gift.

These bigger moments, or alternate realities, seldom fade from our memory. They are anchored more strongly in emotion or feeling than any words we can find. Bigger moments are unexpected boons that grab us, shifting our attention into a greater reality. We all have these gifts from eternity: a breathless ocean sunset, a brilliant swallowtail butterfly lifting the heart, a dream filled with light and insight, or the discovery of the long-sought solution to a gnawing problem. Joy breaks through. We are the better for the experience. We are bigger. Amazingly, we don't feel lonely anymore.

The triggering event may be one we prefer. It may be one we do not prefer, such as a heartbreaking loss. At the points of both birth and death, bigger moments can seize us. If we are aware, we can drink in the expanding vista. The feelings you get from a bigger moment let you know your life has called you, called you in gentle whispers or in loud gongs that ring across the valley. You are being called to expand into a greater self. If you pay attention, you will notice you can step into a higher frequency, a more harmonious feeling through the bigger-moment path that has revealed itself.

Whenever you have one of these notable bigger moments, don't doubt or minimize it. Instead, be in gratitude. Milk it for all it's worth. Here's why. You feel expansive. You feel joy. You may also feel sorrow but you feel authentic and deepened. You get relief from the grind and from superficiality. And the big one—you give yourself permission to say yes to your soul, yes to your eternal self that has appeared.

## Levels of Reality: Frequencies, Dimensions and Planes

Various realities are innately woven into the whole life-death-afterlife continuum. This is the nature of things. As humans, we try to find ways of categorizing our realities. It seems to be our predilection to try to organize the Mystery. The other side or afterlife side seems less interested in these things, but we humans want to better comprehend our true nature. It's our way.

We are using several terms interchangeably: frequencies, dimensions, realities and planes. These are not so much places as they are states of consciousness, a way to understand the consciousness continuum that is a part of our daily lives. For our non-technical discussion they have similar meaning. This consciousness continuum is referenced in all sacred scripture. Masters and teachers exhort us to aim higher, to lift ourselves out of the darker levels of experience. For example, Jesus said, "In my Father's house are many mansions. I go to prepare a place for you, that where I am, there you may be also." He was referring to the higher states of consciousness that align us with our spirit. *Mansion* is a great metaphor because it connotes a wealth of being, a claiming of our higher nature. He lived in these higher states while walking within the human experience. His work, as with all masters, was/is to awaken the many mansions within his followers. To aspire to higher styles of living and transitioning to the next world requires some comprehension of these realities and frequencies. Our earlier discussions have alluded to them.

Being multidimensional is an undeniable part of the journey. We simply can't declare that what we see and touch and hear with our physical senses is all there is. If that sunset over the ocean opened your heart so wide that it brought tears to your eyes, you already have proof of something beyond what your senses were picking up. And if your living room seems to light up with something akin to unconditional love on a spring morning, it is way more than a physical, 3-D experience. So is dying—much more. We have to go beyond this third-dimensional reality to get a handle on it.

Obviously, when you die, you don't have this 3-D body anymore, so you aren't here anymore. But where are you? Since many NDE and PLR folks report that they can look down and see their bodies, their families, their surroundings, they obviously are still in contact with this reality. The same thing happens with those who die. They can see their bodies, families and surroundings. They are here and not here. They now dwell in another reality or plane of existence that *interfaces* with physical Earth.

One way to understand realities is through emotion. Earlier we discussed higher frequencies that include unconditional love, mercy, compassion, joy and clear-mindedness. You will recall that the lower frequencies are typically around negative emotions like hatred, rage, vindictiveness, dark depression and fear of all kinds. The extremes of our consciousness represent a wide range of emotions, from the highest wisdom to the darkest fears. There are many options from which to choose.

Our discussion on dimensions and realities correlates with the light spectrum, which includes infrared at the low-frequency end and ultraviolet at the high-frequency end. Human visual ability resides in only a small segment in the center of this continuum. The lower infrared and higher ultraviolet frequencies are invisible to us. Yet they exist, of course, and are proven with a variety of instrumentation. Besides light and color, what other realities exist alongside us that we deny simply because we don't perceive them? Is "heaven" right there in the ultraviolet range? Is "hell" in the equivalent of the infrared area?

**Light or Electro-Magnetic Spectrum**

Infrared--------------------------------(---------------)----------------------------Ultraviolet

(Low frequencies)           Human Visual Range           (High frequencies)

Even lower than infrared are radio and microwaves and even higher than ultraviolet are X-rays and gamma rays. Though we don't see the greater light spectrum, it is continually impacting us. Let's create a similar spectrum for emotions and feelings and see what happens.

**Emotional-Feeling Spectrum**

Deep Depression, Lethargy-------------------------------------------Joy, Compassion, Light

(Low frequencies)                                                       (High frequencies)

These light and feeling spectrums represent the consciousness continuum quite well. Each emotion has a higher/lower frequency or resonance, a greater or lesser quality of light. Think about that for a moment. Our amazing feeling nature is not limited like our physical eyes are. Through our feeling nature we experience the equivalent of infrared and ultraviolet light. From the depths of negative feelings to the heights of eternal compassion, we taste from the smorgasbord of frequencies. We dance within a wide spectrum of realities.

We are, therefore, citizens of a multidimensional universe existing both within us and outside of us. Within each dimension or plane of existence, certain frequencies resonate. Certain qualities define the different strata. For example, a lower dimension that relished sadistic behaviors would not be drawn to a higher dimension of exquisite beauty and love—nor could it survive. The two are incompatible, vibrationally. They don't resonate. They don't jibe.

If we are galumphing along the unconscious path of a pizza and beer diet, bad TV, drug/alcohol addictions, wrangling an illicit deal, and wallowing in the "life sucks" philosophy, we'd be wading through a lower reality. You could even go to "the pits" but you don't want to; it's the realm of evil in all its forms.

In the higher frequencies, we might find people involved with awe-inspiring art, music, science and spirituality. Here we also find the kindest of hearts, the most courageous of souls, fragrant flowers and exceptional children. We would find enlightened gardeners, healers, businessmen, warriors and spiritual masters.

There are a number of ways of categorizing our multidimensional nature. Here are a few we will consider:
1. Energetic body layers: physical, etheric, emotional, mental and spiritual.
2. Numerical dimensions: metaphysics, quantum physics—dimensions 1-12+.
3. Classic esoteric terms: physical, astral and causal.
4. Psychological levels of mind: unconscious, conscious and superconscious.

## Energetic Body Layers

Let's start with our *energetic body*. You may be aware of the aura or the energy field that surrounds and penetrates the physical body. It is rich and layered and is the wholeness through which we exist. Our first layer is the visible, the *physical* 3-D body. The next is often called the *etheric* layer. It sits in close and if you relax your gaze you might see it as a clear shadow about ¼ inch out from your skin. The next dimension is usually called the *emotional* layer and is ever changing according to our moods, yet it has a predominant coloring due to the general emotional hue in which we live our lives. The next dimension is the *mental* layer, created by our thoughts and beliefs developed over this lifetime, influenced by family, culture and past lives. After that are *spiritual* layers housing our unlimited nature and linking us to soul, higher self, angels and guides. Altogether, it's an oval-shaped energetic bubble within which we dwell.

These energy bodies are coordinated through the seven-plus energy centers or chakras with which yoga students are familiar. Interestingly enough, the chakras play a part in conscious dying because our consciousness affects them. Dwelling in the sacredness of life allows the higher chakras to open. Higher awareness opens the higher chakras that are so helpful when we depart.

Before going any further, let me list the seven major chakras that align themselves along the spine and are associated with the endocrine system. Those who study our evolving multidimensionality say we are developing even higher chakras, so we are unlimited in our capacity here. However, for our purposes, we will work with the traditional seven.

### Chakra System

| Number | Name | Location | Function/Quality | Color | Gland |
|---|---|---|---|---|---|
| 7th | Crown | Top of head | Transcendence | Violet | Pineal |
| 6th | Third Eye | Brow | Intuition/Knowing | Indigo | Pituitary |
| 5th | Throat | Throat | Expression/Sound | Sky Blue | Thyroid |
| 4th | Heart | Center of chest | Love | Green | Thymus |
| 3rd | Solar plexus | Solar plexus | Power | Yellow | Pancreas |
| 2nd | Sexual | Above pubic bone | Sexuality | Orange | Gonads |
| 1st | Root | Base of spine | Survival/security | Red | Adrenals |

Here's where our interest lies. The highest chakras that we have activated during our life energetically assist us in the afterlife realms to which we travel.

So, for example, if you have developed a deep meditation practice in which the third-eye and crown center have been spiritually activated, that high frequency will help you immensely. If you have loved deeply and unconditionally, your heart chakra is activated and aligns you with the love frequency. If your main focus is power, money, sexual pleasure and securing your survival needs at all costs, those lower chakras are humming. You activate those frequencies and in the afterlife may be hanging out with similarly driven souls. Some Buddhist and Hindu traditions teach the importance of focusing on certain higher chakras during the dying process. This helps the soul exit through the most auspicious chakra, creating, therefore, the higher-frequency departure.

Ideally, when we die and let go of our bodies, we also let go of this physical dimension. That includes, not only our bodies which, of course, have died, but our day-to-day *ego* involvement with those we know who are still in 3-D. We aren't 3-D anymore. This often takes a while, as the layers of Earth life fall away. If we are going to be of service in the next stages of the journey, we will want to release the ego and step into our heavenly bodies and their heavenly mindsets, relatively quickly.

When going through their deaths in past lives, clients report that they still have bodies, which keep changing as their personal and physical identities dissolve. It's as if they are letting go of each of these energy bodies and merging their consciousness with the spiritual or higher-frequency layers of the aura. These energy bodies become the vehicles of their identity and travel in the afterlife planes or dimensions. One person may find himself in a garden or sitting on a hillside. Another may identify with Earth-like surroundings but be in another reality that has Earth-like qualities. These scenes are generally created in the astral or fourth dimension discussed below.

When clients look closely at their new bodies, they say they are hard to describe. For some there is no sense of a body at all. Others perceive their bodies as made of light and swirling or vibrating colors. They describe the souls around them similarly—as shades and shadows of energy. Some describe robes with various insignia on them. If they see themselves in human forms, they are healthy, vibrant and less dense.

Imagining this process helps break up some of our concrete thinking. We can practice feeling less physical and limited. Can you imagine how you are still you, only more so as you let go of your body? Can you imagine how okay that can be?

We can embrace that we are multidimensional right here and now on this day driving our cars to work. When we receive intuitive insights, when we dream, when we pray deeply, we are multidimensional. We just come back into our lives and go make dinner. When we die, we don't make dinner anymore; we keep going instead.

## Numerical Dimensions

Giving the dimensions *numerical* names is popular. It has a physics/quantum physics/metaphysics association. We know about 3-D because we live on a 3-D planet—height-width-depth or space-time-density. By the very nature of assigning numbers, we can assume there are many dimensional options, not just 1-3. Twelve is usually the highest given. Those who work with the dimensional realms say that we now have the option to evolve rapidly into 5-D consciousness and beyond. Our bodies are working hard to understand how to "digest" the higher energies. Choosing to expand is the amazing option we have as we move through all the changes we are experiencing. Planet Earth is also evolving, throwing off the limiting fear-based systems that have been so harmful for all. In 5-D, thoughts manifest more quickly and higher intuitive abilities are activated. Dimensions 5-D through 9-D and beyond have inherent qualities of harmony, freedom, compassion and unity with Source.

When our medical and educational systems become more aware of developing the frontal cortex of the brain, the higher functioning part of the brain, multidimensional education will be prized for the highly functioning humans that will result. I see this as being the norm in the decades to come.

Remember, we interweave with all of these realities. Dr. Suzanne Lie (www.multidimensions.com) believes that we are in a period of time when the third dimension is collapsing into the fourth, and the fourth into the fifth. So if it feels like your life is falling apart at times, join the crowd. This seems to be part of the agenda for the next few years as the old energy in our lives wrangles its way into the dust while the more evolved rises. Some of my clients describe their experience by saying, "I just have no desire to participate in the old drama anymore. I have no emotional energy for it. I'm done." Or "I don't think like I used to. I don't want all the busyness and material stuff. I want peace and simplicity." That's the collapsing of old 3-D dramas, distractions and fears. A gentle higher energy is calling. It's happening in ordinary folks like you and me.

## Esoteric Dimensions

In the *esoteric* teachings of the mystery schools, ascended masters and the wisdom traditions, we find the dimensions often broken down into three main levels: physical, astral and causal. The *physical* level is the one we dwell within here on Earth. It is the one we call the *real* reality of daily life in the physical body. Judging it to be more real than the higher dimensions is often our way of trying to stay grounded in this life. It can also serve as an avoidance technique. If we can say this is all there is, then we can remain cynical or cerebral, depriving ourselves of the unexplored worlds of soul and spirit.

The *astral* level corresponds to the fourth dimension and has many levels of consciousness within itself. It is a powerful emotional plane. The lower 4-D or lower astral levels are the darkest, the places of our nightmares and darker side. Here also are the darker "hell" and "purgatory" levels you learned about in religious education. The higher 4-D/astral levels are brimming with ease and heavenly love. Sri Yukteswar, the Indian yogi mentioned in Chapter 4, describes the astral dimension as not simply a layer around earth but as another universe of its own. Instead of the physical planets and stars of our universe, it is even larger with astral planets and stars. Here souls can spend time between lives growing and learning before returning to Earth.

When souls graduate from Earth, they take up residence in the astral universe where they continue to grow and work out their karma. Instead of the delayed effect we have in 3-D, they experience instantaneous results from their thoughts. Here, we can appreciate the importance of our inner healing and inner discipline while in a body, for this effort also serves us well in the astral plane. Some souls, like Sri Yukteswar, do not need to return to Earth because their learning is complete here. They can choose to remain in the astral planes.

The *causal* plane is the highest dimension of consciousness, and like the physical and astral planes, is a vast universe filled with causal planets and realities. To us these realities would seem misty, ephemeral, glorious and very difficult to describe. This multileveled reality is the soul's last series of high-mastery learning from which it melds with Divine Source in eternal oneness.

In the esoteric system, we have not only the physical and astral bodies right here and now but a causal one as well. The physical body's work is within the physical universe. The astral body's work is in the astral universe of feelings and expanding awareness. The causal body is part of limitless creation and houses the substance or energy of all our constructive efforts. I find myself thinking of it as our own personal library of spiritual effectiveness. All our positive work over the eons is collected in our brilliant causal body and becomes a "battery" of light to be utilized throughout creation. This helps us know that in our work of healing and loving, it all matters, it all counts.

## Psychological Dimensions

*Psychological* dimensions are another way of comprehending this layered being that we are. The *unconscious* is a vast part of the mind holding all our childhood, genetic and past-life memories and beliefs. It is instinctive and related to the reptilian part of the brain that focuses on our sense of safety and biological survival. Our fears and traumas rise from the unconscious and become evident through our reactive emotional responses. When we say things like, where did that come from? Or, why am I so upset about that?—we are acknowledging those unconscious forces within us. To our conscious mind, what we just did makes no sense. When frightened, the unconscious has many of the qualities of a scared child. When happy, it shares space with our superconscious as the spontaneous divine child that we are. Dr. Carl Jung has a succinct comment for us on this: "Until you make the unconscious conscious, it will direct your life and you will call it fate."

Research shows us that strong, unresolved fears and impulses still residing in our minds will direct the experience in the afterlife for a bit, or a long time, depending on inner clarity. It's like you can't take all that sludge into your higher consciousness mansion. You can't fake your way. Let's side with Dr. Jung on this and clean it up before we die. Part III, Tools for the Journey, will help.

The *conscious* mind is our day-to-day awareness: what we *do* remember, how we view ourselves and our world, how we identify ourselves as unique. Conscious mind is generally ruled by the ego, gets us off to the meeting on time and holds us responsible for what we value. It judges and feels guilt and elation with little ability to sustain calm equilibrium.

The *superconscious mind* corresponds to the higher fourth dimension and beyond. It is the part of the mind that holds the soul and the unlimited spiritual planes. Here we find our higher feelings, our higher nature and our deeper identity as a spiritual being. Here is memory of our true essence and of the heavenly realms we visit in our sleep and after our lives. We know from this vantage point that we are Love itself, we are heirs to the Kingdom, and we are unlimited beings having the temporary experience of growth through limitation. Our superconscious mind keeps it all in perspective, urging us on to further growth and service to the whole. It smiles often, helping us find the humor in it all.

Sometimes when I chat with someone about our multidimensional nature and that way of being, we may seem to understand each other but it's difficult to put into words. If you were to ask me for more specifics, I'd aim for simplicity. Maybe something like this—the higher dimensions are those states of consciousness where we:

- Are more authentic and soulful
- Have more ego-free moments
- Feel more expansive
- Experience genuine compassion and a sense of joy
- Just *know*
- Give service that includes the *conscious* care of our bodies and energies

I'd add that transcending limitation isn't necessarily easy. It's difficult when everything feels like it's collapsing. It's painful when you buck old systems. But you breathe in the clear light and do it anyway. Or maybe I'd just say becoming a multidimensional person is like opening the shades after what has seemed like the darkest night—remembering that the sun has been shining all along. And that when seen through the eyes of God, the dark night and the brilliant sun are one.

# CHAPTER 8

# Getting Lost

*When people die, they don't know that they have died.*
*...There is disturbing confusion because they cannot interact*
*with other people and their surroundings.*
— "My Descent into Death" by Howard Storm

YOU HAVE HEARD ME ALLUDING to this *getting lost, getting stuck* part of some departures. Now, I want you to walk with me down this path so you can feel more comfortable, travel-ready and on the lookout for missteps. Remember I promised that you would be getting some savvy pointers for going out in style (GOS)? This is the equivalent of the do-not-eat-uncooked-food and avoid-stepping-on-scorpions part of the GOS Travel Guide.

What does getting lost or stuck look like? There aren't any mysteries here. You just don't get out of the mud and onto the road. You dally and mess around, often not realizing that your physical body is gone and a journey of vast adventure lies waiting. If you dally, you will likely get bored. This is a good thing. When you see that no one is paying any attention to you, you will likely wake up to the truth of your situation. Trying to tap your husband on the shoulder, for example, is an exercise in futility because he ignores you worse than he did before! Then there is that new talent of floating through walls and down hallways that seems perfectly natural—almost. It's the same world but different all at the same time. You might find yourself asking, "What's happened here? Oh-h, have I died?" You pause, recollecting yourself, and turn your attention from this world to the unusual light, color or sound rising on your awareness. It becomes compelling and you are off. Goodbye and God bless!

This is the simple version; a short experience of disorientation, then finding your wings and flying free.

But it can get complicated. We can trip ourselves up quite impressively. Remember shamanic teacher Alberto Villoldo's estimate that one person in 10 doesn't have a good departure? This refers to those whose confusion or high drama remains firmly in place after the body dies. They have little sense of the mire they are in, a way through it, or even a thought of trying to find one. So the individual can spin into deepening patterns of despair, anger, addiction or interference.

However, these people don't have physical bodies any longer or the same experience of time. Without bodies, they aren't able to directly affect the people they love, or don't love, but they can energetically interfere. Without the dimension of time to stretch out results, the consequences of thoughts and behaviors manifest quickly—instant karma, if you will. If you think it or feel it strongly, that's what you experience immediately. A lot of confusion can arise in this state. So, as a review, sudden, traumatic deaths and darker, heavier emotions can get you lost. We might call it an *out-of-style* departure experience.

The astonishing vastness of the afterlife realms may be difficult for the human mind to grasp at the present time. But the grandeur, love and beauty can draw the departing soul like a butterfly to the lily. Most of the time, this happens readily. We will explore what it's like when the butterfly doesn't know the lily is right there blooming nearby.

Everyone has a ghost story or wants to hear one. As we will see, there are many souls who don't get off the planet, even though they've left their bodies. Sometimes these people become fixtures in the character of a place. Here in Colorado, stories abound of ghosts who've never left the hotels and saloons of old mining towns. Sometimes they can be glimpsed walking down the stairs in their 19th century finery, or heard rustling in the upstairs bedroom where they met their demise. These rather romanticized stories belie the difficulties inherent in getting lost. Ghosts are spirits who are stuck, due to trauma or strong emotions of any kind. They are unable to move on into the higher realms beyond Earth. It's not a kindness to keep your ghosts around. We needn't reiterate that it's difficult being trapped in a world where no one listens to you and you can't get out.

There are millions of souls who are stuck, lost and confused. They have died but haven't arrived in some sort of heaven or "better place." Their spirits are caught between worlds or dimensions and they don't understand what has happened. This heaviness weighs on us and on the planet.

Let me give you an example of a lost soul experience that came through a dream. My friend, Scott, mentioned one day that he had had a troubling dream. In this dream, his friend R.P., who had died several years prior, showed up. R.P. had been a music aficionado and played in a small band. In the dream, R.P. was complaining about the lousy options for his band, which found itself relegated to practicing in dark, dingy quarters. Nothing was going right—no good gigs or breakthroughs, no matter how much the band practiced. R.P. was in despair.

Scott woke up with the feeling of gray clouds over his head. He felt sad and shaken. He wondered what he could do for his friend, because this dream seemed more real than symbolic. I agreed with Scott that this was probably a call from the in-between worlds. His friend was most likely stuck and had been trying for some time to find a way out of his dilemma. Together we discussed a plan of action. At the appropriate time, Scott would talk to R.P. He would suggest that there was another option, if he wanted to try it, and that there were actually others who were enthused about his music. Soon he would notice a door opening where none had been before.

That evening during meditation, Scott invited R.P. and his band up a dark set of stairs. At the top of the stairs a door opened, and a beautiful blue presence appeared. Scott affirmed with R.P. that this presence was enlightened and would help R.P. and his band get the gigs of which they were worthy. The band walked through the door onto a brightly lit stage and an auditorium filled with appreciative folks.

Scott slept deeply and awakened refreshed and clear. The fog had lifted. He felt fairly certain that R.P.'s door had opened and a loving guide had escorted him, and perhaps others, out of the in-between world.

## Negative Near-Death Experiences

Our road map for finding our way includes a few travel pointers from those who have journeyed across and come back to enlighten us. We might think of these folks as multidimensional storytellers who help us weave the worlds.

Corrections on the path aren't easy. Near-death experiences (NDEs) can provide profound correction and encouragement. In dying and then being resuscitated, our NDE friends tell some transformative stories of love and light which helped them find new direction. They may see beautiful beings of light and experience love so all-embracing, there is no longer any fear of death. They often say they don't want to come back to their bodies because where they are feels like home, but they are told it's not yet their time to die. The experience uplifts their hearts and gives them the bigger view.

But to those of you who may have had a negative NDE, and don't want to share it because the word on the street is that NDEs are all sweetness and light, I want you to know you are not alone. Howard Storm's story in *My Descent into Death* is a case in point.

### Howard's Story

Howard Storm was an artist and an academic caught in competitive intellectual striving. He was aloof, egotistical, anxious and easily angered. Other than his connection to his wife, he says he had few relationships that he valued. He tells of his NDE in a hospital in Paris while there on an art tour.

Howard was shocked to find himself walking around his hospital room while his physical body remained deathly ill in bed. Eventually he heard his name being called and wandered out into a foggy hallway, following the alluring voices who coaxed him along. The deceptive nature of these 'helpers' gradually became clear to Howard, but by then it was too late. Name-calling, poking and prodding had escalated into torment and terror.

He writes, "*How ironic I was ending up in the sewer of the universe with people who fed off the pain of others. I had had little genuine compassion for others. It dawned on me that I was not unlike these miserable creatures that had tormented me. Failing to truly love, they had been led into outer darkness where their only desire was inflicting their torment onto another.*"

Howard felt these beings were people who may or may not have been successful during their lives on Earth, but they had missed the deeper values of compassion, hope and faith. They wanted love and intimacy but found the experience tormenting. It seemed they were reaping what they had sown.

Howard struggled mightily, uttering any sort of prayer that came to mind, finding them all to no avail. Then he remembered something of the children's Sunday school song, 'Jesus Loves Me' and in desperation began singing and calling out for that love. The air around him lightened, growing brighter. As the light strengthened, his tormentors fell back and he was swept into the light which he called Jesus. He returned to his body and embraced the physical and spiritual healing required to bring his life into balance.

Howard's NDE dramatically corrected his path—he chose a completely new direction in life. Another story told to me was that of a fundamentalist Christian minister who also had a corrective NDE. Prior to the NDE, he had been unrelenting in his depiction of God as a God of wrath and judgment. His sermons and life reflected this harshness. After his NDE, folks began to notice that his sermons took on the qualities of love and presented a God of mercy. Though the minister and Howard may appear to be on opposite sides of the philosophical fence—one being cynical and liberal, the other conservative and rigid—their inner dynamic had similar tendencies. For both, it was easy to be critical, unforgiving, angry and controlling. Their NDEs assisted them greatly in returning to their soul paths, for they had lost their way. Had they stayed on that negative trajectory when they died, their afterlife experiences would likely have taken on similar tones. If we were to apply what we've learned in the previous chapter on realities, we could say that Howard's spirit had the experience of being lost in the lower astral plane or lower fourth dimension.

## Battlefield Ghosts

Gordon Michael Scallion (author of *Notes From the Cosmos*) and others have shared their experiences of feeling and seeing the spirits of those who have died on battlefields and other places of sudden and traumatic death. Gordon is a gifted visionary and dimensional traveler. He tells the story of how he and his wife Cynthia were guided to go to Fredericksburg National Cemetery in Virginia. In this cemetery are buried approximately 15,000 Civil War soldiers, mostly from the North but also some from the South, who fought very bloody battles in the region. We can only imagine the traumatic effect of these sudden deaths on the villages, the land and families of that era, and the continuing ripple effect through the fabric of our own time.

During his meditation at the cemetery, Gordon became aware of a presence. Out of the mist stepped the spirit of a very young Civil War soldier, Private Jemison. Gordon recognized him from earlier visions he had had at home, though he hadn't known much detail. This time when Private Jemison appeared, he was not alone. Hundreds of other spirits who had died in that difficult battle came forward. They had called Gordon through his dreams, for they recognized him as one who walked comfortably in the spirit world and who could, therefore, communicate with them. They told Gordon they were stuck between worlds, and sought help in understanding where they needed to go and what they could do to help themselves move beyond the 3-D Earth plane. Gordon began to share with them what he understood of the journey of the soul, of reincarnation and of higher dimensions.

As he spoke, he noticed the spirits began departing. Private Jemison was most grateful. In his parting comments, he said, *"More need to know about these changes. There are many of us...who are caught. We were so young at death. We knew so little. Our lives were gone before we had time to prepare for this transition, and we were caught off-guard. Many at this level are in shock, continuing to replay the battles that took their lives, and those of brothers, friends and lovers. The war forced us to choose sides, and did not leave us time to make choices for ourselves. Your words have helped many here today. Perhaps others will come to help at other gravesites."* (p. 120-1)

Gordon is one of many who have helped trapped souls leave the Earth plane. His experience confirms the difficulties that may rise for those who die traumatically without inner resources to help them navigate beyond the shock of dying. It is a reminder that because the body is dead doesn't mean the drama is over. Imagine, if you will, this Civil War battle continuing to be relived and played out for the past 150 years because those who died couldn't find their way.

## Hospital Departures

Hospitals and other medical treatment institutions can unwittingly become difficult transition sites. People may feel alienated from family, support systems and hope. They may feel imprisoned by the medical setting and by their own painful bodies, thus contributing to high anxiety at what may lie ahead. They may also be heavily sedated. Without assistance to ease their angst, they may well pass on in some kind of foggy thought process that keeps them stuck: "I will never get out of here," or "No one understands my pain," or "I'm so scared. I need to find a safe place," etc. Their bodies may be dead, but they are still in the hospital bed energetically, believing they are still in pain and "will never get out of here." So they don't.

One of my PLR clients died of a massive tooth infection in a past life. She moaned and groaned, holding her face. She had died but in the afterlife was still holding her face in pain. Then she heard someone ask her why she was holding her face. Suddenly, she became conscious and realized where she was. The pain disappeared. Another PLR client died from being savaged by a lion in a Roman coliseum. It took some time in the afterlife before the emotional and physical trauma was eased. By the nature of past-life regression, we were able to release the soul from the trauma and bring in perspective and healing.

When people die in medical settings, we want to create ease. It is important to whisper in their ears and let them know, just in case they aren't aware, that it's over. They can go into the afterlife and rest, being totally free of any physical and emotional discomfort. Go to the Light. Go to the Light. If you sense that the person is not believing you, you can continue to gently counsel him or her to see the truth of the situation.

## Military Post-Traumatic Stress Disorder

The trauma of war and warlike experiences are fraught with the phenomenon of men and women experiencing sudden death with no idea they are dead. They may have felt the explosion or the bullet, but are still wandering around trying to get out of the battlefield situation. This is described earlier in Gordon Michael Scallion's experience. The other part of the picture is that those souls who have had sudden deaths like this may become extremely confused and frightened. Without realizing the complications, they may decide to nestle in close to someone else who is alive for safety and comfort. Their compatriots are familiar and safe. So they hitch a ride. The problem is that that this is not where they belong—in someone else's energy field. They have now added their trauma to the trauma of their living friends. So not only do we have the "normal" level of PTSD sparking the nervous system of the living soldier, but the additional fear and trauma of the one who has just died are added to the mix. This creates a major overload for service men and women returning from war zones.

An acquaintance shared a similar soldier story. She worked in a successful investment company, learning the business from her boss, who had been a young man during the Vietnam War era. Many years after the war, the boss found himself often thinking of a soldier friend who had died in Vietnam. He became increasingly troubled, sad and de-energized. He shared this with my friend. They both noticed a feeling of heaviness and sadness, but only at work. This went on for some time, affecting the workplace atmosphere and quality of their focus. My friend, who was learning about these troubled spirits, put two and two together and suggested to her boss that this soldier's spirit was likely lingering and wanting help. If so, it was time to tell him he was indeed dead, give him instructions to head for the light, and suggest he turn and see others on the other side who were waiting. They both made a commitment to try this experiment. It worked. The atmosphere of the workplace cleared and her boss found he thought less frequently about his friend. When he did so, it was simply with compassion and appreciation.

## Mischief and Interference

Recently I had the privilege of interviewing a dimensional traveler and healer, Mearah Marqua from Hawaii. Mearah described her work as "helping those without their bodies on." At one point in her work, she found herself drawn to assist those spirits she called the ancients or ancestors of Hawaii. These spirits tended to gather at a particular place on one of the islands that she felt held more fourth- and fifth-dimensional energy. It was their best shot at heaven on earth. The ancestors had not moved on because they were attached to the land, an object or a person. The object might be a stone, sacred object or tree. The person might be a relative they felt they needed to be with. For example, the grandmother of a little girl who had died in the hospital was still there, still trying to assist her granddaughter. Some motives of the ancestors weren't laudable. They stayed to get even with someone. They stayed to get retribution and feed off of the fear in the situation. Whatever the reason, they were stuck.

Mearah described this situation as similar to the need for acupuncture. Acupuncture assists the patient in unblocking the energy flow in the body's meridians. Blocked energy is seen as contributing to the pain or illness. The Hawaiian ancestors were blocking some of the "meridians" of the islands. She was guided to work with several "acupuncture points" on the land. On four occasions, she worked with the ancestors, convincing them of the importance of making this transition. Eventually they all departed.

Mearah's stories included helping children who were having behavioral or learning difficulties. She gave an example of a nine-year-old girl who had developed increasingly disturbing behaviors. Her parents were desperate and ready to put their daughter on medication. Mearah could see into the child's energy field. The disturbing factor turned out to be the spirit of a 40-year-old woman who had become frightened and taken up residence in the energy field of the nine-year-old. Mearah called in some spirit guides and together they lovingly assisted the 40-year-old to her place in the afterlife. The nine-year-old became calm and showed no further need for medication.

We are seeing that sometimes someone dies and remains in the location of his or her death, unable to leave because of feeling incomplete. They feel something needs to be done, someone needs to be told or they want revenge. Someone may die not quite knowing what to do, and gloms onto a family member or other loved one for comfort. Or they may choose a total stranger, as with the nine-year-old in the example above. Usually it is someone who is considered loving, safe or comforting by the wandering soul.

Alberto Villoldo tells this story in an interview. (Sacred Mysteries Productions, DVD.) He was beginning a talk with the Random House Publishers sales force regarding his new book on shamanic healing. The audience was less than enthusiastic, prepared to yawn at an unfamiliar, "woo-woo" topic. Shortly into his talk the "editors' boss's boss" walked in the room. Everyone came to attention. "For the last 10 years I have had a problem with alcohol," he said. "After several sessions with one of Alberto's students, I am free of that problem. Listen to what he has to say." Then he left the room.

Later, Alberto spoke to his student and asked her what had happened. She said that when she saw the editor the first time, she noticed that his father's spirit was attached to his energy field, afraid to move on. The father had had a major drinking problem and had died 10 years earlier. She worked with the editor's father's spirit, helping him understand that he needed to move on into the afterlife and that all would be well. The father's spirit departed and the editor experienced immense relief as his drinking problem disappeared. His acceptance of this healing modality was complete and his gratitude profound.

It can be difficult to discern whether you are simply in the throes of the grief process, or if you are experiencing a confused spirit. Certainly the above story is instructive for us. Should your grieving process include unusual behaviors, you can be alert to this possibility. If you take on uncharacteristic anxiety or addictions, such as the editor who began drinking heavily, perhaps your loved one has not moved on. He or she is holding onto what is the familiar—you. You may be able to insist that your loved one depart while giving assurances of being loved and safe. If, necessary, someone knowledgeable can provide assistance .

The editor's father did not mean to create mischief. He simply couldn't figure out what had happened or what he needed to do. He was caught in his own lower astral levels of fear. So he clung to the familiar and attached himself to his son without realizing the effect. He needed some assistance to move to higher frequencies of love where he could find true comfort and healing. Some spirits are benevolent with little interference. Some are unconsciously creating difficulties, like the father above. Some aren't benevolent and create real mischief and trouble.

Should you be interested, these are additional authors who have written of their work in this field: Dr. Edith Fiore, *The Unquiet Dead;* and Louise Ireland-Frey, M.D., *Freeing the Captives.*

Let's explore one more example of how situations like these arise. We are going to return to some pioneers mentioned earlier. Robert Monroe is the man who brought out-of-body experiences to the forefront through his own unexpected journeys. Robert decided to take the approach of the researcher by documenting, cataloging and numbering the levels of consciousness to which he traveled. He called them *Focus Levels.* For example Focus 24, 25 and 26 are called the Belief System Territories. In this area of the consciousness continuum are souls who ascribe to specific religious or philosophical beliefs regarding the afterlife. Focus 34 and 35 are beyond human belief structures and are called The Gathering. Here we would also find beings from other parts of the universe.

Robert traveled the gamut of what we might categorize as lower and higher astral planes; murky places, places of some light and places of great joy where he witnessed souls gathering to learn, share and increase their awareness. When he found confused souls, he sat with them, giving them ideas about stepping beyond where they were and how they might do it; an inter-dimensional counselor, if you will.

Bruce Moen studied with Robert Monroe and became adept at OBE search-and-rescue forays into the lower astral levels, as well as travel to exalted realms. Several years ago, I attended his "Exploring the Afterlife" workshop in Albuquerque, New Mexico. Personally, I was thrilled by this opportunity but had no clue if I could travel into the out-of-body worlds suggested by the workshop flyer. I did know that I wanted to learn more from someone who did it regularly. Our group was impressed by Bruce's methodical training and entranced by his stories. I want to retell one of his wonderful stories of assisting a troubled soul that illustrates one of the ways we can get lost.

### *Chelik's Story*

Bruce received a request from a young woman whose friend, Chelik, had died in a street bombing incident in Israel. It had been over a year and she felt her friend's spirit had not moved on. She contacted Bruce to go check on Chelik. Bruce set out and found him hiding in the darkness of the in-between worlds, refusing to come out. Chelik didn't want to be seen, fearing that he was grotesque to look at, given that his body had been blown to bits in the bombing. He was killed in an Arab bomb attack just as he was completing his Israeli military service. He had no sense of how long it had been since he died.

Chelik was insistent that he needed to get the attention of his fellow soldiers. "I have a message I have to get back to my friends. Forgiveness is the only way. That is the only way this madness can stop...The Arabs and the Jews hate each other. We both carry that hatred around with us every place we go." Chelik was able to see that hatred breeds more hatred and perpetuates its own vicious cycle. He wanted it to stop. He wanted to be an advocate for forgiveness.

As Chelik became more adamant, he stepped out of the shadows appearing as a slender young man in a healthy body. He continued to ramble on about not being able to leave, that he had to get this message to his friends. You and I might say, well if he hasn't been able to contact his friends for a year, this tactic obviously isn't working. But to souls like Chelik, time isn't the same as it is to us; it was not directly a part of his reality. He knew that he had died but was surprised to learn it had been more than a year ago.

Upon arriving in the afterlife, Chelik's forgiveness realization was so profound and earth-shaking that he was determined to get his message back to his friends who were still fighting. It had so gripped him that he felt he must share it, hoping it might save some lives. This had become his mission. Though well-meaning, he was trapped by his obsession to save his comrades.

Bruce put out a call for assistance and noticed an elderly gentleman emerging from the shadows. He appeared in a long robe, holding a staff and wearing a yarmulke. The old man threw up his hands. "Do what you can. This boy is impossible! I have been trying to get through to him since he died." After a bit of clever re-education, Bruce was able to hand a stunned and relieved Chelik over to the old man. As they disappeared, Bruce noticed Chelik's clothing changing to ceremonial robes. Bruce followed. He saw that the old-man guide was taking Chelik to a lovely Jewish village scene in the afterlife, where he was being welcomed.

The old man explained to Bruce that Chelik had been caught in the belief that he needed to make atonement, thinking it meant to show grief and sorrow, but atonement, he added, is simply forgiveness. He thanked Bruce for being the human intercessor and using his skills in turning the situation around.

We questioned Bruce. Why couldn't the elder guide get the soldier's attention? Aren't they all-powerful on the other side? Here is Bruce's understanding. If those who have died are able to shift their focus to the next steps, the next adventure in the afterlife, they release more and more Earth identity, which enables them to perceive guides or angels or family who are in the afterlife. Then they advance in that direction. Awareness takes the lead.

If souls are so focused on the Earth—on family problems, on strong emotions or fears, like Chelik was—that focus is an earthly focus. Again, awareness takes the lead. In these cases, their focus is at the level of physical reality. By being so focused on things in the physical world, newly deceased people are limiting their own perceptual ability to 3-D. Their guides can attempt contact and offer assistance, but they are held back by people's inability to perceive them. Because guides are nonphysical beings, they are often invisible to the new soul crossing over. This can make it difficult, if not impossible, for the guide to be of assistance. They cannot interfere, due to the law of free will, and must wait for souls themselves to ask for help. In such cases, the person will more easily perceive a physically living human. Therefore, the assistance of a skilled human guide, still carrying the human-earth energy, is more likely to be seen and heard by those who are confused. This Earthly counsel can do the trick by helping souls shift their awareness. They can then be released from their bonds and turn toward their particular heaven.

You are getting the picture. The other side is set up, not only by wiser beings than ourselves, but by us. We set it up with our collective and individual focus. That's a big one to swallow. But it is a powerful key I want you to have.

Love—the big capital "L" Love—invites us to press on, to keep going and growing. Love allows us to create whatever kind of heaven or hell we are focused on. Love also invites us to awaken and do it consciously. In the meantime, we are allowed to drift to wherever our unconscious hopes and fears take us after death.

We, however, are not doing this alone. We are surrounded by grander forces than our own limited human minds. We each have a higher self, a part of our complex guidance system that is eternally conscious. This aspect is the superconscious or causal body we spoke of in the previous chapter. It is the higher-dimensional self. It is our divinity that is unlimited. It is our direct line to Source, no matter what. Our relationship to it is through the bridge of awareness and compassion.

In addition, we have helpers every step of the way. They have been called guardian angels, guides, ancestors and masters who respect and deeply love each of us. They acknowledge that the human journey is a most challenging one, and they respect every level of mastery we achieve, knowing it is hard-won. They have been in the dilemmas where we find ourselves and are our cheering section on the other side.

Here is where our power lies. By choosing to be conscious and empowered beings, we are more savvy on these trip-ups that can happen now and then. We know that higher frequencies and lower ones don't get along. So we simply continue our high-frequency work: meditation, joy, authenticity, resilience, sense of humor, good care of the body, forgiveness and blessings to all. We then cancel the energies that don't mesh with ours. Remember this.

Thousands of years ago, much of this information was known and used by many. What a boon for us that we are being gifted once again with these understandings on the departure process. We are seeing more clearly how to navigate the terrain. We are getting smarter in updating, editing and adding poetry to our own Going Out in Style Travel Guide.

# PART III

## *Tools for the Journey*

# PART III

## *Tools for the Journey*

### Introduction

DEPARTURE IS ONLY ONE PART of the consciousness continuum journey, but it is so significant that we want to be inspired. Gathering information and tools can serve our finer exit.

After all, death wants to evolve into our exquisite muse, our most demanding teacher, our finest poem. Departure sits tapping us gently on the shoulder or banging on the window if necessary, but it begs us to embrace life like there is no tomorrow. Of course, there is always a tomorrow; it just may not be here.

Death inspired my client, Nora, many years ago. I've mentioned her story. Her four-year-old daughter drowned during a family vacation. In the ensuing months and years, Nora pursued all avenues of inquiry into Emily's whereabouts and likely experience. She sought answers and solace—and in the process awakened to her soul.

Death, near-death to be exact, inspired Dr. Raymond Moody to research the near-death experiences of patients, and to publish his collected work in *Life After Life*. This small book kindled the flame of a worldwide movement.

Death inspired Siddhartha, a young Indian prince 2,500 years ago. One day while escaping the confines of the palace, he wandered the streets becoming more and more disturbed. All around, he witnessed aging, suffering and death. Siddhartha made a remarkable choice. He renounced all the status and wealth of his position, vowing to discover the cause of suffering and a path to relieve it. By utilizing suffering and death as his motivation, he reached a high level of enlightenment and taught the way of compassion and an untroubled mind. He became the one known as the Buddha.

Though these are dramatic inspirations, our departure muse can be awakened more quietly. Years ago, I began with the romantic desire to explore the afterlife realms through past-life regression therapy. I became intrigued. Though not everyone had a great trip to "heaven," certainly everyone's journey was unique to them. By being so intimately a part of PLR work, departure forced me to look more closely at what was showing up. Death became the inspiration for gathering the stories and material of this book.

In Chapter 9, *Clearing the Path*, we discuss tools for seeing the bigger story and clearing personal clutter. These lighten your energy for your life and your departure. Some of these tools may already be in your back pocket.

For more clarity and tools on the afterlife, Chapter 10, *Bridging the Worlds*, can assist you. A simple summary for departing in style is offered in Chapter 11, *First-Aid Departure Kit*. For those of you interested in creating departure ceremonies, Chapter 12 offers some guidelines.

# CHAPTER 9

# *Clearing the Path*

*I think the most important question facing humanity is, "Is the universe a friendly place?" This is the first and most basic question all people must answer for themselves.*
—Albert Einstein

W HEN EVENING EVENTUALLY ROLLED around, we were more than ready. So was my mother. The dishes were done, pajamas donned and the difficulties of navigating through tempestuous waters in a large family eased. It was story time. Whether I was age five or twelve, with many younger siblings, I couldn't resist one more chapter in *Little House on the Prairie*, or whatever adventure book called us. But we had to earn it. The requirements, besides generally behaving ourselves, were either massaging Mom's shoulders or brushing her hair. We took turns. It was never questioned. Please, one more chapter, please! After promising our allegiance to her requirements, we were granted the delight of seeing Laura, Mary, Pa and Ma Ingalls through another winter snowstorm. Their hard life seemed quite romantic compared to our own.

After mothering my own three daughters, I fully understand the end-of-the-day exhaustion and the desire for a bit of reward. My mother's requirements taught us to give in order to receive, which developed our compassion and sensitivity. Most of all, we learned the power of story. Laura Ingalls Wilder's pioneer childhood, though very plain and filled with struggle, became magical through the well-told story. We knew on some level that since she survived those hardships, so could we. When you are in the midst of your own story, you don't know if you will truthfully survive, but there is hope. Because others have been brave, you can be brave also.

Whether from nursery rhymes, Aesop's fables, fairy tales, or my mother reciting Alfred Noyes' "The Highwayman" from memory, we became steeped in appreciation of a good story. The stories had the usual beginning that started something like "Once upon a time," a middle filled with challenge and adventure, and then an end that resolved into some version of "happily ever after," or at the very least, a lesson learned. I preferred the happily-ever-afters.

Stories moved our mountains. Whatever tensions may have flourished between siblings during the busy day dissolved as the story, under our mother's expert rendition, drew us into itself. Whatever tiredness she was feeling released somewhat as we attempted our best shoulder rubs and our best sitting still. We were inspired by verbs and syntax and history and another way to understand love. We became bigger. We didn't know that, of course. It was simply a story and we wanted more.

Story makes life more real and alive. Story works the whole brain. A good story engages the heart and enlivens the soul. The world grows larger before our eyes and in some sense we feel our aliveness within the cosmic scheme. Our soul wants to discover itself through the story we are living, wants to find its *real* story underneath the noise and tell it again and again, until we stand shining under the noonday sun. Our story tells and retells itself through the rise and fall of our own personal adventures. Perhaps through the retelling, a need is met and we can validate our existence, or better know who we are. We might consider that the story we are in the midst of is trying to make us bigger. It's changing the world as we have known it.

Isn't that how it is when you tell a story of what happened yesterday as you suddenly realized that your lawn-mower boy reminded you of your cousin at that age? That's why you were reacting to his shyness. Every time you tell it from your heart, you have more understanding of your own story. Perhaps the lawn-mower boy is a link to the muddled relationship with your cousin. As you feel more tenderness for his shyness, your tenderness for your cousin grows.

We are meant to hold our story precious while also cleaning up its misspellings and misunderstandings, rewriting it over and over until it's really vital and alive. We want our story to sing. We want to find our authentic voice through our ever-evolving narrative. Until we understand that it's our *own* story that wants telling, we may feel obsessed with someone else's story or the collective dramas espoused through the media. Once we know it's our story we are trying to track, we can smile at our need to see a movie three times. We can take what gives insight and color to our own journey, leaving the rest.

We live in a reality awash in stories. There are the big stories contained in myth and legend, religion and nationalism that influence whole generations. These stories inform our behavior and our psyche as a group. There are the stories handed down from our grandmothers that weave themselves into the lore of our own personal lives. From all these stories, we gather up survival tools and discover how to be a "good woman" or a "courageous man." We decide, as Albert Einstein suggested, whether this is a friendly or unfriendly universe. Is life basically an adventure to be taken, or is it a war of survival from start to finish? Can I trust you? Can I trust myself? Is this a good neighborhood of life for me to live in?

In childhood, we spend a significant amount of energy trying to comprehend the story in which we find ourselves. It takes a great deal of effort. Children are often deciding if they agree with the story. Some brave folks have told me that early in childhood they knew the story they were told was a lie. The teaching on religion, bigotry, gender roles or heaven/hell felt wrong. It made no sense. It wasn't the truth of things. They witnessed how the old story in their family, church or school had become an ascribed truth long after its usefulness had passed. Basically, the story was too small.

We are participating in a grand story of universal proportions. Here, on the edge of the Milky Way Galaxy, the heart of our exquisite planet is breaking with the swell of human upheaval and suffering. We could safely say that we are participating in a swirling story involving about 7 billion individual human realities. We are in the difficult part of the tale in which the drama is heating up to a fever pitch. The heroes and anti-heroes keep changing according to the interpretation and spin of the day. We wonder how to weave a collective mythology that sustains and unifies. We sense that somehow a bigger story is coming into being, one that contains and absorbs the 7 billion smaller stories into itself. Most of us could sincerely say that we long for that story, that greater story, to be filled with hope and joy and a new light rising within human consciousness.

The part of the human story that you and I are delving into, in order to correct misspellings and misunderstandings, is the section on departure. We aren't alone in our search for an updated and excellent departure story. We are blessed by those who have searched the highways and side roads of the departure experience. You have been introduced to a number of them.

If we were to go back in time in order to visit past cultures who valued dying skills, we might hike into the Himalayan Mountains to the highest Buddhist monasteries of pre-Chinese-occupied Tibet (*Tibetan Book of the Dead*). We could choose to be privy to the secret initiation rites of an ancient Egyptian priestly class (*Egyptian Book of the Dead*). We might walk the dusty old paths to the ashram of the great Indian yogi, Patanjali (teachings on yogic wisdom). These excursions, going back hundreds and thousands of years, would yield rich secrets and powerful tools. These tools would include the rigorous disciplines considered necessary for transcending the pitfalls of life, and ascending to the higher dimensions of the afterlife.

If we were so inclined, we could also focus our time travel back 2,000 years to the land of Palestine. Here, we could listen to the radical teachings of the young Rabbi Yeshua and his insistence that the heart holds the path to our divinity—not laws, empty rituals or dogma—and is the clearest bridge to the afterlife. In fact we would be hard-pressed to find any venerable tribe or culture not concerned in some fashion with the afterlife. The conundrums of inhabiting a human body that dies, while simultaneously having a consciousness that transcends death, are not unique to 21st century people.

But we are everyday folks. Most of us aren't in ashrams meditating five hours a day. We haven't been chosen by a ruling priestly class for our exceptional spiritual qualities. We couldn't live in a Tibetan monastery even if we wanted to. We are post-modern earthlings maxing out on uncertainties, health issues, money worries, environmental disasters and relationship woes. We are beset with too much minutiae and not enough substance.

Precisely because of all these challenges, I believe we are learning to be exceptional. I believe we are pushing out of the cocoon of controlled behaviors and limited thinking, and finding our wings, no matter where or who we are. I believe that the breakup of the old ways is here and the vast potential of the consciousness continuum is opening to us as never before.

Massive shifts in consciousness are also precarious times. Often during times of upheaval, many souls choose to leave the planet. Some go one at a time; some in large groups through either natural or man-made disasters. Should you suddenly find that you are one of those who are leaving, perhaps something in our conversation on tools will be of benefit for your departure. May you transcend fear and rise to your highest light. If you find that you are one who chooses to stay, may you know you are a fabulously created being here to bring in the new, more highly evolved human. May you *know* what you know and live from your deepest truth. Perhaps you will find inspiration to help assist those around you who are passing.

I'm excited when I hear people really understanding that death is like the end of one chapter and the beginning of another in their ongoing story. They have no doubt that the adventure continues. Having gone through some sort of awakening or education on the subject, they feel equipped to turn the page when the time comes and fly free.

However, I'm suggesting that all of us—the confident and the scared—can benefit from a few more departure tools. Tools can help in clearing the path. Tools assist in building stronger bridges on the journey to the next chapter called *The Other Side,* which begins immediately on the next breath of consciousness. Tools give us impetus to better monitor tangents and distractions. We can determine if we are staying in alignment with our manuscript, our getting-conscious assignment, our true story.

## TOOLS

### Basic Styles

If you have identified yourself as a Chapter 1, Basic Style person, I know you may have some resistance to this topic. You don't particularly want to dwell on departure or analyze how it works. You may either think it's a morbid subject or you have a pretty set view of how it works. You might feel you are right. And you don't want to be bothered with too much detail.

We will keep it simple. Perhaps you would identify with a student of mine in an "End-of-Life Care" class years ago. This student listened patiently for a while. Finally she asked, "So what's the bottom line? What's the main deal when we are dying or we are helping someone who is dying?" Needing the simple version, she drew her own conclusion. "Can we just say, 'Go to the light'?" Of course. When we need the basics, this is the place to start.

### *Basic Style Tools*

### 1. Light

When you are dying, head for the light. It's the light NDE people usually see. Ask for the light if you don't see it. Call it by whatever name you prefer. Merge with it if you can. Don't look back. Go for it.

## 2. Love

Meld with love, like the most gracious mother's embrace. While we are on the subject, let yourself become really comfortable with feeling and giving love now. It all counts.

## 3. Let go

Let go of fears and negative emotions while you are still alive. This will smooth the way for you. Then when you die you are better equipped to let go of the life that is passing. You can be in the afterlife more fully. Say goodbye and let go of your family. Let go of rigidity and let love and light show you where to go.

## 4. Get help

If you want help, ask for it. You will find that you aren't alone.

**Traditional Styles**

If you are identified more with the Traditional Styles category, you are comfortable with traditional religious guidelines or traditional intellectual approaches. Let's look at tools for you.

## *Traditional Religious Style Tools*

Ask yourself a few questions:
- *What in my religious belief system gives me comfort with departure?* Here you might find gifts like faith, assurance, love and appreciation for the mystical nature of death. Focus on deepening these qualities within yourself as you go about your days.
- *What aspect of the divine do I feel personally connected to?* This may include a mother figure such as Mother Mary or Guadalupe or Quan Yin or simply Divine Mother. It may be a father figure such as Jesus, The Lord, Mohammed, Krishna, Buddha or Divine Father. Whoever opens your heart the most is who you pay attention to. This archetypal energy assists you, links you to the energy they carry, creating the heart-bridge that you travel upon. Grow that heart-bridge by invoking this being in your meditations and prayers.
- *What about departed loved ones and ancestors? Do I believe that I will find them again in the afterlife?* If you do, be aware of their essence,

particularly when the transition portal is beginning to open for you. They can be of great assurance.

- If you haven't yet grappled with the questions at the end of Chapter 6, please do so. They are helpful in clarifying your faith and what fears you may still carry.

## Traditional Intellectual Style Tools

You might consider these guidelines:

- While you are alive, why not commit to being a lifelong learner, if you haven't already? Observe nature, the cycles and seasons, and find the graciousness undergirding life. Release yourself periodically from the noise of the news.
- Use your mind, your bigger mind. Be the observer and experiencer as you transition. Enjoy watching things unfold. However, know that you are the creator as well, so be mindful of your own personal psychology and wise energy use. Do you like to ask questions? Find great answers? This can serve you well both now and in the afterlife.
- Stay open. Choose to travel as far as you can after you have completed your goodbyes and departed. For example, if you are a scientist and are avid about your field of study, you will have the opportunity to learn more in your specialty in the afterlife schools that our PLR clients and OBE friends talk about. Your intention and passion will take you to that particular afterlife place of further learning, when you are ready.

### Conscious Choice Style

The following tools are not only for Conscious Choice people but everyone, whatever your style may be. In addition to the very real work of periodic counseling, bodywork/energy work and psychotherapy that are often necessary, these tools are empowering for us no matter where we are on our journey. Some of them will simply be reminders because you are already on the job of clearing your own path. The more conscious we are, the more we want to get cracking and make a difference.

## Bigger Story Tool

The tool of our bigger story is the tool of perspective. With our bigger story, we are able to gaze out the window and see a path that draws us, whereas before all we were able to see was suffering and helplessness. In the smaller story, it's hard to find the window, let alone the path waiting for us. We may have resigned ourselves to believing it's all God's will or some unknown karmic contract.

To see our bigger story, we often start with suffering and feeling helpless. Eventually we want a way through the suffering and we want to find help. That's the beginning of the bigger story, the first page. We may go through many cycles of suffering and helplessness. This is our psyche's effort to heal past wounds. With each cycle we have the option of becoming stronger and more self-aware. If we keep following what relieves suffering, and finding ways of helping ourselves out of the mud, we discover a bit more energy. It may be the energy of hope. It may even be the energy of adventure because some of the heaviness has been lifted.

The truth of the bigger story is that we are souls on a journey of growth and self-discovery. We seldom bring with us a clean slate when we enter a life. We usually come with something from past lives that we want to clean up or learn more about. We come with some level of growth and mastery in mind. Even that small, fresh-faced infant you were cooing over at the grocery store is on a soul mission.

It isn't unusual for PLR clients to get into the afterlife and make some comment about how they wish they had been more courageous or less small-minded in the life they just finished. They say things like, "That was a waste!" or "Why didn't I speak up?" or "I learned some things about love, but have a ways to go yet." They are relieved to have a break but realize that they missed some key elements in their learning. They want to come back and get that wisdom piece of their story wrapped up.

With that perspective in mind, we can better embrace life's challenges. This takes us out of that helpless victim mentality and gives impetus to be a learner. We start with the situation we are in. We say, I'm in the amazing story of my soul. I don't necessarily understand what this story is about, but it's mine! We commit to getting some tools and tackling what is before us. We join the crowd of other souls who are waking up to their soul's journey. We realize we aren't alone and that self-discovery is compelling.

Did you know that "Earth School" seems to have quite a reputation in the afterlife? Earth is known as a very, very difficult, but highly effective classroom. The wisdom component of the soul can blossom better here than in some more benevolent realms, because of the challenging nature of our curriculum. In her regression research, Dolores Cannon has found that there is a waiting line of souls to register for a place in our school. There are often more souls who want to incarnate here, but the right body or situation hasn't been available. When some people hear that, they say, no way did I want to come to Earth! It's way too hard! So a gentle reminder may be helpful; the ego doesn't choose—but the soul, which has the bigger story in view—does. Once again, we see the value of tapping into a greater perspective so we function more effectively.

Our bigger story can:
1. Relieve us of being victims and turn us into learners.
2. Remind us that we, at the soul level, chose to be here.
3. Give us courage to face the difficulties because finding mastery through these difficulties, and walking through these fears, may be just the empowerment we are seeking.
4. Grace us with a sense that we are part of the Mystery, the greater story unfolding on Earth.
5. Help us realize that it's all about getting conscious, whether we are living or dying.

### *Rewriting and Updating Your Bigger Story*
For this exercise, ponder these questions and jot down your insights:

*Where in my life have I often felt like a victim?*
Have you felt like a victim of circumstances, of loss and betrayal? Or of not enough of something like love, attention, money, respect or security? Perhaps you have felt like a victim at work, on the school bus or in the family. You may have given and given until you are drained and feel as though no one appreciates your sacrifice. You are stretched for time—always. Too much time spent on doing what you hate, and not on what you love, a victim of time and set schedules. You may have been a victim of the harsher realities of war, sexual abuse, beatings, hunger or devastating illness. You may be feeling excruciatingly lonely—a victim of loneliness.

Wherever in your experience you feel or have felt a victim of life's hardships, is an exceptionally important place in your story. You are in the part between "Once upon a time" and "happily ever after," the part where the real essence of your story takes place. It's the part where you become the hero or heroine in the Rumpelstiltskin fairy tale. You find nothing but straw (hardship) and learn to spin it into gold (wisdom/learning.)

Some of the most compassionate healers I know are the ones who, through healing their own abusive childhoods or traumas, come to deeply understand the healing process. They have an innate sensitivity and wisdom they bring to their therapy rooms. That's a straw-into-gold example that creates the bigger story.

Take a moment and list all the types of victimhood you have experienced. Next to each one, list something of gold that you have gotten from it. If you aren't sure, hazard a guess. For example, after becoming a widow, did you gain a new understanding of the grieving process or learn to become more independent? After living with noise and chaos throughout your childhood, did you develop a keen skill for creating order and calm? I understand that it wasn't easy and that you may not be through the pain, but if you continue to do this exercise, over time, I promise you will find the gold within your story.

*What is the gift that I can give because of what I have learned through these difficulties?*

On this one, you might be quite practical, but I want you to enjoy dreaming as well. List all that you have to offer because of what you have experienced. You may be a more grounded and loving friend or you may now have a new book to write or class to offer. You may be able to bring a new pattern of healthier behavior to your family, benefiting the next generation. You can join with many of my clients who say, "The pattern stops with me. No more!" Perhaps you can say that you are a more understanding parent or a more fearless and assertive leader because you have been through your own fiery challenges.

*How am I living my life more consciously because of what I have learned? How is my understanding of life and death evolving because I am living in the bigger story?*

This can be subtle or overt. Are you feeling more purposeful? Do you sense more direction or ease? Are you less fearful? Are you facing difficulties, knowing that they may be just what you are needing to master your life? Can you imagine the value within the work you are doing? And that this is the gold you will be able to take with you to the other side? You might find yourself feeling more confident, wise or free of victim thinking. You may realize that you are stepping out of your fear and really learning to love. Perhaps you are learning to handle conflict and use it to grow. Perhaps there is a new trust of life, of a divine plan or of a greater picture that gives you assurance and joy.

Make a list of the ways you are living your life more fully because of what you have experienced.

**Tool #1.** We rewrite our story from a larger perspective, a higher state of awareness. As we do so, this adventure tale becomes more than confusing piles of straw with no value. We better comprehend that the straw needs the focus of our love to turn it into golden threads with which we reweave our life story.

## *Unhooking Addictions Tool*

To be human seems to include a propensity toward addictions. To have a sensual body that enjoys eating and drinking and sex, to have a nervous system that wants to slow down or rev up, to have a mind that wants to experience altered states, to have an emotional nature that wants to feel secure, loved and familiar—all these carry the potential for getting hooked in some way. If you come from a heritage of addictive patterns, you are all set up for the addictions journey. It is then part of your story and you can make it into gold if you choose.

I have mentioned addictions in the context of our departure conversation, and here's why: Addictions can hold us back in the afterlife. During our life, they become a substitute for love, security and the lift we want from Spirit. It's a familiar cycle. At first, the addiction gives us something of a high or blissful feeling. But as many of you know, this wanes and the feeling becomes harder to achieve. Addictions are often an attempt to numb out "unacceptable" feelings such as anger, fear, loneliness, abandonment, etc. Addictions then become a side trip we take in hopes of getting that "good" feeling without having to experience the "bad" one. They are an understandable self-medication attempt to survive difficulties and traumas. But they've not shown themselves to provide the real goods. They are distracting to our focus and hold us back. They become an escape hatch and deplete us of our wholeness. It becomes difficult to really get conscious. But if we work it right, addictions can be a great venue for getting conscious.

Addictions include:
- Substances: Alcohol, drugs, nicotine, food.
- Stuff: Money, shopping, collecting, "bigger and better," etc.
- Relationships: Fear of being alone.
- Sex: From insatiable, unconsciously driven sex to compulsive, warped sexual predation.
- Religion: Escaping into religious/spiritual groups and belief systems.
- Drama: Needing upheaval and chaos. Uncomfortable with quiet and calm. The victim habit with habitual anger and/or blame.
- Power over others: Needing to manipulate, control, feed off of others' weaknesses. This may include thieving, conniving, striving for control over others.
- Power over self: Perfectionistic obsession with body image, cleanliness. Excessive need of control over some part of one's life.
- Technology: Compulsive and habitual use of computer games, cell phone messaging, television, etc. Feeding the jittery surface mind. Avoiding calm and depth.

One of the most powerful addiction-healing tools I know is facing and feeling all of our emotions. We don't escape by intellectualizing or grabbing for another addiction distraction. Instead we enter that place of genuine, what-am-I-truly-feeling courage. The body is a crucial part of this emotional work; therefore, good nutrition and endocrine balance are also important.

Here is the afterlife part. If our energy field holds a lot of addiction energy when we depart, our spirit is drawn to that particular area of the afterlife where others who share that addiction are still trying to work it out. For example, a power and manipulation addiction would take you to the "power hell" that fits you and you would only be with those who strive for cruel power over others. The game would continue for you until you'd had enough. You would indulge until you reached some state of boredom or dismay and wanted out. Then the addiction energy would drop away because it wasn't being fed. You could then be escorted into higher-frequency heavens.

Another option is that you get a break in the afterlife from all your addictive tendencies. You experience a great deal of love and support. Then you return to another life in which you will work on the unfinished issue/addiction. All we are saying is that it's simpler to deal with addictions now, given all the support groups, treatment programs and growth potential we have available on this side.

**Tool #2:** We commit to overcoming our addictions by facing them and letting them be the vehicles of our growth in consciousness. There is a lot of good support out there. We don't have to do this alone.

## Forgiveness or Letting Go Tool

Sometimes I've looked back at my earlier life in dismay. How could I have been so blind? How could I have behaved in that manner or not seen the pain I was causing? How could I have been so self-absorbed? Why did I focus on things that didn't matter? Why was I so shy about speaking my truth? The list goes on. Only as I am able to shift into the bigger story, can I place my life in more perspective, understand that I was doing the best I knew to do, and let go of that self-blame. It's a journey of dropping the finger-pointing and opening the heart. Life is an ongoing class in cultivating forgiveness and gratitude. This helps the story become bigger. Complaining and blaming keeps the story small. Forgiveness is an evolving experience of letting go that we do for ourselves.

One morning in our meditation group, I was feeling some sadness that I was less than robust in my courage toward life. I flashed on my paternal grandparents for some reason. There I saw my deceased grandmother Anna, shy and reserved, speaking mostly German, always in the kitchen with wonderful smells. She was pregnant before they married, so the story goes—a totally unacceptable state of affairs in her time and culture. For this offense, she and my grandfather were properly shamed by family and church. I can only imagine how that stain of guilt must have colored her life. I sensed that shame this morning and the subtle emotional lineage rippling into the generations that followed. My father brought with him some of that shame, and though never mentioned, it was palpable enough. Unsettled sadness, such as this, weaves itself into the fabric of the following generations that we may carry unawares.

I doubt that my grandmother felt forgiveness from her family or was able to imagine forgiving herself. She and my grandfather went on to raise a large, strapping German Mennonite family and for all intents and purposes became normal and productive citizens. The fact that my grandmother came to me and that I sometimes feel the weight of my own imperfections, tells me that another layer of forgiveness is calling my name. There is something that I carry of her, in not only my genetic stock, but in my emotional makeup. By letting go and offering compassion to myself, I can also extend this more gracious way of holding life, back through the generations. She would no doubt smile in amazement at the very pregnant brides walking down aisles today—with no guilt.

The places where we aren't forgiven, where we still feel guilty or hold someone else guilty, are the places where the weeds grow. When I can hold the wonder of the bigger story, I realize that being a student of life changes everything. Anything can be forgiven. Anything can be healed. The weeds become wild roses growing along the fence. I learn by experience and part of learning is not understanding the nature of weeds until I've dealt with them a few times. Finding my way through the weed patch is the learning part. Healing is when I can embrace the whole shebang in some kind of gratitude. Healing is when I can find the gift in the pain. Then I can grow roses.

Helen Denning, Ph.D., author of *Life Without Guilt,* researched the guilt phenomenon. She accessed past-life memory with her clients that related to their crippling guilt in this life. PLR therapy brought to light situations from the past that the soul had carried, about which he or she still felt guilt and shame. The guilt was unconsciously repeating itself in their present lives through their present experiences. It was difficult to release. They had built a legacy of guilt spanning the centuries. What we learn from Dr. Denning's work is how the power of unresolved pain/blame/guilt/shame continues with us, life after life, until we can release it. "Aaron's Story" in Part IV is an example of this legacy.

Forgiveness is the act of letting go. And letting go again. It is embracing the lessons, finding gratitude for that growth, and feeling less and less emotional charge around the experience. Whatever happened, happened. It can't be undone. It may not have been right, and we needn't condone those behaviors, but it is now a part of our story. What shall we do with it? Our power and freedom comes from changing our orientation to what happened. The more we can find meaning in it all, the more likely our recovery. Meaning comes with some sense of service, and compassion for the suffering of all concerned, including ourselves. We are aiming for a more empowered and kindly inner landscape. Whether your finger has been pointing outward or inward, either way we are looking for that tendency to subside.

**Forgiveness Exercise 1**
a)   Take a moment to consider a difficult relationship or situation in your life.
     Notice the blame and resentment you feel toward this person or situation.

Note all the things about this person or situation that really gripe y̆. It's okay. Spell them out.

b) Now, ask yourself, where in me are these same qualities or behaviors? For example, if your list includes someone who is immature or irresponsible, ask when do I behave like that? If someone is arrogant and annoying to you, ask do I have a secret desire to have that quality she has, i.e. confidence? Or where am I arrogant and superior? Don't hold back. Your ego can handle the probing and will be stronger in the end. Find the parts of yourself that are similar, either obvious or repressed.

c) You may begin to see the way in which your criticism of someone else mirrors the way you are unconsciously in judgment of those same qualities within yourself. Or, if you are very astute, that your blame of another may be envy that you don't have what they have. Keep working this until you can find the lost parts of yourself, the rejected parts, the shadow self that has been pushed aside. Perhaps a small orphaned inner child will rise from the depths of your soul. All that rises is important.

d) Lastly, take a moment to find some compassion for the way that these patterns have tried to help you. These blame/shame/guilt beliefs are often old ego patterns that have become convoluted. In a similar way to healing the victim pattern that we did earlier, see the way that your guilt has tried to serve you. Perhaps, you have hurt someone so badly that your guilt is trying to keep you from ever hurting someone again. Or perhaps you have been hurt and are bitter and blaming. Your blame is trying to make someone else wrong so you can feel less hurt. Thank your patterns for trying to protect you from either getting hurt or from being the cause of someone's pain. Begin to know that blame and guilt are survival tools but not thriving tools. Allow some tenderness, some compassion toward yourself, much like you would a small hurting child. Let your heart soften. Be in compassion as you embrace the many challenges you have faced. Know that it is the same with everyone you meet. They may be facing quiet hells of which you know nothing. As your heart softens, notice some of the judgment falling away. Your inner space is cleaner now, your story more alive and authentic.

My Grandma Anna would be astonished by this option of self-compassion and its obvious link to compassion for everyone's suffering. She would be somewhat befuddled. The possibility that her suffering and self-condemnation

enough food, water and shelter to survive. We have options for stability and security that are greater than many past cultures provided. Therefore we can do more than simply survive; we can heal, thrive and contribute to the greater good. Our access to information, education and spirituality is limitless. Add to that the complex challenges so many are facing and you have a formula to bring forward vast inner strengths and skills.

To shepherd myself means that I include all the various parts of my nature. I include all past lives, even though I may not know about them. I embrace the opportunities to grow. I decide to include all the parts of my story, like a shepherd who guards and guides his entire flock of sheep. I say, "All this is my life—completely, uniquely and amazingly mine."

**Tool #4:** We clear the path by holding our entire life as precious. Through containment and shepherding, we provide a compassionate embrace without loose ends.

## Practicing Goodbyes Tool

Whatever you are doing, notice the beginning and the end. If you are going for an evening jog, notice that you begin at your doorstep. So say "hi" to the beginning of your jaunt down the trail. When you are coming up to the end of your workout, say "goodbye" and give thanks to the Earth and your body. Be aware that the sun has gone down a bit more and that you are ready to call it a day. Note the end of things as well as the beginning. Practice elegant goodbyes, no matter what they are. Your heart will find most goodbyes simple—the end of the day, the end of lunch, the end of a phone conversation. No-sweat goodbyes. Others are more challenging, like seeing a child off to college or moving to a new location. Goodbye to the child or the old home can still be accomplished with elegance and class. Say goodbye with clear intention and compassion. Through your tears you turn your heart to what happens next, being as fully present as you can. We practice goodbyes by releasing roles and identities that are past, like husband or boss or householder. We practice by releasing whatever is no longer necessary, from possessions to culture.

Of course, you know what we are aiming at here. It is important to embrace hellos and goodbyes as innate to life. There is a strength that comes with accepting the impermanence of things. Every goodbye is a practice for whatever grace we bring to our own planetary departures—and an opportunity to root out whatever heebie-jeebies we still have about dying.

Saying goodbye is a practice in being intensely alive to the present and the realization of the truth of our existence in these time-limited bodies. We can be like my friend Mia's father. After a near-death experience in the hospital, Robert Curtiss said matter-of-factly, "Well, that was a trial run!" He knew he was practicing for his final farewell.

At the same time you are saying goodbye, do you get better at realizing that an end is also a beginning? This is our practice in playing the consciousness continuum game. Life force doesn't stop; it changes form and expression. We ease from one part of the day to another, from one role with our children to another with our boss. We ease from yesterday into today more seamlessly. Our consciousness has continued from that Now to this one. In like manner, we are consciously intending a seamless easing from this body and life to the next steps of our soul, the next Now. When your departure time has arrived, you will have no need to resist or drag it out, for you will be well disciplined in the art of completing, then releasing and courageously smiling at what comes next.

This tool, combined with departure education and a deep stillness practice, supports us in staying conscious through our transition. We are paying attention. We are as calm as possible. We are present to all that we are experiencing. There is less clinging because we have learned to let go more readily. Included in our emotions are those of a calm, anticipatory and courageous nature. We transform death from a dreaded necessity to a sacred goodbye. And though we may feel sorrow, we can also smile at what happens next, for our soul is slipping into the driver's seat.

**Tool #5:** We clear the path by practicing gracious hellos and goodbyes. This firms up our core self and empowers our departure.

Our box of tools allows for a bigger story. It allows for growth through all the difficulties of life and an awakening of compassion for all who suffer. We gather gratitude and forgiveness, healing and empowerment. A greater spaciousness enfolds our journey. Conflict becomes a catalyst for growth, rather than a cause for war. These seemingly simple disciplines are effective in dissolving the traps of our common reality. Our toolbox then allows for another wonderful tool—joy. In activating our own innate joy, we launch ourselves onto the high-frequency journey of the soul.

# CHAPTER 10

# *Bridging the Worlds*

*When I die, I might as well die alive.*
—"Too Late to Die Young: Nearly True Tales from a Life"
by Harriet McBryde Johnson

*There is no death and there are no dead.*
—"Soul Shift" by Mark Ireland

SOMETIMES WE HEAR SOMEONE SAY, "Well it's all conjecture. We don't *really* know about the afterlife. We can't. All this is theory." While there is truth to these sentiments, I would counter with two questions. Are we limiting our options by validating only that which we can experience with our eyes, ears, nose, tongue or touch? Are there other senses and skills by which we can actually *know* about the afterlife while alive in these bodies? Perhaps perceiving the reality of the afterlife rests in expanding our consciousness rather than expecting truth to arrive upon the five physical senses. This may be a stretch for many. However, stretching consciousness is the name of the game we are playing.

How many people need to go to the other side before we have a consensus on its realities and variations? We have a quandary on our hands. New research is raising questions about our past assumptions. Will we open to it or continue to demand more proof—or both? As I write, I am thinking of the flat-Earth philosophy and how challenging the new discoveries were to that belief system. The stunning information that Earth was not flat after all, shattered the social, political, religious and psychological structures of 15th century Europe. Explorers had ventured beyond the known world and returned with new concepts. With this information, the old "truths" crumbled and a vibrant world of possibility was born.

We are participating in an even more remarkable shift in possibilities. Consciousness explorers have gone beyond the safe known world of Western thought, religious teachings and medicine. These are the inner landscape, multidimensional explorers you have been reading about. As Christopher Columbus and Amerigo Vespucci returned with treasure and tales for Queen Isabella of Spain, so too are our consciousness explorers returning with treasure today. To accept these gifts means further exploration of the trails into the inner worlds. Unlike the power struggles between the Spanish, French, Portuguese and English for a power hold in the New World of the Americas, these inner realms belong to everyone. No one entity owns the inner life and afterlife real estate. No one group or religion, no matter what the teachings have been, has first dibs. As we let our own flat-Earth-style beliefs drop away, the bigger story of reality becomes our priceless gem. How many more afterlife stories do we need to hear? I'm amazed by the swelling tide of those who've faced the prevailing and contradictory afterlife teachings and found a direct way to their own truth. We are becoming the Queen Isabellas of our own turf and receiving the gifts of "proof" coming our way.

After conducting PLRs, reading case studies and hearing stories, I would be remiss to conclude that we simply can't know. I haven't had an NDE, but I have touched the numinous and felt whisperings from those/that which I cannot see with my physical eyes. Though my skeptical mind is alive and well, there is a growing joy with this expansion of "real." Nonphysical means of perceiving—our inner senses of seeing, hearing, touching, feeling—are coming alive in us. What we call real is expanding every day. With our inner senses, the multidimensional worlds are most often *felt*. Because our 3-D time, space and density break apart on the other side, our bridge to the afterlife is via internal experience.

## UNDERSTANDING THE AFTERLIFE

To support your further education and your heart, here is a summary of afterlife experiences and information. It is encouraging to find the cross-correlation between authors and researchers. It is confirming to see how the experiences of PLR clients also mirror this treasure-trove of material. Those of us working quietly in our private practices hit many unexpected twists and turns with regression clients. It's never boring. But we wonder how we are doing. Whether through support groups, colleagues, clients or written material, it's rewarding for us to see the commonality of the information coming through. I hope this review of what we are learning about the afterlife will be helpful for your knowledge base, as well as encouraging to your heart.

### Common Descriptors of the Afterlife

- The afterlife has many layers or dimensions. A few are heavy and dark. Some are remarkably similar to a higher-frequency Earth. Others are brilliant, luminous, ethereal and filled with the indescribable consciousness of love.

- The other side interweaves with 3-D. It is here now. For example, we travel there in our dreams and daydreams. We might sense someone we love who has died. We have images and feel energies that are not of this dimension. We can leave our bodies and access the other side while still living this life. We can learn to shift our perceptions so that heaven presents itself.

- The afterlife experience differs with each person because it is a continuation of the unique consciousness that each has developed. We glide across on the frequency we have built during our lives.

- In the afterlife, we continue to inhabit a body, only it is a lighter energetic one. It may be seen as similar to the physical body we had, only in its prime. This energetic body changes as we let go of Earth identity. The higher into the dimensions, the more variety with the body. The energy body can expand from one that appears more human, to one of luminous light, to one of geometric shapes, to one of sound and beyond.

- We may reach the afterlife immediately after the body dies and find ancestors, soul groups or master teachers. We may reach the afterlife in stages. We might remain on Earth a while, for example, and watch over our burials and families. Then, we might drift about, eventually moving from the lower physical realm to higher vibrational areas. Most people notice a light of some sort and arrive in an area that feels familiar or has familiar beings.

- We can be in the afterlife but not realize it. We can inadvertently still be involved with Earth life, not realizing our death has occurred and we are without a solid physical form. We may see our form but haven't realized it is only etheric or energetic.

- In the afterlife, communication is through thought. Thoughts are instantaneous in their effect. Thoughts are not hidden. Neither is there any snooping into our thoughts by others. There is simply much more transparency of mind.

- There is a period of adjustment after leaving the body. For some, it is very short, and for others it is longer, depending on their consciousness and the type of death they experienced.

- The afterlife has many places for rest and recuperation after difficult lives and deaths. These places are designed to fit each soul's needs and personal psychology and often resemble something familiar and comforting. After recuperating, the soul moves on to its next steps in the afterlife.

- The level of our spiritual development while on Earth guides our afterlife travel. Nothing is forced in the afterlife. Souls go to where they are most comfortable, i.e. where their energy fits the best.

- Restrictions and limitations in consciousness that we bring with us from our Earth experience are gently eased by the higher afterlife energies.

- Small amounts of negativity can be transformed by the Light of God/ Source/Love and the soul can be lifted into more radiant levels. High amounts of negativity are too dense and draw the soul to areas that fit its energy. Like attracts like. Personal volition is important. Any soul can release negativity at any time by deciding to change and request help.

- There is no one-size-fits-all in the afterlife. We all create our own experiences.

- The only judgment in the afterlife is self-judgment. Self-evaluation, with the help of guides, assists the person in understanding what has been learned and not learned from the life just completed.

- Time and space are very different in the afterlife. Time passes yet seems to stand still. PLR clients comment that what seems like only a day or a year in the afterlife can be centuries on Earth. Space is infinite because consciousness is infinite. We move through it by thought.

- We only go where our awareness levels or frequency fit. We would not go higher or lower unless there was protection, service and learning involved.

- There are many opportunities to learn in the afterlife. Souls can gather in beautiful libraries, temples or schools of learning. Learning is multidimensional. Understanding is shared by "downloading" full concepts or experiences. Teachers are those who are somewhat ahead of their students. Teachers have teachers and those teachers have teachers. There are many levels of learning in the higher realms of reality.

- Earth School is considered one of the fastest and most challenging learning institutions because of the sharp contrasts and many changes that are innate to physical life. In the afterlife realms, there is less experience of change. There is more a sense of being in the present or the now.

- If you believe you can grow and change in the afterlife, you will. If not, you stay the same. This would include those who only planned for "a better place" and therefore have a nicer home, nice neighbors and enjoy the company of others who have similar beliefs. When they get restless or want change, they can go to whatever higher learning fits their frequency. They may also prepare to return to Earth.

- If you strongly believe that you must sleep in the afterlife until the return of Jesus, or if you adamantly believe there is no part of you that survives death, that will be your experience. You will sleep a long time or you will shut down your consciousness in order to not experience awareness. Loving beings will check on you periodically to see if you are ready to awaken.

- Some people feel so tied to the Earth because of trauma, grieving loved ones, or wanting to still be involved in family/business affairs, that they have difficulty lifting off. They may remain earthbound as "lost" or "restless" spirits. Whether understood or not, the choice is theirs as to when they change their minds and therefore their locale.

- Helpers are always on standby. On this side, we help by our positive thoughts, prayers and encouragement of the departing ones. On the other side, the helpers can be angels, ancestors, soul group members and master teachers. Guides/spirits have the ability to adapt their appearances to fit what will be most comforting to the departing soul as it arrives on the other side.

- Your soul is energy—so is your personality. So is your body, only in denser form. When you are done with the body you take your beautiful energetic consciousness and skedaddle. It can be clean and simple if you so desire.

- Anything you can visualize can become real—here and there. So if you want to practice visualizing your departure, why not? Do you want angels to meet you and guide you? Do you want to ascend a golden staircase or cross the Jordan River? What about the boatman who steers your boat through the clouds to the light? These beautiful images and metaphors are bridges to the afterlife. Enjoy building your own.

- Many afterlife amenities are available to us. As well as the temples already mentioned, we can ask to receive healing in the healing centers. Healing centers are available to us when we have died in a manner in which there has been much degradation to the body. Although the physical body is gone, the energetic body may still feel the effects or be in the mind-set of illness/injury; therefore, you can request further healing. This can be a very speedy process. Afterlife amenities are also available to us *now*. We can ask to receive healing in the healing centers or visit the temples during dreams and meditation. You are likely already partaking of these services, though you may not always be aware of it.

## UNIVERSAL LAWS

Knowing something of Universal Laws gives us real girders to shore up our bridge to the afterlife and get the most out of each incarnation. They may be given different names throughout the ages, but Universal Laws remain in full operation, whatever the name. In a sense, they summarize the nature of how consciousness works and evolves. These energies have been used by groups in power for eons and often kept secret. Within our human family, a significant percentage of us are ready to consciously use the power of Universal Laws for the higher good. The following fundamental precepts stand out as priorities for us at this time.

### *Law of Attraction*

The Law of Attraction is popular in the personal growth movement. This law is so powerful that it is sometimes referred to as the Law of Life. Most of us know what it means at some level. Like attracts like. What you sow, you reap. What goes around, comes around. Basically, it is the way in which we attract our reality through the frequencies we give off with our thoughts and feelings. What we are thinking and feeling most frequently and strongly, both consciously and unconsciously, magnetizes that same energy back to us. Our actions reflect our inner psychology. Thought is empowered by feeling and the two together create action/reaction.

On Earth, we may be clever at concealing our real feelings. This may serve us in some situations. What we want is a generally experienced integrity between our inner thoughts and feelings and our outer expression. Our inner and outer selves want to be in harmony. That higher integrity adds higher vibration—less sludge and more empowerment.

In the afterlife, the Law of Attraction is immediately experienced. In the higher dimensions, thought manifests immediately. Because nothing is hidden, the predominant energy you bring with you creates the attractive force toward your group of similar souls—your particular heaven. I don't want you to be dismayed by this in the least. Just smarter. Think how nice it will be to feel truly seen and understood. The challenges you have mastered on Earth will show through, adding luminosity to your beautiful soul. Your light will be free to shine as the hardships of Earth fall away. No more secrets. No need to hide or protect.

Knowing the Law of Attraction, and applying it effectively so that the highest good manifests through us, takes a while. Think of the Law of Attraction as the *magnetic nature* of Creator Source allowing us to experiment with it, learning how it works—and becoming co-creators.

## *Law of Karma*

I like to think of the Law of Karma as swirling waves of energy wafting through universal creation. Karma is like a breeze blowing through tall grasses and as it moves, other grasses move and bend into the mountain stream. Eddies swirl around the grasses. Water becomes diverted into quiet pools that allow the fish to spawn. New things happen and old things disappear, the result of karma's cause and effect. Some of creation lives and some dies, but learning blesses all dimensions.

Karma is the great cosmic breath of energy from which we are born and set foot on the journey, and the great breath that draws us home again. It is evolutionary energy, not punishment and retribution, though at a personal level, it may feel that way at times. Karmic law is a gift of balance and learning. It keeps us on track. It keeps us from getting lost forever in a morass of unfinished business and loose ends. It gives us another opportunity and another. It allows us to reap what we sow and be loved every step of the way—and it intimately intertwines with the Law of Attraction.

This law is our firm but caring teacher in the classroom of the cosmos, i.e. it is active in all dimensions and in all universes. We might as well be friends. We might think of the Law of Karma as the great *breath* of Creator

Source, inhaling and exhaling through all that is, allowing us to experiment and learn how it works.

### Law of Love

We love the Law of Love, but it befuddles us as well. Our understanding of love is given continual opportunity to stretch-h-h. That's because the difficult roles we play with each other may seem unlike anything remotely related to love. We are regularly reminded that this is a classroom of both tough and tender love. A broken heart may be breaking open to more compassion. An old relationship may need to pass so we can grow. Under the Law of Love, entrenched and limiting beliefs/cultures/institutions end up crumbling so new light can shine through.

Love intimately involves itself with our dance of life. Many of the things that could go wrong or endanger us don't because of caring, protective forces that we do not see. Love steps in at times to lift us up and then steps back to give us space when we must find our own inner strength. Often more people love us here than we are able to see. And certainly many people on the other side are lovingly cheering us on. All the while, Creator Source holds us in such love that we are granted whatever we focus on, even though it may take us on a side road. Giving us free will and a perplexing classroom in which to practice it, seems an ultimate gift of love. Creator Source trusts that all creation is learning, expressing and finding its way into its own likeness, which is Love. As we amplify our love quotient, love draws near and radiates in our reality. Unconditional, limitless, breathtaking love characterizes higher dimensions. At a fundamental level, love of self and others are entwined.

Within the Law of Love lies the beautiful *Law of Grace*, which, simply put, is the gracious aspect of Love. It is the ultimate Divine Mother energy, easing us off the wheel of endless suffering. Grace is the warm breeze longed for after winter's chill. It rests beneath all our illusions and carries us when our reality crashes. Grace fears no sorrow and avoids no wrongdoer. It is summoned by the humble heart and offers light in the darkest night.

We might consider the Law of Love as the great *heart* of Creator Source, the fabric of all creation, becoming visible in each of us.

### Law of One

The Law of One holds that energy can never be created or destroyed; it simply changes form. Every fiber of creation is connected to every other fiber by gossamer threads. Whether we experience connection or loneliness, we are a part of it all. No one is left out because there is no "out," really. Everything and everyone are a part of the whole. We can feel each others' pain and joy. We can intimately sense the shifts in the Earth and in humanity. As God can sense the fall of a sparrow, so can we. We feel and sense and know because we dwell *within* All That Is. Embracing our eternal oneness soothes our lonely places. Despite how disparate life appears to be, we are wrapped in the Law of One. We are Universal Consciousness in expression. The same life essence expressing through you is also singing through stars, flowers, microbes, your children and ascended beings. This essence comes to remind you that you are more than a mere human slogging through the workday.

We might think of the Law of One as the great *embrace* of Creator Source, allowing us to discover our oneness within the divine scheme.

Universal Laws enfold us from beginning to end. To consciously participate with these forces is to be alive to the *magnetic force, breath, heart* and *embrace* of God.

## Breathing

With this tool, we begin with a reminder to slow down. Slow down… Surrender to this moment…Take a nice deep breath right now as you are reading. Take another. Let your exhalation release that old air from the very bottom of your lungs. We tend toward shallow breathing which keeps the body on alert, and often tense. Continuous tension inhibits our sense of well-being and ability to change. For the physical body to be receptive to higher energies, it needs to experience periods of deep relaxation. Conscious, deep breathing assists us in receiving the higher frequencies. Breath is the bridge between spirit and matter, between soul and body. Breath activates latent evolutionary energy that uplifts us.

In one of my favorite books on the afterlife experience, *Testimony of Light* by Helen Greaves, the suggestion given from the afterlife is to learn to "relax into God." Here, while in a body, relax into whatever you call God on a regular basis. Let go, take a deep breath and relax into acceptance. Relax into all-is-well. Relax into gratitude. This develops spaciousness, trust, openness, and the ability to perceive the greater reality that is actually breathing through us. The vast blue sky becomes our consciousness. Our breath is the way we drink awareness into our bodies. The clouds are simply like the thoughts we notice in passing. No attachment, let them go.

Perhaps you have been through a lot of difficulty and suffering. After such challenges, we can feel so overwhelmed and devitalized that we might think we can't do it. How can we relax into God? And anyway, who is God? My friends, it doesn't matter. Put on some quiet music and allow your breath to deepen and your muscles to relax. Simply breathe deeply to whatever extent you can. Allow yourself to feel, to rest. Surrendering is therapeutic. Allow yourself to listen to the tenderness whispering around you. Let trauma be interrupted with a gentle breath…

*Breathing Exercise:* Notice your inhalation, then the slight pause at the top. Notice your exhalation, and the brief rest at the bottom. These are the four parts to breath. As you are relaxing, notice these four parts; inhalation, pause, exhalation, rest. Repeat often. In yoga, relaxation and stress management, meditation and childbirth, focused breathing is an essential component. We are wise to gather an assortment of breathing tools.

Someday you will inhale, pause, and your exhalation will finish on the other side. Or you will exhale, rest and your next inhalation will be in your new light body. With *conscious breathing* we build an intimate, gentle bridge upon which we can walk to the other side.

## My Own Room

We can create a welcoming place on the other side for ourselves, starting right now. Paramahansa Yogananda spoke of meeting the Divine in our inner room, the room of our heart. Jesus said he was going "to prepare a place for you…In my Father's house are many mansions." St. Germain meets with his students in lovely, elegant rooms complete with beautiful light, furnishings and sound. Part of the out-of-body travel work some students learn is to create their own place in a higher-frequency area on the other side. They go there to rest and rejuvenate, among other things. The inner room or personal safe place has a long lineage.

In hypnosis or guided imagery work, I suggest the client go to a beautiful, quiet place such as a mountain, a seashore or a meadow. Once in a while someone goes to a cave or a room, but it is a place in which they feel very safe with no worries or concerns. Many of you are familiar with this technique in some form. We are expanding this procedure, extending it for our bridge-building to the other side, so that you can develop comfort with it now and utilize this place for your afterlife arrival, should you so choose. It's like investing in afterlife real estate, if you will.

As previously mentioned, the results of thought are immediate in the afterlife. We go to the place befitting our own desires. Imagination activates these higher-dimensional worlds which we can access now. We can be proactive and direct these energies for our own well-being, no matter which side of the veil we find ourselves on.

One PLR client created a place where she could go to meet her guides. The more she imagined it, the more solid and real it became. It included a soothing pool of water, beautiful flowers and a sunny indoor room. She had fun designing it and even more fun noticing what had changed in the intervening time between her visits. Even when she wasn't there, her guides evidently enjoyed coming there and left their "calling cards."

Another PLR client recognized a lovely serene room in the afterlife "where I go to rest and reflect after my lives." She had been there before. It was familiar. Her room appealed to her sense of order and calm with large windows looking out over hills that dropped down to the sea. She enjoyed sitting at her desk, which faced these windows. Here, she could easily write and reflect on her journeys. She also mentioned that her guides came here to chat and check on her. As I sat with her, the serenity of this place was palpable, permeating my 3-D office.

Examples such as these have convinced me of the value of creating our own place on the other side. The other side, in this case, is not far away. It is coexisting within our own hearts and minds, and in higher-dimensional reality. This place of serenity and beauty is developed from the ethers of our own consciousness. It rises from the imaginal realms that we can imagine/perceive through our third-eye chakra. What we imagine or focus on is what we can create. We are using the power of the mind and the passion of the heart. We are activating the Law of Attraction.

Your place or room is one in which you can:

1.  Go for replenishment.
2.  Clear your mind and meditate.
3.  Invite your angels or guides to come speak with you or comfort you.
4.  Receive answers to questions.
5.  Invite loved ones who have passed over to come and meet with you. (This may also include pets.)
6.  Receive higher understanding by simply resting in the energy.
7.  Offer to be of service on the other side or clarify your service here on Earth.

8. Experience the "peace that passes understanding" promised in scriptures.

### Specifics for "My Own Room"

By now, you have likely begun to consider what your personal place might include. Your room may have four walls and a ceiling. Or the blue vault of heaven and the four directions may be your room. Having your own room affirms your place of belonging in the scheme of things. What settings do you find awaken you? Calm you? Have you hiked to a breathtaking mountain meadow or strolled along a seashore that you loved? Have you entered a mansion, a monastery or a chapel that felt like home? Do you love adobe or stone or wood or marble? Do you prefer an expansive vista that stretches into forever or a secluded green valley with a cozy cabin and a fireplace? Perhaps your own present home has just the room that represents you well. Do you want just the bare minimum of a room with no distractions from the serenity you crave? Are you drawn to books of wisdom that you can pull from an ancient library shelf, or only the book of your soul? Do you want to snuggle into a comfy chair and gaze quietly out onto the water? Do you simply want to be in a circle of loved ones and angels? Whatever the design of your room, it will also be a feeling place in the center of your chest that is the connection to your authentic heart self.

Trust yourself as you design the room where your heart feels truly alive, safe and serene. Within this aliveness, your quiet place will evolve and change with your own process.

### My Own Room Meditation

(Note: This exercise requires a quiet outer world as best you can arrange it. Quiet music or none at all. Turn off the phones and radio and TV. Children and pets need to be elsewhere or quiet.)

Give yourself permission to create some time for yourself to go inward... Take some deep relaxing breaths...Notice each breath, with an inhalation, a slight pause at the top, a full exhalation, and a brief rest at the bottom... Follow the flow of your breath with this awareness. Let your body rest into its own breath, its own natural, relaxed rhythm.

Now, shift your attention to your inner awareness and begin to imagine the most relaxing, comforting, safe, beautiful place for you...where there are no worries and no concerns. It may be a mountain, a seashore, a meadow or

a beautiful quiet room—a place where there are no tensions or problems…
So peaceful…Continue with your deep breathing, letting the sense of your
own room, your welcoming place, rise in your mind. Begin to notice the
colors, the light and textures around you. Details are emerging…Knowing
that walls and ceiling are loosely defined here, enjoy becoming aware of your
ceiling and what your walls are like…Somewhere nearby is a comfortable
place for you to rest. As you become more comfortable you notice clearly
what you are sitting or lying on…and the particulars of all that surrounds
you…

It is easy to feel the energy of this place which is inviting and welcoming…
Your home, your place in the higher dimensions that may resemble a higher-
dimensional Earth where there is no pain, no sorrow. Here, nothing can
harm you. Any sorrow or pain that you may have been feeling is held tenderly
here. Cleansing tears may fall, releasing the love that you are. There is no
judgment. The difficulties of your life are understood. In this place you are
accepted as you are. As you become more comfortable here, love rises to
meet you…

If you like, invite someone to join you. It can be a loved one who has
passed over; it can be an angel; it can be a guide or master. Notice them
gradually coming into your awareness…You can commune together as you
receive whatever you may need. The difficulties of your journey are deeply
understood. You are fully witnessed…You needn't rush or hurry…No effort,
just allow yourself to be here…All that you are is enough…Here you receive
anything that you need to live your life on 3-D Earth, more empowered and
with grace…And all is well…Allow yourself to be fully here in your own
room, the place you belong.

Be in the spaciousness and ease for as long as you like…When you feel
complete, bring yourself fully back to waking consciousness refreshed and
relaxed.

You may want to write down your experience.

My Own Room exercise takes the power of the mind, which is already
imagining what the afterlife experience is like, whether we are aware or not,
and gives the go-ahead to do it consciously. Knowing that we are eternally
part of the consciousness continuum gives weight to our focus. Not only will
loved ones greet us, but we can have a place to gather with them or adjust to
the changes we have been through. While alive on Earth, we also benefit by
simply enjoying this altered state.

## Staying Conscious Through Departure

What if we could die noticing and experiencing each change, knowing where we are and what is happening? What if we could stay conscious through the entire crossing over? Wouldn't it be grand to be able to mitigate the disorientation so common in departure? And how about not getting lost? Let's be done with that. All the things we have been talking about are aids in this quest for skillful navigation. Staying conscious through departure means that we know we are about to set foot on the bridge to the afterlife. We know the body is dying, but we are conscious of that. We have enough inner awareness to stay alert to the process of our soul pulling itself upward. We notice the changes in what we are hearing/seeing/feeling. We have addressed worries, pain and fears. Final grief and other emotions are expressed. Now, we set our intention to arrive in good form, focusing on that which is the highest spiritual love and light we can imagine.

What are the common guidelines for conscious departure? Our appreciation grows for the older traditions that emphasize staying conscious through the death process. The mystical branches of all spiritual traditions teach some form of conscious departure.

Some commonalities in the conscious departure traditions include:
- A daily practice of inner stillness, usually meditation.
- Disciplined focusing and concentration skills.
- Familiarity with one's own energy field—chakras, energy flow, emotional and mental and spiritual energies. Accurately assessing one's own energy. Sensitive awareness of another's energies.
- Breathing techniques for focusing, directing, calming or increasing one's energy.
- Primary identification with that aspect of self that is eternal, infinite or conscious—often called higher mind, superconscious, soul or spirit.
- Study of the dimensions or states of mind/consciousness and gaining skill in accessing them at will. Knowing those states that are beneficial to conscious departure.
- Full participation in the world but non-identification with it. The 3-D world is seen as a dream, an illusion or a classroom in which to develop mastery. Pain and suffering are viewed as part of that mastery, as are compassion and gratitude.

- Practice in leaving the body, learning about dimensions and returning. Death then becomes one more experience of leaving the body, but without the return.
- Specific teachings on the conscious dying process usually include some sort of overview of the afterlife terrain plus techniques for quiet mental focus, breathing and chakra awareness—particularly the crown chakra as a departure exit.
- Handling contingencies such as disorientation and physical pain.

Daily practice and further education strengthen whatever of these has energy for you. The tug from your soul will guide you into your own personal program for staying conscious through departure.

## Practicing Altered States

I was recently talking with a colleague who shared the events surrounding her mother's last days. Her mother, Aileen, was dying and in great pain—pain compounded by botched medical care. The final part of the story is important for our discussion. Aileen's son, my colleague's brother, was seated at her side in the hospital. Highly distressed by the pain, Aileen cried repeatedly, "I don't know what to do! I don't know what to do!" Overwhelmed by his mother's suffering and in a moment of brilliance, her son asked, "Mother, did you and Dad have a favorite place you liked to go? Did you have a place in the mountains with trees and a stream? Why don't you go there?" That was the trick. Immediately Aileen latched onto the suggestion and took her consciousness to the Wyoming mountains she so loved. She was more than ready for an alternate reality. She relaxed into her favorite place, then fell asleep. Within 30 minutes she had departed in peace.

We are blessed by Aileen's departure story, for it lends affirmation to the importance of practicing altered states—healing states of consciousness where the whole world of pain and dysfunction can be turned on its axis. In an intuitive flash, her son suggested a simple guided imagery technique that allowed her consciousness to step out of limitation and into her greater self.

One of the tenets of hospice care is sufficient pain management to create ease for the dying person. Of course. If we are not distracted by pain, we can die in greater ease. This is a tricky balancing act when we add in conscious dying. Some relatives and friends of dying patients have voiced concern to me about too much medication. Did their loved one become so woozy from the pain medications that they couldn't have the option of a more conscious transition? Does the dying person comprehend that they have died if they are knocked out with morphine? Did they pass on in confusion? These are relevant questions for those wanting to have a conscious death. We are refining this work; enough pain management to give ease, not too much to dull our fortitude and equanimity of spirit.

Actually, altered states aren't complicated to us. We move in and out of consciousness states throughout the day and night. For example, spacing out, daydreaming, watching TV, meditating, dreaming, or being emotionally triggered by some event and going off on a tangent are common altered-state experiences for us. The altered states that assist us in conscious departure are the ones that also assist us in conscious living. Given Aileen's experience above, we are witness to the power of being able to shift the mind to another, more pleasant state. Redirecting her mind to a peaceful place in nature provided her the altered state of consciousness necessary to shift from the despair of pain to the miracle of a graceful passage.

Simply put, while we are alive, we enrich our lives in 3-D with altered-state experiences. When we pass over, the altered state *is* the reality. 3-D dissolves. Most likely, you are already allowing yourself some of these experiences. Many books, tapes, clinicians, teachers and resources are available to assist you in exploring different tools. Here is a list of the common altered-state healing and consciousness tools I highly value:

- Deep prayer and stillness
- Meditation
- Guided imagery
- Hypnotherapy
- Dream incubation and interpretation
- Shamanic journeying
- Afternoon naps
- Past-life regression, age regression
- Practicing compassion, forgiveness and gratitude
- Creative expression and art
- Yoga
- Working with angels, guides, master teachers or ancestors
- Out-of-body experiences

If your altered-state practice includes some of these tools, and most particularly the practice of stillness, you are spanning the worlds.

Bridging the worlds makes us Earth dwellers par excellence. We can shift from one state of consciousness to another, learning to increase our frequency. We better comprehend the nature of the afterlife, we learn to cooperate with Universal Laws, we are breathing consciously, and we choose techniques and tools that expand our options and our journeying skills. We have become multidimensional travelers, knowing that our earthly departure can be a smooth continuation of this extraordinary journey.

# CHAPTER 11

# *First-Aid Departure Kit*

*This is what death should be;*
*a quiet choice made joyfully and with a sense of peace,*
*because the body has been kindly used to help...*
*along the way...to God.*
—from "The Song of Prayer—An Extension of the Principles of a Course in
Miracles"

LET'S TAKE WHAT WE'VE TALKED about and create a first-aid kit for you and your loved ones. Let's take a clear and practical approach so you can transition into the afterlife without confusion. Despite how assured you are of your belief system, or that a belief system is unnecessary and bogus, your actual inner discipline and awareness is crucial—as are your conscious-dying street smarts. Remember that you might be old or young, ready or unready, but the *when* of your departure is usually unknown. A first-aid kit is good self-care for birthing yourself more happily into the next world.

## For This Side

1. *Live consciously NOW.* This includes:
   a) Learning to forgive and be grateful.
   b) Developing compassion for all beings.
   c) Practicing mental discipline and clarity.
   d) Fostering an inner life.

2. *Walk with your death.* It's here, just over your shoulder. Turn and say hello often. I'm serious. As you take your evening walk along the river,

smile and look over your shoulder and say, "Hi there, my dear Departure. How's it going?" See what happens inside you.

3.  ***Focus on what you want to grow.*** Your inner thoughts and feelings match what you magnetize to yourself here and in your passing. Hone your ability to consciously create more joy, forgiveness, grace, courage, empowerment, etc.

4.  ***Release guilt. Release guilt. Release guilt.*** Take whatever you are, whatever you've done or not done that you hold guilt and shame about, and ask, "What can I learn from this? How can I think about this in a bigger, more soulful way?" Ask for help in releasing the heaviness you carry and, no matter how flawed you may feel, commit to being a learner on the journey of life. If you grow from this, all is not lost. Release the guilt and step into your worthiness as a child of the Universe. Unresolved guilt draws us back lifetime after lifetime to try to rectify our guilt feelings. So do that now. Then you can come back with a cleaner slate.

5.  ***Get comfortable with altered states.*** Develop your inner perceptions: inner sight, inner hearing, inner feeling/knowing. Remember you won't have your physical eyes and ears and body. You will be perceiving with higher senses. Meditation, guided imagery, bodywork, relaxation, dance, yoga and deep prayer help you let go of the limited, rational, pushy left brain. By whatever means, allow yourself to drop into your deep feeling nature, your true self.

## For the Other Side

6.  ***Simply be with the experience of passing over.*** Watch sensations, noises and colors if they arise. *Keep praying with a gentle grateful heart. Keep your mind focused on loving kindness and gratitude.* The noises and sensations and colors can be your consciousness separating from the body. Don't attach to any of it. Tibetan Buddhists describe the sensations of dying as sometimes intense. For example, every hair on the head may feel like a tree and you are walking through that forest with the trees falling around you. Some people experience roaring or buzzing as soul force pulls itself out of the body and the separation process unfolds. Some hear music. Some just move quietly up and out. Let it happen. It's surprising, but you are okay.

7. ***Know how to tell if you are already on the other side.*** This is important. If you become confused, ask yourself these questions:
   - Am I walking through walls or furniture?
   - Are people not listening to me, no matter how I try to get their attention?
   - If I walk by a mirror or reflective surface, is there no reflection of me?
   - Am I getting from one place to another as if by flying or by the power of thought?
   - Where is my physical body? Can I re-enter it?

   (Note: If you can get back into your own body and it feels like it's truly yours, then you're an astral traveler and have had an out-of-body experience—OBE. If you almost couldn't get back in, or didn't want to get back in but were told you must, and have experienced talking with guides or light/dark entities, you've had a near-death experience—NDE.)

   So if you:
   a) Can't get back into your body
   b) Can't get people's attention
   c) Can't see your reflection in a mirror
   d) Are unhindered by physical matter, or time and space—you have died.

   You can then say to yourself, "Oh, now I remember reading about this. These are clues that I am dead to that body and am now very much alive in the afterlife!" Remember, many people die not realizing that they have died. They may have known they were going to die, but don't realize it has happened because they feel the same. They linger here and sometimes get into trouble. You needn't go on that detour.

8. ***Release your body, and your life.*** So let's say you've discerned you are dead to this world and have arrived on the other side. If you want to go check on people you love and say goodbye, do so. But remember, you are now done with this chapter. You are okay. Get acquainted with your new world. You will probably find it quite pleasant and familiar.

9. ***Focus deeply.*** Once you have determined that you are on the other side, follow the Light. Follow the Love. You can meditate and use the mantras, prayers and chants that uplift you. You no longer have a body to help you get grounded, so any and all spiritual and mental focusing abilities will help you navigate to higher realms.

10. ***Aim high.*** If you are Buddhist, invoke the Buddha of Infinite Light. If you are Christian, invoke the risen Christ to guide you. If you are a follower of the Kriya yoga path, invoke Yogananda or Sri Yukteswar or Babaji to lift you to the high astral realms. If you are of another mind-set, invoke the highest beings and highest consciousness within your system of understanding to escort you to your afterlife home, such as angels, guides and ascended masters. Call on your higher self. (Some believe that the great light seen by some souls is their higher self coming to meet them.) Use your tools but release a need to have a certain outcome, or you may trip yourself up. Let heaven show you around.

11. ***Be honest.*** Be willing to see your own karma as it rises and you evaluate your life. The afterlife winds of karma may blow upon you. On the occasion that fearful visages show up, take them as representative of your own fears and love them into calm. Don't be blown away. Stay neutral and let them go. If there are heavens you long to participate in, let your devotion to the Divine swell, and your beautiful heart open so that love leads you there. Here's where we really experience the power of our thoughts. And our hearts. Don't settle. Call for the Love you long for.

12. ***Let yourself be taken to a place of reflection on your life.*** If your life has been tiring or you die from a long illness, you will be given a time for rest and recovery. Remember, your body is gone. You are recovering in spirit and it needn't take long. Here is where you can be as thorough as you like. Learn as much as possible from the life just lived. Ask for your guide to assist you in seeing what you have gained and where you might like to improve yourself.

13. ***Set sail!*** At some point, you will feel unfettered and complete with the life you have left. Let that happen sooner rather than later. You can still be in contact with loved ones on Earth in a healthy way while being free to experience your unlimited divine nature. You are free to study, to learn, to go to higher dimensions or return to Earth for further growth and service. Or all of the above. Relish the light, the incredible love, the wisdom granted you from your sojourn. Now you can KNOW you are a being of Infinite Light.

# CHAPTER 12

# Creating Departure Ceremonies

*We want to bring our dying home,*
*make it our own,*
*and as deeply sacred as possible.*

EVERY BELIEF SYSTEM HAS ITS own unique contribution to ceremonies and rituals that seek to aid the dying and support them into the afterlife. Even though it's a risky business to simplify these complex rituals into their common themes, I feel it is essential. We want to bring our dying home, make it our own, and as deeply sacred as possible. The ceremonial guidelines we will discuss are for the dying. We do not say that the ritual is for the living, though it may grant the living ease or a sense of purpose. Neither do we assume that somehow the departing soul has it all figured out, with or without the aid of mysterious helpers on the other side. That may be the case, but we do not assume this. Because, as we have learned, many souls have found out otherwise, our goal is to help our loved ones get to their highest realm, unconfused and loved.

It is important to make certain someone else is assigned to care for the comfort of the dying person's body. Your work is the care of his or her mind and heart as you provide uplifting support on their behalf.

Although these guidelines assume you are able to be present for the one you are assisting, they can also be effective for long-distance support. You may set up sacred space, as suggested below, and work with the spirit of the individual, adapting the rest of the guidelines as needed. The same applies to those who may have died suddenly. You may not be able to sit beside their physical body, but you can be in contact with their spirit and lend support.

## 1. Establish Sacred Space.

*Inner Space*. Practice in creating sacred space can be a daily ritual. The more we do it, the more prepared we are to offer sacred space in departure ceremonies. For this, we deepen our inner life so that we can drop into the sacred more readily. Quietness, deep breathing, firm grounding in your role as guide, firm grounding in the system of thought/belief that you and your loved one share, and confidence in your death midwife role—all support the calm that blesses this time. You will find much of the ego falls away and you may experience the relief and joy of becoming a servant of the Mystery. This is sacred *inner* space.

*Outer Space.* The room or space where you are with your loved one, the *outer* space, can also be cleared and brought into sacredness. Make the room as beautiful as possible. Fresh flowers, fresh air, lovely vistas and quiet music increase the higher energies. Creating an altar with those things that uplift such as candles, flowers, pictures, feathers and crystals can be very calming. If you are familiar with feng shui or space-clearing methods, you can utilize those techniques. Intention and prayerfulness are pivotal in both your inner and outer space work.

Your prayer or invocation might include:
- That the room be filled with love and great light.
- That those celestial escorts waiting in the wings draw nigh.
- That all fear and negativity the departing one has held, be lifted up on the wings of love and dissolved completely.
- That all disease and sorrow be cleared from the soul matrix/energy field.
- That wholeness and perfection of spirit reign supreme.
- That the crossing-over be timely and auspicious.
- And that the soul be fully aware when it has crossed over, find its "home," and be at peace.

## 2. Establish a clear and heartfelt connection.

There are two important connections for your heart.

(1) One is the alignment with Highest Source by whatever name you call it. Remember, we are looking for high frequencies: Infinite Light, Limitless Love, God, Allah, Buddha, Omniscient Wisdom and Compassion, Powerful Protection and Guardianship—and beings who embody these energies. You

may invoke names, or you may simply invoke place, i.e. the Place of Infinite Light, etc. Use all your gifts of imagery to evoke the *feeling* and image of Highest Love.

(2) Your second heartfelt connection is to the beautiful soul you care for and are assisting. See him in his highest functioning, his most gallant and loving nature. Feel her heart shining brightly as all clouds of suffering melt away. Affirm her arrival at her highest heaven with ease and gratitude. The way of the open and loving heart is the way of magnificent grace. Let your higher nature rise to this occasion. Your positive connection to the one you are assisting deeply enchants your work.

### 3. Use chants, prayers, music and meditations that empower the departing soul.

These can be innate to the system of belief shared or may be unique to the individual. They carry guidance, comfort, exhortation and inspiration. The use of sacred music, chants and prayers used by many over time creates a powerful energy to which you connect. In this way you are joined with all others who have blessed those words and songs. You aid yourself and your loved one to ride those waves of sacred power. Musical suggestions include very quiet bells, chimes, relaxation music, gentle hymns, mantras and chants. Nothing that distracts or jars. Silence and gratitude are also lovely music.

### 4. Assist with emotional release.

Your work may also include supporting your loved one's cathartic emotional release. Lama Zopa Rinpoche says, "It is okay to medicate pain in order to help the person to be able to think. But medicating for mental anguish is not okay. Sedation before death prevents working out bad karma. Anguish becomes fruitful if the individual can experience it." ("How to Benefit the Dying and the Dead," www.lamayeshe.com) It can be a great relief if sorrows and worries are released before passing. You can assure your loved one that it is okay if he or she needs to cry and wail, or express anger and regret. This frees up energy that was stuck. Then, you can guide them to breathe deeply, surrendering into Love.

### 5. Use icons or images.

You can suggest that the soul depart through the crown center at the top of the head. It can be helpful to have a picture/icon of Buddha, Jesus, Mohammed, an angel, a star or whatever image of higher consciousness fits for your loved one. Place this at the head as a symbol to draw the soul from the body at this auspicious chakra.

## 6. Avoid loud displays of emotion and loud noises of all kinds.

In the same way that we can positively affect the birthing of a soul onto our planet by quiet and peaceful surroundings, so do we provide the same for those departing. Minimizing distractions in this world supports the sacred space we are creating. It promotes an easier crossing. So even though your heart may be filled with many emotions, breathe into your calm center and quietly hold the torch of an excellent passing for your loved one. That's love at its finest.

## 7. Honor the uniqueness of each soul.

Each soul has its unique karma, which influences its experience in passing to the other side. Despite all our preparations, support and planning, the deaths of our loved ones may or may not go as hoped. No matter what takes place, we can celebrate the amazing work of those on both sides of the veil— the whole transition team—and the soul itself. We can affirm that at a deeper level, all is perfect for the learning acquired. We have done our part to hold the space of conscious dying. As we affirm that all has occurred for the highest good, we release the outcome and surrender to the miracle of departure.

# PART IV

# *Journey into Love*

# PART IV

# *Journey into Love*

## Introduction

IN THE END, I REALIZED I WAS WRITING a love story. A love story that was bigger than the one we've been told. In this love story, everyone can win, even the losers. In this story, pain can't last forever, but while it's around it's a fast way to get to the bones. In this love story, separation seeks togetherness. Darkness seeks the light. Heaven beams upon Earth and Earth adores Heaven. Opposites long for each other, unawares. Suffering keeps trying over and over to find a way through to morning. In this love story, our inner being is grasping for its own awakening. And death shakes us loose so we can live.

I started out with concern for my human family. I felt such a longing to see my beautiful planet in better hands, people who understood the love story. What called me was the burden of unconscious living and dying over the millennia that created a dark cloud in the ethers of Mother Earth. I felt I intimately understood what Robert Monroe called the *wave of disorganized human thought*, a difficult and distasteful band of energy around the Earth that he had experienced. I felt I knew what Gordon Michael Scallion described as *the borderlands*, whose lower layers appear as dark clouds filled with troubled beings. I heard the sadness in the mental fog that has clogged up our ability to see the truth. When I first saw this, it broke my heart open. I determined to write and do whatever was in my capability to wake up the sleepers who were ready to see, including myself.

So it seemed more of a wake-up story for the first 12 chapters. This wake-up story was about hitching our star to the vast forces of consciousness that rise through our bodies every day, waiting for permission to be activated. But then my mother, who made her transition in 2001, began showing up and the

157

story became even more personal. I would be looking in the mirror and think of her. I would be gardening and want to show her the gigantic garden spider eating a fly in its newly mended web. My psychic friends began to see her and relay her messages to me from the other side, some of which I've shared with you. I felt her interest in this subject of consciousness, something she had little sympathy for while alive.

I woke up one morning recently, saying to myself, "I miss my mom." I just missed her. My heart was soft and tearful. I appreciated anew her strength and humor. I appreciated the love of learning and nature she passed on to us. But most of all, I just missed her. "It would be so nice to be able to chat with her," I thought, "to get her perspective on things, now that she has had several years in the higher planes. It would be nice to know that she understands." Then I smiled, realizing that to wake up missing my mother meant that she and I had likely been chatting. Only my body was sleeping. The rest of my consciousness was visiting with her in the nighttime realms.

This, I want to tell you, is a small love story in and of itself. Although both my parents' ways were hard for me to comprehend at times, this was especially true with my mother. Throughout the many years we had together, my heart was both uplifted by her praise and crushed by the harshness of her criticism. I felt confused, befuddled, loved and amazed by her. In nearly 30 years of psychotherapy practice, my mother reigns supreme as my most significant case study.

As you know, the parental bond is pivotal in forming our sense of self. The good parenting we received rests quietly in our psyches. It assists us in being comfortable in our own skins. Whatever parenting hasn't worked for us is a wound that becomes grist for our mill. We develop coping skills, compensating behaviors, avoidances and talents rising from that empty, wounded place inside.

From the grist in my mill, I developed a deep need for harmony, stillness, beauty and order. The hypersensitivity and anxiety of my earlier years became honed into the ability to sit quietly with a troubled soul. I also came away with a gigantic curiosity. I dived into consciousness and spirituality, wanting to know who we are from the inside. I thank my parents for all of this. Without that wound around which something akin to a pearl could grow, and the curiosity to explore it, I may not have become such a motivated explorer. I can't say for sure.

I can say that it's all part of the unfolding love story. From my perspective as a PLR therapist, it's likely that my mother chose to play this difficult role, not only for the learning it would bring to her, but so that each of her children could learn what we have needed to learn. That's an act of love. Perhaps my soul work entailed the challenge of a significant healing process. By continuing the journey into wholeness, however muddled, things have worked because of the choice to grow. And, I can affectionately say that I now have the best relationship with my mother that I have ever had.

The stories in Part IV represent our amazing soul journeys. In *Zetta's Story*, we witness the courage it takes to face imminent death wrapped up in the courage to face life again. In *Aaron's Story*, we straddle the worlds and learn more about the dark side, suicide and redemption. In *Crossing-Over Stories* we share the experiences of PLR clients as they peer into the unknown, blessing us with insight and courage. Then we push *The Future of Death*.

A moment ago, I stepped outside for some sunshine and fresh air. My gaze became riveted on a large, yellow, swallowtail butterfly. It fluttered above some orange-red day lilies and then folded its wings and deftly pulled itself deep into the blossom. After claiming all the nectar in each flower, it brushed about six inches from my arm, circled over my head and was gone.

Again, I thought of my mother, her presence so near. The journey, it seems, is *into* love—by choice, by courage—leaning into the blossoms of life and death, on deeper into love.

# CHAPTER 13

## *Zetta's Story*

*I will not die an unlived life.*
*I will not live in fear of falling or catching fire.*
*I choose to inhabit my days, to allow living to open me,*
*to make me less afraid, more accessible,*
*to loosen my heart until it becomes a wing, a torch, a promise.*
*I choose to risk my significance;*
*to live so that which came to me as seed*
*goes to the next as blossom*
*and that which came to me as blossom, goes on as fruit.*
—"Fully Alive" by Dawna Markova

**PART 1:** *The Beginning*

YOUNG PETER STEPPED INTO my counseling office one day, full of angst. He was struggling with what he called the "death demon." In the midst of his parent's separation, moving to a new school, and other adjustments and losses, Peter's friend's horse died. Peter had come to love this beautiful mare and cared for her on a regular basis. It was all too much. He told me that there was an angel of good, but the death demon was a really maddening bad guy. In his grief, Peter was angry about death.

Actually 10-year-old Peter was onto something. The death demon, the "demon" created from our misguided understanding of departure, *is* too much. We are more than weary, especially during this time of so much change and loss. The "archetype of death," as I choose to call it, is so laden with terrors and sorrows that people everywhere are choosing a new road map of proactive, conscious choice in departure-related matters.

We are participating in a phenomenon emerging just below the radar of our culture. Tucked away in the conscious-dying movement is a rising wave of everyday pioneers. In addition to the innovative work of professionals in the field, these pioneers are breaking through entrenched death beliefs by transforming their own departure experience. Unnamed courageous souls are shattering their old death map. Some are accomplishing this through gradual re-education of their entire psyche. Others are catapulted by crises into confronting their own version of Peter's death demon.

Jan Tober, co-author of the book *Indigo Children*, speaks of this work as clearing the "death phantom." According to Tober, this phantom is a collective of experiences, beliefs and agreements about death which we have gathered over the span of our soul's journey. In other words, our past deaths often unconsciously influence what we expect for our death this time. With each lifetime we live, we also carry some sort of soul agreement that includes what we hope to accomplish each time around, and the hows and whens of our departure. However, what we haven't always understood is that this plan can be changed. Zetta's story is a prime example of casting off the death phantom and changing the departure plan altogether.

## Zetta

I learned from a mutual friend that Zetta was dying. I also learned that her dying was coupled with some transformative events. Because of my work in the conscious-dying field, I was eager to interview her and hear her story. Zetta was most obliging and so, in the autumn of 2007 I drove to Boulder, Colorado, where she lived in her quiet, simply furnished apartment. Zetta, then 54, had spent years working as a social worker in hospital chemical dependency and psychiatric units, as well as agency case management. An Illinois native, Zetta left the Midwest for new adventures in Colorado in 2001.

The adventures awaiting Zetta were beyond anything she could have imagined, for in May of 2006, Zetta came face-to-face with her own death phantom. For many years, she had known she was infected with hepatitis C, but she continued to lead a normal life. Then, one night without warning, she woke up from a deep sleep and ran to the bathroom, vomiting up "a sink full of blood." She was rushed to the hospital in Albuquerque, N.M., where she lived at the time. Before being given a shot of Haldol to stem the bleeding and pain, the doctors asked her if she wanted to be resuscitated should it come to that point. Always in the past, with different medical procedures, Zetta had declared, "Let me go." This time as she heard the question, she opened her eyes and saw the worried face of her partner, Jane, gazing at her. In that moment, Zetta knew that she had not finished her work with Jane and changed her answer to, "Yes, bring me back." Had Jane not been there, Zetta says that she would have asked to be allowed to die, a likely event since her physicians gave her only a five percent chance of surviving the severe loss of blood and liver damage.

For four days, Zetta remained unconscious in her hospital bed, but she retained almost no memory of her experiences during that unconscious state. Eventually bits of memory surfaced. Zetta began to recall traveling to a spiritual "Council of Seven" in the higher realms. She remembered saying to them that she didn't want to leave her Earth life yet; she needed time to clear up some things and learn a bit more. When I pressed Zetta for more details of the Council, she described them as immensely wise and evolved. She felt showered with an indescribable, unconditional love. While reflecting on her experience with the Council, Zetta's face softened, and her voice quieted.

In stating her case to the Council, Zetta outlined the matters that still felt incomplete: One was an awakened desire to learn more about love; the other was the age-old quest—how to be human *and* experience the freedom of spirit. The day that Zetta went before her Council is the day she believes she had contracted to die. It was the original soul agreement, the old map for this life's completion. In asking for a change, she received approval for a renegotiated contract, adding more time.

Much of this perspective submerged itself in the recesses of her mind as Zetta returned to consciousness and her hospital room. Her predominant sense was that she had 2-3 months left to live and so she set about doing all the practical end-of-life tasks such as medical power of attorney, updating her will and giving away her belongings.

As it happened, about one month after leaving the hospital, Zetta and Jane moved from Albuquerque to Boulder to be near their support system. They struggled, loved, learned and struggled again. With the weeks expanding into months, Jane became exhausted and overextended, given all the demands of her caregiver role. Eventually, they reached a mutual decision to live separately, with Zetta being accepted for affordable housing, Medicaid and hospice care. At this highly vulnerable time, Zetta found herself living alone. Ironically, she was learning to receive care and love from a wider support circle.

As the 2-3 months lengthened into 4-5 months and then a year, Zetta understood that the extra time she was given had less to do with practicalities than with the deepening growth of her soul. She also began to remember more about the beautiful Council that had blessed her choice.

### Disease as a Vehicle of Wholeness

Though ill and often exhausted, Zetta's soul-learning was rapidly expanding. She continued, "In the past, I could always give love. I knew how to be generous and caring. However, I never quite believed that I was lovable, that I could just receive love from all the people who love me. It's the metaphor of the hand in a bucket of water. If you take your hand out, if you are gone, it looks like you have made no difference. That's how I'd always felt. I had to keep giving to others to make love happen for me. Now, for the first time in my life I have been able to be open and receive and know that I am inherently lovable."

During her four days of unconsciousness in the Albuquerque hospital, Zetta experienced another level of love. Her intuitive friend, Bonnie, in Colorado Springs, shared her own story. At the time of Zetta's hospitalization, Bonnie was teaching a healing class. Zetta's spirit came to Bonnie during the class saying, "Tell Jane that I'm coming back. I'm just having a hard time getting back into my body." Zetta then gave Bonnie the specific things she needed, including changing some of the medical equipment so she could return. The attending nurse was amenable, made the changes and Zetta crawled back into her body. Besides the nursing help, Zetta is convinced that the prayers and love of her friends and spiritual family are what she utilized to pull herself back into her body and her life. Had it not been for this collective assistance and outpouring of love, she would not have been able to return to carry out her mission.

Though her desire was to return to this life for further learning, Zetta was frank about the difficulties in living so intimately with one's own death. Is it worth the $75 to buy a good pair of walking shoes in October if you might die in November? What about getting that new winter coat? With death hovering in each physical discomfort and each hospice nurse visit, how do you decide these things?

Some days left her completely exhausted. On other days, she felt a mysterious level of energy. Several times over about a 16-month period, she revisited the door of death. On one occasion, she went to her acupuncture appointment and said to her acupuncturist, "It seems like I'm getting ready to leave. I couldn't care less about food, friends, going out. Nothing here has meaning for me." As he checked her chi, he agreed, for her energy was unusual—different from his patients whose chi was flowing within the more familiar fluctuations.

Then, somewhere within Zetta a shift occurred, a mountain moved and she stayed. "One day the sun came out, like spring, and I woke up and felt good, felt energized and positive and I said, 'Oh shit! Guess I'm not going to die today!' I knew that at some level I had made the decision to stay. Among other things, the problems in the relationship with Jane made it obvious that there were still some things I hadn't learned.

"There have been a lot of times in my life when I've wanted to leave, to die, to get out of spiritual and emotional pain. After the hospitalization, I had a long talk with Spirit. I said, 'I'm so tired. Everyone says I should enjoy life. What does it mean to live life if I'm not working, not productive and have a lot of time on my hands?' I have come to know that I do not want to leave this body because of wanting to escape. I want to die in love, clarity and feeling spiritually complete. This 'time on my hands' is my time to deepen and heal.

"Now, I understand that living life is about following my heart on a moment-by-moment basis. *Since I'm here, I may as well live until I die.* With that realization I really got it, and with it I felt a huge relief. I started living out of an inner freedom. I have freed myself from a lot of fear; fear of trying to take care of Jane's anxiety, fear that I am unlovable, fear of not having control. *There is something about the dying process that has given me a unique sense of myself.* This whole process that I've gone through, by being open and conscious about it, has given me a new freedom and purpose as I share with others.

"My journey is also unique in that I have chosen not to take the medical route. One of my doctors stood over me and shouted that I was a fool to not try the drug Interferon, that it was my last chance. I still chose to say no. My doctors didn't understand. Some of my friends didn't either. When it is my time to die, I will. Dying is a viable option. It's just an option society doesn't necessarily want to accept. The whole goal is for the ego-self to surrender. At the level of dying, my ego-self has no control."

Zetta had ample opportunity to contemplate the meaning behind contracting hepatitis C. She felt that the disease was born of self-hatred and was a way for her to end her life, though she wasn't aware of it at the time. "I was 23 years old when I shot heroin with a dirty needle. I loathed myself then. When I found out 20 years later that I had contracted this disease, I asked why I had called it to me. They say the liver is the seat of anger. I've sat with that. It didn't make sense to me. I don't have an angry personality. There is no one I carry anger toward. I couldn't figure it out. Finally it hit me; it was about my hatred and anger at myself." By letting the disease show her where she was not yet whole, Zetta was utilizing hepatitis C as a vehicle for psychological and spiritual wholeness.

### Further Reflections

As we continued to chat and reflect, Zetta returned to her chosen lesson plans—experiencing more expansive love and freedom within the restrictions of being human. The relationship with Jane felt pivotal to her healing. "I believe, for many of us, relationship is how we come to love ourselves. When people would tell me, 'You can't love another until you love yourself,' I couldn't see how that works. A mother's love is what reflects its lovability to a baby. Why wouldn't that also be true for us as adults? Why wouldn't the love of an intimate partner help heal our lack of self-love? Until Jane's love, I never knew that level of love. Jane has loved me for exactly who I am, loved me unconditionally."

Paradoxically, by her and Jane choosing to live separately, another layer of lovability would fall into place for Zetta. She was in hospice care and living alone. The nature of her living situation and her health now required her to be open to support and love from others. "Before, I often felt lonely. Through this process, I have come to *know,* for the first time, that I truly am not alone. My heart has opened. I am more willing to be honest and vulnerable with friends. I am allowing people to see me, not my defenses. I no longer have the overwhelming fear of being unlikable. I know the truth of me. This is really me. This core of who I am is permanent.

"Now, even if I were to be alone, it wouldn't matter. My core, my essence, is in place. I have had a fear of living alone, but the longer I live alone, the less alone I feel. It's freedom. I no longer feel bound! It doesn't matter where I die, who is with me when I die, or how it looks when I do. My belief is that it's going to be perfect. In truth, as I look over my life, it has been perfect and my death will be also. It is all about what is best for me, for the people I'm closest to, for the world, and for the Universe as a whole—whatever will bring the greatest healing for all.

"I went through a period of saying goodbye, of feeling the grief of the last book I would read, the last morning I would see, the last hug I would feel. It was very sad for me. Then I started thinking of what it's like on the other side—the love, the freedom, the continued growth, the continued learning, and more understanding of the spiritual worlds.

"I have a sense of the home planet that I will return to. It's been thousands of years since I've been there. Once during a workshop, I saw the tall, beautiful blue beings from my planet. Long ago, something happened and I left my planet to come here to Earth. I believe I have a core soul family. We work together and act as guides to one another when one of us is on the Earth. When I depart, I believe I will experience divine connection to a greater extent than I have been able to experience while on Earth. I think this connection is multidimensional and I know very little about it. However, the part of me that is always in Spirit is very much at work helping with the Earth changes we are in.

"The people that I am closest to—I feel and hope that my process will help them in their own passage. By me going through this process as consciously as possible, it may help the journey for all. That would give me joy. There is no right or wrong way to die. *There is just your way to die. Dying is a very individual path.* You are the only one to know your path. You can't do it anyone else's way.

"The main thing is, there is really nothing to fear, including death. Our greatest fear has been death. In my life, the focus was all outside of myself, though I worked with getting in touch with myself, with Spirit. Today, I know that who I am *is* Spirit. Everything I need and desire is available to me. Both love and freedom live in me. I realize now that the things that have happened over the last 16 months are what the Council and I talked about. I feel that I most likely am completing my incarnations on Earth. This 16 months has perhaps given me the opportunity to clear my slate. Though difficult, it has all been a great gift.

"Over the past few months, when I've thought I was on the verge of dying, I've felt joy. Then when death left me and I stayed, I came to feel joy as well. It doesn't really matter now. Both sides have something wonderful to offer."

Zetta's new embrace of love and freedom, and her sense of her impending departure focused her life. She still felt fragile and often tired, but the new goal had been declared and the deadline of dying brought her into the sunshine. She was dying, but also living as if for the first time.

## PART 2: *Past Life and the Council of Seven*

At the conclusion of our interview, I mentioned to Zetta that if she wanted to further explore her connection with her Council of Seven, she might be able to do so through a past-life regression session. I couldn't guarantee what we might discover, but if she felt adventurous and strong enough, we could experiment. Two months later in December of 2007, Zetta arrived on my doorstep—strong enough to drive alone from Boulder to Pueblo, adventurous enough to risk a PLR in the hope of procuring another meeting with her Council.

In addition to the hoped-for Council meeting and clarifying her agreements with them, Zetta's intention for the PLR was to access more support and enthusiasm for life. She also wanted to plead her case before the court of heaven regarding her ongoing financial struggles. Things still felt really hard.

Zetta was uncertain that she could attain a sufficient level of hypnosis to be effective, mirroring her anxiety of the process. This is not unusual with clients who are experiencing their first PLR, and the vast majority are surprised to discover they are "successful" after all. Zetta did, in fact, return to a past life. She has given permission for this work to be shared for the benefit of others.

### *Past Life as "Borgan" (summarized)*

Zetta stepped through the veil into a past life as a man named Borgan. "It is daylight....I see a small village that I am looking at. I have on leather boots, plain pants and a heavy chest plate that goes over my shoulders. I'm a man, a soldier. I feel proud and strong. My skin is dark, like Hispanic skin, dark hair and eyes. I am about 30 years old. I feel protective of my village. I have a sense of joy just standing here looking at it and the people moving about. It is home.

"The buildings are made of mud with thatched roofs. It is the marketplace. The people are happy, bickering over prices and joking with each other. They know me. The men are in shirts...I feel that I don't stay here all the time, but everyone knows me. I travel a lot...This is my respite place. I am in the army. It is hard living on the go, in tents, never feeling settled, yearning for home. It is hard seeing the battles, seeing men killed, killing many. I serve the King... All the killing and the lifestyle—I'm so tired of it (begins to cry)...But I have to help protect the people...The year is 1736...

"The friends I serve with...Micah. Micah is a jokester. He has served for a long time. I trust him more than most of the others...Jeran. He is more steady, steadfast and dependable…. L__?___ *(This name was hard to hear)* who is dark and is a good soldier, but he doesn't have the heart, the compassion…

"We are preparing to go into battle again. I am scared…We are outnumbered…I draw on my strength and my power…I don't want to die in the battle! I'm scared! There is fighting…men are falling around me. I feel a stab just below my rib cage in the back right side. I fall to my knees…………. ……..I continue to want to do battle…and finally…just….*(Borgan is dying)*

"…I am thinking of my mother and of my family…Just seeing them and loving them…I feel sadness. There is a little girl, my daughter…It has been a good life because of the relationships that I have had. I fought well. I did my duty…I'm picturing the scene of standing at the doors looking at my village…I'm feeling the joy of being a little boy again…The tip of the spear went through my body into my liver. *(Remember, in this life, Zetta suffers from hepatitis, a liver disease. A wound/illness from a past life can continue as an influence in this life.)*

## Afterlife

*Marcia:* Now Borgan, be aware of taking your last breath and of your spirit leaving your body. Share with me what you are aware of.

*Zetta:* I'm aware of myself looking down at the battle…I'm floating up and away…Getting lighter…I have chosen to go to a park-like area. It is open with trees, but not like Earth trees, not as solid…I am resting…

*Marcia:* Let's begin reflecting on your life, as you are ready.

*Zetta:* I learned how to suck it up and do it anyway. It was a lot about not doing for myself…Always putting the higher good before myself. I learned that killing doesn't solve the problem. I don't know that I knew that then. When I was younger, I was all for the battle, the kill, the righteous anger. But the battles kept happening and none of the problems were changing. In one battle, my best friend was killed—Marone. That changed the way I viewed fighting. I started seeing the senselessness. After that I started losing the lust for the kill. Yet I stayed faithful to my commitment to being a soldier…

*Marcia:* You learned some valuable things in your life…I wonder what you have learned that you might like to share with Zetta?

*Zetta:* Don't make yourself do things that you really don't want to do. Love is different than loyalty. We think that we have to be loyal to a cause, to our village, to our king. However, with that loyalty comes a price, which is self-sacrifice. Love doesn't demand that…

*Marcia:* What does love demand?

*Zetta:* Love demands being vulnerable, showing feelings, even the tender ones. Love brings joy. Loyalty brings obligation. Let your heart be free.

*Marcia:* What if the village, or king, or relationship wants you to be loyal anyway?

*Zetta:* You must find your limit. Find that line. You can have love and loyalty, but you must learn to say no. There is a natural loyalty that comes with love and it is not all bad. But commitment that takes your heart and soul is harmful. It pushes you beyond what you know is right to do…It's harmful… Trust your own wisdom, your inner knowing. Selling your soul doesn't make the end any easier. (*Borgan is keenly aware of this dawning realization. He struggles with the complexities and difficulties of discerning the fine line between loyalty and the need for self-care, soul-care, particularly in the role of a soldier.*)

*Marcia:* So now that Zetta knows about you, how might you stay in contact with her, continue this connection?

*Zetta:* Whenever she feels the wind, a soft breeze on her cheek, I will be touching her. She may even feel it when she is not outside…

*Marcia:* Before we move on, I want to check in with both of you now, Zetta and Borgan, and see if you sense anything else that needs to be seen or released from that life.

*Zetta:* It feels complete.

### Council of Seven

*Marcia:* Now we will release the life of Borgan and prepare to go to your Council of Seven. Begin to be aware of a guide who will come forward and take you to where we need to go…

*Zetta:* I see an Asian man with big energy…We've been together a long time. I am enveloped in his love. He knows me, he knows me deeply. He sees me… (*Zetta is deeply touched upon meeting her familiar, loving guide.*)

*Marcia:* As you are reconnecting and merging with his love, take some time to ask for any healing you need with your liver, both past- and present-life healing… (Pause) Then let us ask if it is now appropriate for him to take you to your Council.

*Zetta:* He says yes. (*Zetta was having some trouble with nausea. This was likely a result of both the healing she was experiencing and the increased frequencies of this higher realm. Because of time constraints we needed to move on as soon as she was comfortable. With much encouragement and affirmation, we proceeded.*)

I am floating to light… (*This process required encouragement and coaching.*) I am at a building, a big, white, formal marble building. The Council is

169

inside….. (*Zetta's voice became quieter and more reverent as we continued. She was obviously in awe and wonder at the beautiful architecture of this building within its celestial setting. I asked her to enter as she was ready, sharing with me all that she is aware of. She continued.*) The Council is sitting in a semi-circle. There are angels behind them and around the room. They appear large and radiant, sparkling and magnificent. Each one is different.

*Marcia:* Describe each of your Council to me.

*Zetta:* They have taken on a more human form for me. The one starting on the left is an elderly gentleman. The second is also male……There is a feeling that they aren't human, the human form becomes translucent…The third is female, fourth male, fifth female, sixth male, seventh female……There is a different feeling to the feminine than the masculine. There is a lot of love…..

*Marcia:* Thank you, Zetta. Take a moment and describe the angels that you are seeing.

*Zetta:* One on my left is more masculine. He wears a maroon robe that goes over his shoulder with a gold band, shoulder to waist, very elegant. He is very present and with me a lot of the time. He guides me and is teaching me about letting go of judgment. There is another one on the right end of the Council, a female, beautiful and glorious. She has been helping me a lot with the dying process. We have been pretty clear with each other through this process. She knows and I know.

I am getting ready to face the Council. I'm standing in the middle. The ones on the end are in my peripheral vision. I am very honored to be here. (*Zetta was crying.*)

*Marcia:* Letting yourself receive all the information that comes to you, all the love and energy from these beings…..Sharing with me as you can…

*Zetta:* (*In reverent tones*) I want to thank them for their presence and for allowing me to come…I feel that I have been told so much over this past year about this journey…I want to ask what was agreed on and what else needs to be done with this life I have been given…I feel very humble in making this request…

(*Zetta's tone changed as the Council spoke to/through her*)

*Council:* When you came last time (*during the coma*) it wasn't completely decided you would die. It was your chosen date. You asked for more time and we granted it. It was clear when you came to us that you still had a lot of unanswered questions and turmoil. You didn't understand what death meant. Because of this confusion, we granted you longer life to learn how to be free within the limitations of the human body…You have done well…You have learned much since that day you came to us. You have the freedom to make your life whatever you want it to be.

*Zetta:* I am asking if we made any financial agreements regarding my continued life. I tell them that it is difficult when you have to worry about having enough groceries, when you don't see where the money can come from.

*Council:* Zetta, we have given you many signs that you have been taken care of, that abundance is yours. We know it is not coming as you want. But it is coming from what you need. Open your heart. Abundance can come from any direction, from sources unknown to you. *The only suffering you will experience is that which will help you open your eyes to your patterns.* For the most part your life is complete. You have done a good job! Your karmic connections are complete. The end of your life is now your choice.

We see that you are not happy, except for moments in this life—and that is the belief in suffering that you have carried throughout lifetimes. You needn't suffer anymore. There is no price you can pay for the abundance we offer you. We know that you still desire to die, to leave the world. There will come a day when you will know in your heart when it is the right day to let go. In the meantime, continue to do what you always do: Explore the issues that rise and find healing. You do that so well. You are so courageous."

*Zetta:* I am asking my Council if there is anything else that I need to be doing with my life while I am here...

*Council:* We know it is hard for you to experience joy and fun and laughter, but that is all you need to do; allow yourself to open and see the humorous all around you, the delight that is in everything, the joy that is abundant is all for you! There is nothing specific that you need to do. You can't earn your way to the other side.

With that profound statement, there was a pause. The session was almost over and both of us were tiring. We conveyed our deep gratitude for the time with these beings, then checked in to see if Zetta felt complete. Still feeling the great reverence, she affirmed that she was finished and we closed the session.

Rather than neatly tying up all loose ends, our visit to the Council of Seven gave Zetta new enigmas to ponder. How do you live abundantly when you need groceries and your bank account is almost empty? How do you open to abundance coming from any direction? What is it like to embrace non-suffering and joy? When your karma is complete and your life goals are fulfilled, what's next? Even if you've done a good job with your Earth School homework assignments, twiddling your thumbs is not an option. Neither is dying—quite yet. The MapQuest route to death showed several possibilities. Rather than taking the expected, shortest route, Zetta opted for the scenic one. Not only was she shattering her death archetype, she had evidently chosen to liberate herself from any remaining joy-limiting patterns.

Zetta returned herself to the world of daily life with a few more learning options and the gift of consciously knowing she had a pretty impressive, exacting and generous support system in the higher realms.

**PART 3:** *"I lost my death."*

Fifteen months after our last session, Zetta came to share an update on her life. It was a sunny afternoon, February 5, 2009. She radiated a deep peace. I was prepared for another PLR but, intuitively, couldn't get a handle on whether that was the likely direction of our session. It wasn't. Instead, for the next hour and a half Zetta recounted the remarkable events of her life since our last session.

Much to her dismay, the day of our last session, December 14, 2007, proved to be a most unexpected rebirth. Zetta was catapulted back into life without ever seeing it coming. Her whole ship of state had been sailing blithely toward the sunset of eternity for several years. Closing up shop, releasing belongings, handling health needs in the way of basic comfort, finishing any legal matters. Responsible end-of-life behavior, we'd call it. However, upon her return to Boulder, Zetta discovered she was being discharged from hospice. Her blood tests were indicating greater, not lesser health. The concerns about dying from hepatitis C had waned as far as the medical community was concerned. You are well enough. You don't need us anymore. Support system dissolved. Case closed. With no plan whatsoever to re-enter life, once again she found herself totally lost. No money, no partner, no job, no Plan B, and an apartment she hated. When everyone, including yourself is onboard to get you through the closure of your earthly timeshare and on to your blessed afterlife, what are you supposed to do with your return to time?

Zetta spent months grieving the loss of her death, tossed on the sea of the unknown. Death was the gift she was prepared to receive. Life was not. It felt like a punishment, another grievance to deal with. "Now I'm going to live?! Who do you talk to about this? Where's the map for charting a new direction? I still had morphine and other drugs in the fridge and I seriously considered suicide. How can I possibly fit in again? I felt stretched in all directions unable to find my own center."

Alone at sea, scattered and despairing, Zetta called a friend who came over and listened deeply. Her friend sat with her and then said simply, "You need to move. Go to where you feel loved. You have friends in Colorado Springs, Canon City and Guffey, Colorado. Go where you are loved." By the end of April, Zetta had found a home to rent in Canon City. It felt right. It felt like the home she had been wanting. The move roused her back into her life. The stretching process required for her new life had begun.

Through the ensuing months of adjustment, Zetta found herself facing fear upon fear. With the loss of her death, how were others going to respond to her? They had gone on with their lives. "I did not know how to talk with others about what I was experiencing because I didn't think they could understand. I felt incredibly alone and no longer knew where I fit into this life now presented to me. I still did not know where to begin or how to put my life back together. I knew I was expanding spiritually but didn't have a clue how to integrate it all. And the big bugaboo: What if I couldn't really sustain the positive changes I had experienced? What if they were temporary? What if I would regress back into the fearful, small, protected, victimized woman I had always been? How was I to do this?"

Since there are no manuals written for this major predicament, Zetta was thrown into the deep waters of her own life with only the very basics to keep her afloat—instinct; a still, small voice; and trial and error. New friends began to show up. She started gardening and found odd jobs that fit her energy level. Life was getting easier to navigate.

### Autumn of 2009

Nine months later, Zetta attended a gathering at my home. It was the autumn of 2009 and we'd had no contact since the previous conversation. She was quietly radiant. As we went around the circle introducing ourselves, I was immensely curious as to what Zetta might share. She kept it simple, "I am from Canon City. I am a hospice social worker. I sit with people who are dying and I love my work." Only two of us in the room knew Zetta's full story. We held that truth—a woman who died in 2006, was brought back in order to die better, now sitting among us radiantly alive and perfectly placed in her world. And earning money to put groceries in the fridge!

How did Zetta shatter her death archetype? How has her death demon or phantom been transformed? As her story unfolded, it became apparent that death was losing its sting for Zetta. She no longer ran from it—or toward it. It was her near and dear companion, helping her hone the rest of her life, reminding her to be present to the inherent joy of the moment. In some sense, she was the shaman of her own journey, the one who had faced the unknown terrors and returned empowered. It was scary, but wonder of wonders! Little, if any fear, remained.

Now, Zetta knows, at the deep cellular level, what she "knew" with her rational mind. As she mentioned, she had sought her deeper self throughout her life. Greater authenticity and compassion arrived on her doorstep as she surrendered to her heart and faced her fears and her death head-on. Her heart is soft and open. Her words are real and honest. Her fears are no longer snarling tigers at the door but meowing kittens in her lap. The energy previously used to handle fear and push tigers away is available for reflection and fun and friends as she so chooses. Simplicity has become her necessity and her guide. Gone are all but the essential possessions. Gone are the insatiable emotional needs that often burden our days.

From Zetta and the many others who are utilizing the near-death experience, past-life regression and their own imminent death we learn that:

1. We can change the contract. We can go sooner or leave later with no repercussions, if the highest good is served. There are highly evolved and compassionate beings to help guide us in these decisions.

2. Preparing to die more consciously is also choosing to live more consciously. They are inseparable. By embracing our own death, we embrace the impermanence and preciousness of life.

3. Surrender of ego-based fears brings great relief and peace.

4. Physical illness can be the vehicle of immense spiritual healing.

5. Death is our earthly companion. Then it's gone. Over and out. LIFE is our *eternal* companion.

6. Clearing our slate and adopting the higher emotional frequencies are great goals for a good death and a free spirit. This work is self-love of the highest order. As Zetta nourishes these qualities and clears the drag of fear, she is fueling an extra rocket boost into higher frequencies, both now and when she slips through the exit door.

Dethroning the death demon or phantom is not for the timid. Zetta exemplifies a hard-won inner strength no longer shored up by emotional armor. Ironically, we seldom know our strength until these opportunities present themselves. We are grateful that, through the very personal and quiet labor of thousands of people like her, the old archetype of death is being reconfigured and liberated.

# CHAPTER 14

# Aaron's Story

*It is quite possible that forgiveness is the most important word.*
*It is like a cool balm, a refreshing rain.*
*It oils all the wheels and everything comes into flow.*
*Forgiveness is an experience...*
*The door to freedom is forgiveness.*
—Aaron

## The End is the Beginning

AARON'S STORY BEGAN ARRIVING on my doorstep several weeks after I learned of his suicide, and has unfolded over the ensuing years. With the help of several gifted colleagues and his own beautiful spirit, we've gathered up pieces of his journey that have helped us comprehend the pitfalls he experienced within the dualities of Earth School. Aaron's complex story relates to our earlier conversation on getting lost in the afterlife. It also speaks to forgiveness. It is a teaching story, worthy of being brought to light so that others might benefit. I never met Aaron, but he gave me permission (from the other side) to share his story.

In 2006, Joy, a dear friend of mine who lives in a distant state, met and fell in love with Aaron, a beautiful, sensitive man. During our numerous phone conversations, Joy and I chatted about her life and new love relationship. I came to understand that Aaron had moved across the country nine months earlier and that he was trying to make a new life for himself. He had recently been through a difficult divorce and was the father of two estranged adolescent daughters. This was a profoundly troubling time as Aaron battled to regain his equilibrium and hope. Those who have been through similar experiences understand the recovery process intimately.

However, Aaron had another layer with which he was struggling. He had been raised in an extremely controlling, conservative religious sect and had remained a member until several years prior to his move. Part of the belief system espoused by this group was that leaving the church was a sin; should you dare to leave, you would be shunned. Then you would go insane and/ or commit suicide. These extremes of control were designed to activate fears of social isolation, hell and the damnation of God. As Joy and Aaron grew closer, he shared his struggle with these inner demons. Though he hadn't given credence to these extreme teachings for years, the toll on his spirit was immense. One morning, Aaron was found dead in his parked car.

The tidal wave of his suicide washed through Joy's heart and the hearts of those who had come to love him. The days passed in shock and sorrow, with many unanswered questions still rising within his community of friends.

In the midst of all the unknowns, Joy became more and more aware of a phenomenon: monarch butterflies. She noticed their chrysalises on her railing. When they hatched, they fluttered to her hand, where they stayed for extended periods of time. She found comfort, delight and assurance in the companionship of these winged ones, for Aaron had painted monarchs and written poems about them. Through her days of grieving, Aaron and the spirit world felt nearer because of their presence.

## Entering Aaron's "Heaven"

I began to feel a prompting to check on Aaron. I wondered how he was doing on the other side. I called my intuitive friend, Christine Peters, to see if she wanted to be the interdimensional traveler while I played the role of therapist-scribe. She was excited and came aboard. Then I called Joy to see how this dimensional travel research would feel to her tender heart. Joy was enlivened by the prospect and asked that we share what we discovered.

Christine and I began in earnest. We talked with Aaron four times, three times in 2006 and one final time in 2010. I also asked another intuitive friend, Denise Chicoine, to track Aaron, which she graciously did. What unfolded was the long story of a troubled soul.

Both Christine and Denise dealt with the suicide issue immediately. The wisdom from the afterlife, at least as regards to Aaron, held no judgment for his decision. These are Denise's words: "I saw that as Aaron left his body, he realized what he had done and there was deep grief. I saw the shackles binding his ankles, what he had carried—the burden of the brainwashing. His guides appeared wearing gray trench coats, reflecting the lower astral energy they had taken on in order to reach him. They were trying to assist him. I sensed he had a historical relationship with them and that perhaps they were a part of his soul group. (Note: Here is an example of how helpers and guides take on a form that will best assist the one passing over. Aaron's helpers came in trench coats, like undercover cops getting someone off the streets and out of harm's way. Aaron, being confused and despairing, acquiesced.)

Denise continued, "There is a message about him being a follower. They had difficulty getting him to the light because of his huge despair. But his despair may have been incentive for him to follow them. My higher self began talking with him and we showered him with love and light. Because of his great tenderness of soul, he immediately felt the love and went on with them to a higher realm. He took a fast getaway…but there is no karma with his choice. It is okay that he took this path to break the pattern. He is still pondering it all in the afterlife. He is a delicate, beautiful soul. His sensitivity is a double-edged sword, both a gift and a hardship…People should not spend a lot of time with the whys and whats of his suicide. It doesn't matter. Suicide was a part of his journey. For him, the fast getaway was purposeful and not a cop-out."

Travel into the troubled, lower, astral realms is not without its difficulties. Denise experienced pain in the back of her heart chakra and general low energy after her work with Aaron. She later worked with an energy healer who felt that Denise had taken on some dark energy that not only Aaron but Joy had been carrying. The energy was released. Denise's only comment on this service she rendered was, "It's okay. These are soul agreements that we have made to assist each other."

Christine Peters also struggled to handle the negative energy once she connected with Aaron. She saw dark colors in the region of his heart and had a feeling of being squeezed. It was hard for her to continue. After stabilizing and bringing in more protection for her, we proceeded together. The heaviness and darkness in Aaron's energy field was confirmed by the similar experiences of both of these dimensional travelers.

## A Peek into Childhood

Christine started by gathering information of Aaron's childhood. She saw the likelihood of very early satanic ritual abuse by several older men. This was not necessarily related to the church but was associated with his home. By age three, he was already shielding his heart and difficult to reach emotionally. Understandably, he had begun building layers of suspicion and protection at a very early age.

Aaron participated in this whole exploration from his vantage point in spirit, sometimes guiding us with comments, sometimes sitting back and learning more about his long soul history. There were events that he didn't understand from his past. Christine could see things that he hadn't been able to see. She became aware of numbers, rituals and words that were difficult to interpret. As Aaron moved from the lower astral levels into seeing himself as a soul, he said, "It all fits together if you understand my past incarnations."

## Past Lives

His past lives then began to make themselves known. There were lives dealing with medicine and healing, where he was both the healer and patient. One lifetime was during the plagues of Europe with desolation and smoke everywhere—no beauty and no hope. In that life, Christine saw Aaron was very ill.

Then the word "contract" showed up—a heavy, burdened contract. Christine moved through layers and fragments of information. It appeared that somewhere in his past, Aaron had stumbled into a sort of "contract with the devil" or negative energy. Christine said, "It's like Aaron feels he is totally tied to this contract with no escape. It has followed him through these lifetimes and he has not gotten a break. He feels like he is caught in an eternal loop. Once it was created, he couldn't break the stranglehold. He has always been trying to find answers through medicine, healing and even the dark arts." What was this all about we wondered? What was this contract?

## Links with Joy

We searched to find the places where Joy and Aaron shared the journey that culminated in the present-life situation. Christine saw that sometime around 1560 AD in Europe, Joy and Aaron set out on a dangerous mission. She described the glimpse she was given. "I see a life where Joy is a woman, dressed in a long cloak and hood. She is holding a sword or weapon, with a lantern in the background. Aaron has used the dark arts in the past, but in this life I see he is using the light. Both of them understand what they are doing. Both have a clear vision of their previous work. Aaron felt that this might be an even match with fighting the negative energy. There are those two and the third, that dark one. They are like warrior and warrioress going to battle."

After that scene, Christine moved further back in time to an earlier life in which they were together. "We can see where it started…The starting place is earlier than the 1500s in the region of France, I think. I see them both practicing the crafts. In this life they are both males. They are somewhere high above, shut off like apprentices. They are associated with an order or fraternity called something like 'The Order of the God-Wave.' They have climbed to a high old church, very big like a fortress. In the lower levels of the church are hidden legends and carvings. It appears to be a power place. At some point by accident, they opened to this darkness. This feels like the first place. Initially, the energy was clean, then this event happened and the contract came through." This was the beginning, the mistake, the contract.

Aaron then revealed to us his sense that he had continued to carry the dark energy of the contract in this life. He had a real fear that Joy would be harmed by it. He knew her to be a courageous soul and that she would once again fight the dark forces if need be and that it would be a real battle. He knew she had fought before and lost. He acknowledged that her strength is greater now than before, but he didn't want to be the cause of her suffering. Because of his deep love for Joy, he chose to take the darkness with him in death rather than endanger her again in any way. I was touched, feeling the heroic energy behind some of these difficult choices.

At the end of this session, I asked Aaron if he was comfortable with this story being shared with others for teaching purposes. He replied, "Oh yes!"

## Forgiveness

Aaron's suicide decision had many lifetimes behind it and we were beginning to understand his underlying soul history more clearly. Two months later, we checked in with Aaron again to see how he was doing. Christine described him as more quiet, timid, humble. We showered him with love and support and he warmed to our arrival in his world. But he said, "I have so much resting to do." The energy was foggy around him as he woke up, and it became apparent he was still deeply burdened. The burden was the tremendous guilt he still carried from the misuse of magic in the church fortress basement that mistakenly opened a dark portal, 500-600 years ago. This had brought harm to himself and others, an unforgivable and heartbreaking event for him. There appeared to be a shroud over him. Aaron was unsettled to have his fog disturbed. He just wanted to sleep. It didn't appear that he had made much progress since we last talked and that he was still adrift in the foggy worlds of self-recrimination and despair.

Christine and I worked with Aaron therapeutically on healing, release and forgiveness while gently extending love and building rapport. He was alerted by the word forgiveness. He feared forgiveness meant shoving it all under the table and forgetting. In his mind, it must not be forgotten, for if unguarded, the negativity would escape. He felt responsible for the evil that had occurred and didn't want it to ever be unleashed on the world.

It seemed to me this burden needed witnessing, so I said, "Aaron, we see that you have carried this very difficult burden for hundreds of years and even into the afterlife, that you never felt you could let it go. We understand that it feels so heavy. Because you never wanted it to cause harm to anyone, you are holding it very close. This has been a brave thing you are doing...Perhaps there is something we can do to support you here..." I hoped empathy could be the first step in shifting him from his centuries-old dilemma.

Christine heard Aaron say, "The love you take is equal to the love you make." He was beginning to think in terms of love. She noticed some slight shifting and softening and he agreed to consider what we had suggested.

Then Christine noticed someone in the shadows behind Aaron. It was a Catholic cardinal. Aaron evidently had been a student of this man and bitterly rued the day he failed his teacher. Aaron's guilt was palpable. However, Christine was able to see something that Aaron had not been able to see; the cardinal was in on it! The cardinal was secretly practicing the dark arts in some fashion and Aaron and Joy had been the unknowing pawns in this orchestrated event. As Aaron heard all this, his remorse turned to shock.

The three of us conversed together for a bit before closing the session. Aaron was considering the possible truth of his ancient teacher's deception. Christine and I made certain Aaron was well-placed in his reality. He appeared to have a lessening of the fog. We blessed him with affirmations and love and he agreed to see us again.

Later in the evening, I spoke with Joy and shared our experiences with Aaron. She confirmed Aaron's responses and energy. He had recently come to her in a dream and his presence was heavy and shrouded. She felt this matched the foggy place in consciousness in which Christine saw him. After her dream, Joy also put a boundary up with Aaron; no more dream visits in that heavy energetic state. Interestingly, she was particularly affirming of his trouble with the idea of forgiveness. She recalled that throughout the several months before his passing, he would frequently draw the *Forgiveness* Angel Card—to the point of being frustrated and discounting the cards. Perhaps the depth of forgiveness being called for was toward himself and could not be comprehended with the consciousness he held at the time.

## Releasing Guilt Allows for Help: Phealoh Appears

Approximately one month later, we checked in with Aaron. We found him better rested and able to be curious about the troubled past life with the cardinal. He was able to see that the cardinal did not have his best interests in mind. Though it shook him to the core, at long last he was seeing the betrayal of his teacher and mentor. He seemed somewhat clearer and was beginning to imagine the possibility of putting this burden down.

As the guilt lessened, Christine noticed a comforting presence over Aaron's right shoulder. We both became hopeful that Aaron's guide would be able to make himself known. But first, there was one more piece of work to do in order to release the painful memories. I suggested to Aaron that he would be able to go to the original event that caused so much pain and that he could watch it now without difficulty and that his guides would be there to support and protect him.

Christine reported what was shown to her and Aaron. "I see that Aaron is practicing with ancient energies. The magic he was to create was the culmination of much work and schooling. It was very positive in his eyes. He was happy to be doing it, but unbeknownst to him, the cardinal had something else in mind. I want Aaron to clearly see that it wasn't his fault. This had all been purposely planned by the cardinal. Aaron is witnessing the deep greed and hunger for power surrounding the cardinal. Aaron thought it was the Order of the Holy Word. The cardinal was in love with the 'holy world.'

"The energy that was released in the magic ritual was an energy used to divide and conquer. For instance, I am being told that over the course of history this energy has been released and used. I am shown the event that Aaron calls the 'night of the broken glass,' and four or five other times it was released and had this negative influence. It creates illusion and confusion for people—the sort of distortion where white seems like black and black seems like white. It was released in the Crusades and in Nazi Germany, for example. It is used to weaken and destabilize the light of great beings.

"I see how Aaron has tried to contain it. There have been times when he has been successful and times that it escaped from him. I want to tell him that this energy was not created by him; it was in the world before him. He feels so, so guilty about this...He is saying that he kept the energy contained in a certain kind of mirror, but I don't think that is the broken glass he speaks of.

"There is a general sense of lightening. His guide, named Phealoh, is now able to come forward. He knows Aaron very well. Aaron is able to see him; he couldn't until now. All this is healing for Aaron. The image of the cardinal is weakening and doesn't have as much power. The guide is not a Jesus figure but has a lot of light. My sense is that we are privileged to witness this. A benevolent blessing and knowing is being transmitted to Aaron. We can soak up this awe-inspiring energy if we would like...Aaron is waking up more and more, becoming more whole."

There were a few more ends for us to tie up. We invited healing throughout this timeline—all the historical events for which Aaron still carried grief and regret. Aaron's spirit was releasing its remaining heaviness. His gratitude was apparent.

He turned to Phealoh, many questions bubbling to the surface. He wondered, for example, if being born on Earth was a dream and the present, higher awareness was real reality. Phealoh explained it by saying that it's as if when you blink your eyes closed you are here; when you open them again you are in another life on Earth. Aaron pondered what the role of magic is on the soul's journey. Phealoh conveyed that life is magic. You don't have to conjure. We are creators within the magic of life. Aaron soaked up love and acceptance as Phealoh continued to answer his questions. He decided he wanted to swing and a swing appeared, the back-and-forth movement providing the playfulness his spirit craved.

As we concluded our session, we received thanks from Phealoh for our assistance with Aaron's release from his own particular hell. We felt gratitude for the privilege of witnessing this process. Aaron once again affirmed that his story could be shared. He gave me a branch with tiny white flowers as a gift, saying stories can be told to help people. Christine then noticed people lining up behind him wanting their stories to also be told. This was quite touching. The longing for healing, for validation, for compassionate witnessing of our lives may sometimes be as compelling on the other side as it is for us here. We concluded the session. Assuming that our work with Aaron was complete, Christine and I went on about our lives. Four years passed before our next contact.

## Other Clues

Meanwhile, more clues arose regarding the complexities of Aaron's recent life. Friends began to speculate. A sexual addiction that he struggled with became more apparent as the stories mounted. To some, his troubled behaviors signaled deeper mind-control issues than was likely with the church. Joy was wary when two men-in-suits showed up on her front step, flashed IDs, and claimed they were from the IRS. They said they wanted some information on Aaron's IRS tax records. Not only were they intimidating, their behavior seemed odd. After refusing to cooperate and telling them to leave, Joy collapsed. Instinctively she knew they were not from the IRS. She was tempted to call the IRS to double check, then realized that she might kick up more dust than she could handle in a fragile time. She knew what she knew; they likely represented some secret group or organization associated with Aaron's past. No need for further confirmation.

Friends and folks who were familiar with covert mind-control programs wondered if Aaron had been one of their "trainees." Mind-control programming devastates the body, mind and spirit, as those who have managed to escape and recover can attest. As more became known about his family of origin, his early suffering with ritual and sexual abuse and his present patterns, it seemed plausible. The men-in-suits on the doorstep was the last red flag waving over a sea of deception that had been part of Aaron's inner life. These secrets had attempted to reveal themselves through his addictions and pain. Only after his death, could some of the truth rise to the surface. We were all, in some sense, witness to the long karmic trail of Aaron's journey with good and evil.

## Another Meeting: Higher Dimensions

Then, in the spring of 2010, while checking on an acquaintance who had passed on, Christine and I visited with Aaron again. Why not? What might a soul be doing four years after leaving the Earth plane? The last time we spoke with Aaron, he was feeling light, full of questions about reality and swinging on a swing as his guilt and sorrow dissolved.

We discovered Aaron had moved into a much higher frequency in the afterlife. His past life as Aaron, with all its troubles, and all the other difficult past lives were now distant memories. So distant in fact that he could scarcely recall them. He said that it was important for him to gain the understanding and healing from those experiences, but once achieved, he had moved past them. It all didn't matter in the same way any longer.

He talked with us about his new passion: *focus*, the power of focusing your attention or consciousness. This was his particular learning and fascination in his present dimension. "It really is about focus here where I am. Anything you don't focus on, you don't see. Your focus is then what you see and experience. I thought being in the afterlife was about the end of pain, but you get to experience the *ecstasy of fulfillment*. Memory is scarcely present when I am in this focused ecstasy. It's like the focus that the lens of a camera gives you."

He offered a new perspective on forgiveness, that difficult concept intruding upon his last months on Earth. "It is quite possible that forgiveness is the most important word. It is like a cool balm, a refreshing rain. It oils all the wheels and everything comes into flow. Forgiveness is an experience. It is to be *experienced*. It is the door to the freedom of being absolutely at peace but eager, content but excited about what unfolds next. Here, it is not quite the same connotation as on Earth, but is a quality of being, a door to your greatest rest. It is how you keep your frequency high in order to remain here and grow. Forgiveness is an amazing rest, a mathematical equation for trust and rest. The door to freedom is forgiveness." Certainly, Aaron had evolved in his understanding of forgiveness.

Aaron then shared more specifically what his present work in this higher-frequency heaven entailed. He showed Christine a beautiful grid pattern that was his responsibility to keep clean and functioning. This grid pattern was related to the field of Mind, of universal patterns that influence and sustain multidimensional reality. Along with being a grid "superintendent" he also described himself as a "way-shower" at times, going where he was needed. He was thrilled to be working with the grid patterns because this "is a harmonious place. There is purpose in what I do and no feeling of another life."

Arriving at this place of consciousness and this work was a gradual process for Aaron, as his soul awakened to its true nature. "Imagine your soul looking toward the divine, finally getting a bead on a growing feeling of ecstasy. This pulled me forward until I fully joined my soul in divine ecstasy." Christine likened it to a field of sunflowers that joyfully face the sun, their ecstasy. Our entry into his domain caused him to turn briefly away from his sun, a bit of a distraction for a soul sunflower.

We discovered Aaron to be content and dwelling in this beautiful expectancy. He adored the clear Mind, the universal patterns he helped to maintain. If, for example, the grid became tangled with emotions, he was able to release them, thus contributing to the harmony of Universal Mind.

I asked Aaron if he might be working with the great beings called Creator Gods or Creator Spirits under which many serve in order to keep the worlds and dimensions coordinated and functioning. It sounded as if he might be a part of that effort. Christine reported that, "He says he helps individuals as well as working with the grid. There is a ministering unto in which he takes someone aside, assisting them to shine more brightly with clear light, clear mind. It is like bringing a beautiful orchestra into harmony."

I asked if Aaron had by chance served in helping those souls crossing over from their Earth lives. He said that he had done some of that work but now was in service to those coming into the present realm where he worked. If someone came and asked assistance in a clear, focused manner, in the energy of grace, he helped them. This support looked rather like an activation of their soul, their consciousness. He saw the healing given as an activation of faith.

I then asked about his take on conscious dying. Aaron became succinct. "Just get here! I don't care how! Just do it! You have a skewed perception on Earth. Whatever you think it's like here, it's so vastly more amazing. You don't really have the full idea of being conscious. Though what you have isn't much, it is, however, all you need. Consciousness is quite limited from the human perspective. I keep learning. Even where I am now may not be my eternity. If something greater shows up, a different dimension, I'll go, I'll be there."

We were receiving a sense of Aaron's journey. The movement he made from where we started with him to the present conversation involved some major steps. We sensed that with each change he experienced, another light or guide stepped forward to assist him forward.

I wondered what Aaron's level or dimension was. Christine had no name but described it this way. "By comparison, if this dimension were on the Earth, it would be on a very high mountain. On this mountain would be a sacred temple. You and I would not be able to go inside but would be in the courtyard or garden around it. This temple looks like a symbol for the Masons, only sideways. It is a sacred structure involving a sacred structural matrix or blueprint."

As we closed, Aaron had a last bit of reflection. "While the clear Universal Mind is beautiful to behold, on Earth—where you are now—the vehicle is the heart. Humanity is on the cusp of evolving/dissolving into the other chambers of the heart, into the true structure and blueprint for which the human heart is designed."

From a soul who had experienced unimaginable suffering, suffering weighted with guilt and spanning the centuries, we receive higher guidance on humanity's journey. Christine, Denise and I felt privileged to have been of some assistance to Aaron as he waded through the lower astral levels after death. We also know many are being blessed by the wisdom and service he now showers through his part of creation.

# CHAPTER 15

# *Crossing-Over Stories*

*So peaceful…Soft, warm, gentle…floating…*

AS WE PERCH ON THAT EXQUISITE, sharp edge of departure, we are on hallowed ground. Those delicately balanced moments between this world and the next are places of awe and possibility. The Mystery rises before us, like a new, uncertain dawn. What will happen next? What will it be like? In the presence of humble and loving hearts, miracles and blessings can arise. A client, Bev, and her family shared with me their hallowed ground experience as they attended the departure of their beloved, 98 year-old matriarch, Aunt Mary.

After breaking her pelvis, Aunt Mary had been transferred to the nursing home associated with her assisted living facility. Her body was weak, her heart rate and breathing labored. She requested no intervention except pain management, and commented wryly that in her R.N. training many years ago, pain was managed with one aspirin. Higher pain—two aspirin. Now here she was the beneficiary of morphine as needed.

Aunt Mary seemed to be practicing for her walk across the bridge, for at one point when wakened, she asked, "Am I alive?" Somewhat disoriented, she wondered which world she was in. Bev, her brother Ted and sister-in-law Dora assured Aunt Mary that she was indeed alive. Aware that she was still on this side, Aunt Mary began her own quest to understand what might be awaiting her when she crossed over. After learning what day it was and that there was nothing she needed to do but rest, Aunt Mary said, "I'm so confused. What am I doing? This is not living! Do I have a choice?"

"What kind of choice, Aunt Mary?" Dora asked.

"I'm so confused. I want to go see my family and I'm ready to go the shortest way."

"What do you mean, 'the shortest way'?"

"Dora, tell the doctors the shortest way, okay? God will understand."

Dora, touched by Aunt Mary's questions and readiness to depart, began to cry, leaning her head on Aunt Mary's shoulder.

"It's okay Dora, I love you...Listen, do you hear the music? It's beautiful!"

Later in the day, Aunt Mary lifted her hands as though she was directing music. With a lovely smile on her face, she stretched out her hands, palms up as if receiving a gift. Then she fell asleep.

In a conversation a short time later, Aunt Mary picked up where she left off; this time Bev was included in the quizzing. With her death at hand, she had lost her inhibition. All the questions that had never been asked came flooding to the surface, mirroring her fears and hopes.

"Am I going to go to sleep and not wake up?"

"How long will this take?"

Bev replied, "I don't know, but I believe that you are not your body and that your body holds your spirit. I believe that when your body dies your spirit goes to be with God."

Aunt Mary nodded her head, musing, "...I see God in the dew on the roses..."

The questions continued and included who she might see on the other side and what she might need and what she would be able to do. "Will I eat? Will I have pain? Does God know that I love Him? Will you be able to talk to me? Can I talk to other people? Will it be like this with day and night? Will I be on oxygen and need glasses? Maybe I'll be able to hear!"

As each of her concerns was lovingly addressed by Bev and Dora, Aunt Mary came to her own conclusion. "Well that doesn't sound so bad. I don't know how you know all of this, but I'm so glad that you do. So what's the problem!?"

They replied, "There is no problem."

"Well then let's go to bed!" said Aunt Mary. Laughing through their tears, Aunt Mary's support team called it a day. These conversations seemed to bring her ease for, other than one restless episode, she rested well after that and died peacefully within 24 hours. The exquisite, sharp edge of departure was fully embraced by Aunt Mary and her loving crew, no moment wasted.

I wonder if Aunt Mary would have found comfort in some of the following crossing-over stories. We can be assured that she would have had more questions, and very pragmatic ones at that. Actual stories bring ease to our spirits. These vignettes are excerpts from some of my past-life regression clients as they crossed into the afterlife. They give us a flavor of departure experiences. In some, I've included a hint of the further support and wisdom waiting in the wings. Once they are fully across the bridge, clients are often able to reach deep into Soul or Universal Mind for amazing wisdom and perspective. Because that material is beyond our focus here, just a smattering is included.

In these stories, you will glimpse what clients see or feel as they leave their lives behind and discover their own bridge. Though you may read each story in a matter of minutes or seconds, keep in mind that the story unfolded quietly and slowly over many minutes, sometimes an hour. I want you to appreciate that seldom is the experience instantaneous, because the departing soul needs transition time as he or she moves between worlds. There are helpful insights tucked within the simplest of phrases. I recommend that you read each one slowly, imagining the journey. Then take a deep breath and read it again. Perhaps a part of you will be remembering your own crossing from another life.

The rational part of my mind has wondered if the PLR death is accurate. Is the reported PLR death influenced by the present self and the therapist? With my current understanding I would say—yes and yes. It is accurate and it is influenced. And it is all authentic from the present state of consciousness. To relive a life brings it to consciousness. We hear the historical story, and we are offered the opportunity to see that life—and that death—from another perspective. Our purpose is to gain understanding and bring healing. This graces the soul. It benefits the whole of the journey. The soul, not being limited by time, space or personality, assimilates the new awareness. By existing both in the eternal and 3-D, the soul absorbs the new perspective.

## Common Themes

*Changes in light and perception.* You will notice prevailing themes. For example, clients mention a change in perception and the quality of light. They generally say they feel lighter or see more beautiful lights and colors. Some hear celestial music, like Aunt Mary did. They are surprised to not have a body yet be able to perceive and experience. They may pass through heavier dimensions before they feel lighter. Though they seldom use terms like dimension or purgatory or darkness, for some it is apparent when they are passing through these areas. My role is to encourage them to notice their helpers or the light and continue on. If rest is needed, as is often the case, those needs are honored once the soul has reached the other side.

*Changes in awareness.* Often a larger view of that life opens up. Difficulties are given a more philosophical bent. Triumphs are seen where none were apparent before. Most of all, there is the perspective that comes with a spacious, love-filled vacation. "Ah-h, now I can rest, reflect and remember who I really am."

*Helpers.* A particularly beautiful commonality is the experience of helpers. I call them angels or escorts. We are told over and over that the soul need never be alone in its journey to the other side. There are always escorts. One need only look, or feel, or solicit their presence. Some clients see them, some feel or sense them. Some are too unsettled or awed to notice. But they are nearby. They may show up as angels, family members, masters or mythical figures. True helpers are always benevolent and kind, and take on forms that bring comfort to the dying soul. Different helpers have different roles, so it isn't uncommon for one helper to show up at the beginning to provide the initial assistance and then for another to come forward for the next steps. Many helper variations are necessary given the uniqueness of each soul.

A gift we can give ourselves, our children and other loved ones, is the simple guidance to "Look for your angels" when crossing over.

## STORIES

### General Tales

There is actually little to warrant the term "general" with these stories. They range from long lives and easy deaths to shorter lives and harsh deaths. They are better labeled a cross-section of human experience. Could I have justified a lengthier chapter, you would have been privy to even more wonderful tales such as these. As you read, remember—take a deep breath, read slowly. You are entering sacred space. Seek to put yourself into the expanding new world that opens as the body falls away. You may experience, along with the client, the struggle with language that is so woefully inadequate for describing his or her release.

"I'm happy, like I'm going to float. I'm not scared. I'm in my 20s and ready to die. Floating...Sparkles...Stars...Getting lighter and wider and bigger. I'm slowing down, floating. There is a garden and flowers everywhere. White benches everywhere, beautiful. Sometimes something or someone floats in and out, like shapes. They look at me, but I tell them I don't want to talk. It's just feelings. They are waiting for me to communicate with them...."

*C.J. after short male life with a Mediterranean group, 800 BC.*

"Peace, joy, anticipation because I know that this is the time I get to go and understand. I'd rather look forward than back. I feel a tremendous freedom. I'm zigzagging and it feels wonderful. The weight is lifting...The joy is that there are people here who care, who have genuine concern for helping you learn from your experiences. It's almost like a big party where there are lots of different souls. It's the place to be when a soul comes back, the place everyone wants to be. They show support and appreciation for your journey. I'm experiencing this. There is an understanding that not all souls choose the physical. The physical is the hardest way to learn. Maybe there is an element of curiosity as well...."

*G.K. after short male life as reluctant, troubled mariner on a slave ship.*

"So peaceful, feels like home. Soft, warm, gentle, floating. There are a lot of lessons...I keep thinking of lessons. I have to learn to forgive...I've always been scared...I'm tired of being scared...."

*A.G. after long restricted life as traditional privileged wife who died in 1929.*

"I am comfortable, about 60 years old. It's getting lighter. People are around me who are sad. And I'm trying to comfort them, but I'm not sad... I'm wondering what it will be like in five minutes! Kind of a white light, gentle and floating...There are people here I know. I have joy and relief and am being welcomed back. Someone, a woman is here...I was married to her somewhere, sometime, but that's not important now...I am very happy to have had that life."

*J.B. after life as a rabbi in Scotland, late 1800s.*

"I'm happy because something will change and will be better than this suffering. I am remembering my parents and assume they are now dead. I am remembering the ocean, how peaceful it was. I am remembering that adventurous girl I was. I feel very old and broken. Death is a relief...I feel like mist rising, cool but not cold. Like a vapor rising. I'm formless and drift through the walls into the light. My body below is gray and broken and folded in on itself, in the corner in rags...Now I am formless, a mind and spirit without a body, moving on the wind..."

*M.A. after life as a free-spirited young woman born in the British Isles who traveled by ship to a Mediterranean land where she was punished for flamboyancy. She died in a dungeon from beatings and starvation at age 30. 1400s or 1500s AD.*

"I am out of myself, looking at myself. There is warmth at the center of my chest. I want to drift up...I want to leave after all the fight and the pain. I feel that my wife and child have passed over. The doctors below are trying to resuscitate me. I'm laughing, 'You can't get me now!' I look at the scene but am rising up. I'm swelling and etheric...It's almost like I have gone up onto a ship, like it's all clouds. I'm sitting and waiting, basking in the lightness of it all. Two lights have come into my energy field, like a welcoming hug. Feels like my wife and son. I am almost turning into that light. The last remnants of my earthly essence are leaving...

"I feel very small and that I am looking up at some huge beings with large cloaks, but the cloaks are a part of who they are, not like separate material. I am focusing on the features of one of them and then they blend away. Blue, then green...Almost like they are showing me something...You can be anything...But they are big and expanded and there are a lot of them around...My wife and son are waiting and we are going in together. We passed at a similar time.

"The fight to live has been so strong in me...Now it's okay to die. They are saying, 'Merciful kindness.' I don't understand...Humility and love, love for my captors and perpetrators. Compassion and understanding...I achieved this at the last moment of my life. When my kidney was taken, I saw their (doctors in the lab) pain and it was greater than my own. I was very angry and I only got compassion in a flash at the end. That's why I was released (died). They are satisfied with that. Memories of that life are fading and they are bringing me into a pure state..."

*H.O. after life as Wang Ghin, age 36, who died in a concentration camp in Cambodia, 1964. Died because of starvation, torture and kidney removal without anesthesia.* (Note: The profound nature of suffering and the resulting anger in this life was mitigated and transformed into a gift as Wang Ghin saw the suffering in the eyes of the lab doctors and felt compassion toward them. Compassion released him from his body in that last moment and he was free.)

"There is a flood, a great flood. Everything sinks. The whole island is gone. I have tremendous anger! I had plans, but I die in the flood. As I'm dying I am avenging, "I will return!" I look at the bracelet I am wearing, an amulet of some kind that says "By the power of Euripides." I see the land, some of the columns, some of my warriors, beautiful jewels, a child with outstretched arms—all at the bottom of the sea. It was such a beautiful land. I wonder who will rediscover it…I am now in a place with inky black sky and stars, a place of rest and closeness with spirit. A sweet, serene sense of carefreeness.

*C.P. after life as Paschinna, a powerful woman warrior and leader during a "golden time with a Greek feel."*

"We are being attacked by Indians! I get knocked off my horse. They jumped us and I am knocked out. That's it…I am floating up…I feel confused…There are people in robes, long, light-colored. It's very peaceful and quiet. Two of them have come to help me. One is bald with a beard, middle-aged. The other is younger and taller…They lead me to a building with lots of glass and a big open room with benches. They help me to sit down and are comforting me. I'm feeling better…Others are gathering. They are welcoming me back…I'm starting to recognize them. I'm not Carl anymore… It's like I'm many people, all these people. (Carl is then shown his many lives.) So, so many lives…male and female, dark and light, old and young, lots of opposites. I feel an older woman, a younger boy, a young girl, a married woman, and a servant…I am in a circle of guides. There is a new one! I've been waiting for her!"

*A.P. after life as Carl Mason who served in a U.S. cavalry division, 1870s.*

"Something attacks me, a big cat, a strange cat. I run and it catches me. It grabs my stomach and throat…I feel peace. It's over. I'm gone from there. I walk but not really walk—It's quiet and soft…I float and it's foggy and I can't tell where I am anymore…I hear voices. I don't know those voices, yet I do. I am new (new soul), I am young. I have to go back, but why? I can't see but I can hear. It's about the running. I have to go back (into another life) because of the running. They say go back because I ran away. It's not bad. No one is mad. But I have to go back because I'm new (new to Earth life.) They think

I'm funny…I ran away when my mother needed me and I ran away when my father was killed."

*T.S. as a young man named Sudak, in a very early tribal culture. This is her first incarnation.*

(T.S. immediately dives into a quick series of lives. Many past lives flash before her. She begins to notice that she doesn't run away as much and that she is less fearful with difficult death experiences. She isn't "as lazy" and continues to have a highly intuitive/psychic gift. The final life she was shown follows.)

"I am a midwife…There is a freedom to knowing things. It's okay this time. This is the first time that I am not afraid to die and there is no violence at death. I am old and happy with white hair and brown skin…It is light and soft. I go up. I am happy to be here (in the afterlife) and not scared. I am wiser and now there are more choices. I see now why I have had so many violent deaths; to know pain and not be afraid. Pain is not to be feared. It is simply another tool of consciousness. Consciousness is not what I always believed it to be; it is deeper. I have been given a gift and pain has been necessary. But all people are gifted and all are afraid… I am only in the last of the habit of being afraid and being lazy…I see the four angels that are with me all the time…They say that I can't come home until I'm done, but I have the key now. I know the answer…"

*T.S. finishes the session as a midwife in 1620 AD, having been shown the long journey of her soul and the weaknesses that she has sought to overcome and the gifts she has gained.*

"It's like exhaling from the bottom of the lungs, only when you inhale on the other side, you have left the body behind and breathe in freedom. It's such a rush! So unburdened! Colors! Luminescent colors that are so alive. Glowing pinks and purples and golds. So fine that they glimmer…A hooded monk of absolute wisdom is here now…"

*D.C. after female life as an energy healer serving in a goddess temple on a Greek island. About 10 BC.*

"…A big shower room. I'm very thin, bony. We are having trouble breathing, burning, each breath is blistering. We try but cannot get out the door. I hate them! Not so much them but what they are doing! I hate that they believe what they are doing is right. I hate that I have moments of wondering if maybe they *are* right, like well, what do I know? Then I feel an odd sense of relief and sadness…I feel my spirit rising…I see our spirits rising out of that shower building rejoicing together that we are free.

"I see many dimensions. Layers and layers of dimensions…I see myself before I went into the camp dressed in nice suit and hat. If I had gotten out sooner, perhaps I could have saved the children…I see a bunch of white light…I see energy forms that can talk to me. They look like drops of blue iridescent water that morph into images. It's peaceful and so good to be out of there. I had hoped to learn to love and be loved. I did pretty well. I loved my liebchens (begins to cry as he refers to his children). I wish I would have thought more flexibly. I wish I would have talked to God more often… I'm being lifted up by a golden-haired angel…

*J.M. after life as Franz Liebovich of Munich, Germany, who died in the Auschwitz concentration camp.*

"It has been such a wonderful life, very, very joyous. Light is streaming in the windows…I feel like I am being lifted up, being carried, like someone is holding me in their arms and carrying me. I see others, translucent…We are traveling in a tube and I am being lifted up and traveling past them. I can see the little tube and the light at the end of it…Now I am lying on a bed, a cloud bed or mist. People are all around, mist people. They are saying blessings about things to me and I am saying blessings about things to them. There are about eight of us…"

*K.K. after a deeply spiritual and scholarly life in a Cathar community of southern France. 1549.*

"I've had a long life and am by myself…Nothing is in this room or on these walls. I can't breathe but am not in pain. There is discomfort, a weight on my chest like an animal resting there. Eventually, my chest can't push the animal off and I stop breathing… Elation! Freedom! Satisfaction…I have lived a good life. I'm believing in heaven. I'm believing that life really is everlasting. Don't know for sure but seems I am on a journey…I am part of the Earth. I am everywhere. I am a leaf, I am a tree, I am a cloud. My personal identity is both gone and amplified…I am everything and everything is me…That life helped me understand people's suffering and frailties. I learned about giving, selflessness, honesty. I am pleased that I could improve in the area of being unselfish."

*S.S. as the priest Father Gregor in the British Isles, during a famine, 1317 AD.*

"I made a difference! I think I did all I wanted to do…I see my body. It looks peaceful. It's time to move on. I feel sorry for the girl, Dorothy, who is attending me. She is hurting…I just want to hug her and tell her it's okay…I'm floating like a feather…It's light, yellow and blue, a real warm feeling. There are sparkles everywhere…I'm laughing. I have friends around and we are laughing and gossiping…There is a male presence. He's explaining to me that I did what I was supposed to do. I was a great help. I've known him a long time. He helps in choosing lives."

*B.O. after life as a teacher named Cassie McDougal on flat land, possibly Kansas. Died at about 75 years of age. 1840s.*

"I feel like air. It feels so nice, like I'm flying, like very silky cloth. There are more here like me… (Immediately begins to describe her soul group).…..I was afraid of dying, but death itself was okay. I feel relief."

*E. after brief painful life as unwed, imprisoned young mother. Israel/ Palestine, 1800s.*

"I'm laid out on the hot desert sand. I've tried to create shade but the sun is oppressive and I know that I won't last until nighttime. So exhausted. The only shred of desire I have left in my heart is if I could somehow find my sister. I know it's impossible for where would I start? But this is holding me in my body…I rise up and hover above my body, which looks like a tent of ragged cloth; concealed under the tent is my body. I feel a great deal of failure. We thought we could do some good by seeking revenge…It's been completely fruitless. If only we had not listened to our egos…

"I am moving up, like moving up inside of a pyramid. There is a bright blue light shining through the square at the top. I'm a little anxious as to what will happen when I pass through the square of light. I pass through the hole and feel a great wave of peace. I'm kind of alone but sense other spirits, like pockets of energy…One steps forward, my guide…She welcomes me and assures me that it wasn't all in vain and that I will learn from this. I am ready to go back and try again."

*P.W. after short life as Turkish man from a small village overrun by "unconquerable people on many horses" in the 15th century.*

"I feel at ease. I'm not worried. I'm ready to take a nice nap now. I'm glad I didn't die that night on the bridge (when much younger.) It feels so light and nice. My joints don't hurt anymore. I'm about 90 years old, or maybe

I just look that old. I'm drifting away. There is warmth all around. I can't really see anyone but there are a lot of people around. I see Maggie and Nana and Arthur, who is still kind of grouchy. The kitchen maid is here. We are merging together, it's nice and comfortable. I don't feel any age. I don't sense a body—just brightness and light and air…My guide is off to my left. He is wearing sandals and something like a feathered headdress. I wouldn't dare make fun of him. He's strong…Now he has uncrossed his arms and is smiling. I ask if I have accomplished what I wanted in that life. He laughs and says that I learned a little. It would have been easier if I hadn't waited until I was scared out of my wits to change!"

*A.B. after male life as Griffin Braun in London, England. Died about 1920 after a long life.*

## Children and Adolescents

Perhaps one of the most difficult deaths to experience is the loss of one's children. Not only do we grieve the loss of an unfinished love, we wonder if they found their way. We pray that their angels or grandmothers caught them and swept them on over the rainbow bridge. Past-life deaths as children don't come through as often for clients, but there are some. The experience, as with all departures, is defined by the soul and the events around the death.

"I just go away…Seems there is no lag time." (She immediately dives into another life.)

*A.L. after a medieval European life as a very poor and neglected servant boy.*

"It was very scary. Then I became small, very small, a black dot…There is light….I'm looking at the light. I don't think I have a body anymore. I'm small like a dot. Feels like the light might suck me in….Oh…I'm a light too! I'm not a black dot anymore. I'm a light and it's warm…I'm just resting now…"

*C.J. after traumatic death as young girl in early 1900s in a "land of green rolling hills."*

"I keep seeing spirits above me. They are light and flowy. They want me to come somewhere where we float. It's a tunnel, shiny and bright. I'm little, 5-6 years old. Now it's light like air with an outside scene—beautiful. A sunset with purple and orange and flowers…One of the beings with me has long blonde hair with a silvery-white robe, belted. She's barefoot and wants to take me to a room....She wants me to know I have to help people..."

*J.D. after Native American life as small girl who died in a fire, "somewhere where there is red clay."*

"My spirit is floating. I'm looking down and see me, the sky. Serenity and peace. Someone is helping me..."

*T.A. after life as Caucasian child adopted by Native Americans and never quite belonging.*

"I don't know where I am. I feel lost..... It's a little dark, gray clouds at my feet. Still dark...I don't see anybody. I feel alone. My legs are heavy...Still heavy. Don't see my legs or arms. I just feel like I'm floating. It's dark and warm and thick. Can't see anybody. Can't see anything. Can't feel anything.... I keep thinking back to that girl on the floor and I have a headache on the back of my head. Keep seeing the girl. Keep feeling the headache....I feel lighter now and head doesn't hurt anymore. I'm here again." (She recognizes her place in the afterlife.)

*C.M. after short life as beloved daughter who became dizzy, fell backward, hit her head and then died. 18 years old. No date.* (Much coaching needed to move her spirit through the thickness and pain and into a lighter state.)

## Suicide

Philosophies abound on suicide and whether it's ever acceptable. Religious teachings vary and are sometimes confusing. Unless the suicide comes after extreme trauma or at the end of a long life, we may find it hard to comprehend. Here are several examples of crossing-over experiences after suicide.

"There are clouds...I'm talking to someone who says, 'Why were you so unhappy? I love you. I love all my people...Don't be unhappy. Come into my fold and I will take care of you. I will watch over you, I will take care of you. I am the Holy Spirit. The Holy Spirit will take care of you.' He has white flowing hair and a long beard and is not smiling."

*C.A. after life as young Catholic woman who committed suicide at age 21, 1899 in Colorado.*

"I looked for them all through the night and now I am by myself. (Referring to her two children who seem to have drowned.) I feel dark inside. I know they are not going to come back…So I go into the ocean to be with them. I am feeling nothing. So sad…I just keep walking, walking into the ocean, keeping my head down (Makes drowning noises, screaming and crying as she forces herself under.)

"Now nothing, nothing but sad…Just a grayish mist that flows into a solid blue. There is mist everywhere. There was a very bright light, but now it's just a part of me, only dimmer. I feel like I'm moving backwards, being pulled backwards, like a vacuum. Peace…"

*T.S. after life as woman named Neeva in an early Native American life.*

## Fairies

On rare occasions, clients regress to lives other than human. These can be simple animal forms or more complex animal bodies. From these lives they migrate into becoming human and do not return to animal lives. Sometimes, they may find themselves on another planet or dimension. Once in a while, we also discover lives as "wee folk" who are ready to take on human embodiment. They approach the human incarnation step with some trepidation. Here are two examples of fairy-like beings.

"I am a fairy—'Robby,' like the robin… I feel very heavy and sad. They say that it is time to leave the fairy realm and become a human. I am told that I have mastered the fairy world and to grow I must take the next step. I can fly and can listen with my heart. We are holding hands going through a green tunnel inside a large tree. My body begins to feel heavier.…"

*B.B. being shown a fairy life in Italy or France, 1600-1700, and understanding why as a child she had nightmares of feeling trapped and heavy in her body.*

"I am old and should pass on. We are the wee people…This is what I can tell you about this life. This is the beginning. It is where I learned and from where I will integrate into other lives. In my next life I will be a giant (human).

*Gnome woman named Yodina in Ireland, 1317 or 1319.* (Immediately enters into next life as a "pretty, frivolous girl," which follows.)

"It takes a while to die, though I couldn't move. There is a place I'm going to where I will know what this life is for…Ah-h, now I am in a happy place…I died because my legs were broken and I couldn't move. It took a couple of weeks to leave the body, so I looked at the sky. I am remembering the happy times of that life. It was joyful. I was the instrument of someone else's learning. Life would have been empty if I had continued. I learned about the human body and its functioning. I danced.…Someone has come, an essence of a robe of light silver. I am not solid either. I am going to where a judge would sit on marble or stone. I see one person, a man. He says, 'How did you like that life, Adeana?' I say, 'Just fine, and I would like to try another one…' "

*N.N. after being shown life as gnome-type woman, then short human life in which she was able to dance, yet died of abuse by the man in her life in a "principality, an island." Died 1569. And she is ready to "try another one."*

## Ghost-Busting

Sometimes the PLR crossing-over is an opportunity to rescue a part of the soul that has been lost or stuck in time. Earlier, we discussed the phenomenon of getting lost. The following story is a clear example of this.

"I am standing here because I will NOT feel! I am fearful of seeing it all. Grandma and Grandpa are waiting for some word from me. I am sad. I gave my heart and soul to them and now when they need me, I'm gone, dead! I don't want to see their suffering. I never even got to have an adventure! I was standing on the edge of the river (with other new recruits) and I was shot by a renegade rebel. I'd rather not run into him again!

"…I've stood here too long—the war is over. There is no relief that I didn't kill anyone…I want to know about Grandma and Grandpa, but I *don't* want to know…I am standing on the same patch of land I died on…People walk through me and say they feel cold, but I don't feel cold…I've been here a breath or two or 20 years. Who knows?

(Grandparents came onto the scene.) "Grandma and Grandpa are in the same shape as me, it appears. Grandma keeps trying to take my hands from my eyes. Grandpa takes my shoulder. Grandma says, 'Let's all go together. It's Thanksgiving Day because we are all free!' …I think I'll go…I'm happy to be with them. All they have is happiness. They were surprised to find me standing here. When they were both free (had died) they came to get me. There is nothing better than a grandma and a grandpa in the whole world!

"I jump into the stream of souls, the spiral of souls that never ends. People are always flowing back to the heart of God (from the Earth)…The journey is long for me because of the acclimation needed. Some just step through to the other side, others flow in the spiral. The tube/spiral is bringing about adequate soothing for me so there is no need for remediation. Now I see a pure white shining light, like a door, a portal. I slip through to the other side. Here is my soul group…"

*B.W. after life as Leonard, a Civil War soldier, "standing with Lincoln." He had become frozen in time by the shock of his death, and the terror of facing the suffering he believed his death would cause his grandparents, the only true parents he had known. Leonard resented my intrusions into his protected world and told me to leave him alone! But by shifting his reality slightly, he was able to perceive his grandparents on the other side and get himself into the afterlife. Rather than "a breath or 20 years," Leonard was stuck for about 150 years.*

## Releasing Confusing Departures

The departures that are hard to understand often bring up anger and make it difficult for us to dream a new dance with death. You have just read some of them. Confusing departures often leave us unprepared. We are surprised, bitter and angry at God or someone else. These departures may create heaviness in the way we perceive death and add more baggage to our own death archetype. If we are to lift departure up, it can help to know more about soul choices in these matters. Therefore, I want to speak briefly for the *soul* perspective on those ways of departing that confuse and trouble us—suicide, death of infants and children, abortion, untimely and violent deaths. Soul perspective is essential in our healing and our ability to step into the future.

**Suicide.** We have had some reflection on suicide in the story of Aaron's life. There we learned about the seeding of the suicide idea via his religious group. We understood the inherent difficulties of interacting so intimately with dark energy. All these, we learned, influenced his choice. We also learned that those on the other side held him in love. It was his own heaviness that waylaid him.

In the crossing-over stories above, some examples were given from clients who, in the past, had ended their own lives. With these and other soulful materials available to us, we can say that human embodiment is precious, and human experience is incredibly hard. Sometimes, despite the individual's best efforts at managing despair, the pain seems beyond his or her capacity to cope and an early exit is taken. The energies we are dealing with now are so intense and disparate that many are taxed beyond what their nervous systems are prepared to handle. Lacking hope and sufficient fortitude, they may exit prematurely.

Generally, the guidance as it comes through the PLR literature is that the soul who chooses suicide will be guided to return to pick up where it left off. If an essential piece of its mastery is still needed, it will want to return and try again, for the Earth School exam is still waiting to be taken. However, if you don't finish all of fourth grade, so to speak, at least you have three grades under your belt and next time you'll want to go on to finish high school, and maybe college.

Without knowing the nature of any particular soul's journey, we must drop judgments on suicide and hold such decisions with as much grace as we can. Given what we have learned about the importance of our focus at the time of death, our gift to the one who chooses suicide is to lift them up with our prayers and loving thoughts. This helps them in rising out of despair into a higher plane where they are assisted into love. We suggest to them that they look for their guide or angel. We remind them that there is no judgment, only learning.

***Abortion, Miscarriage, SIDS***. Another quandary we often have is how to understand abortion, miscarriage and SIDS (Sudden Infant Death Syndrome) and the soul's part in these early departures. First of all, we must declare unequivocally that it is beyond human capacity to destroy a soul. The soul is the bridge between the body/personality and the higher self or spirit that we are. Soul-spirit is not destroyed. It is energy and, as you recall from the Universal *Law of One* in Chapter 10, energy cannot be created or destroyed; it only changes form.

Abortions, for instance, do not kill the soul, for the soul is eternally connected to spirit. Soul is the part of our spirit that tries out various adventures for the sake of learning and evolution. Sometimes, the adventure is to tippy-toe into human life, and then make a quick departure. Most souls know ahead of time that the pregnancy they are associated with will unlikely be full term. A short dip into life is a way of getting a sense of physicality. It is a way of checking out different families and energies. Sometimes, the soul says, "Wow, this is harder than I thought!" or "That's enough for now." It then leaves via a miscarriage, abortion or SIDS.

Some souls don't fully enter the physical form until birth. Others attach during fetal development. Keep in mind that the fetus is small and delicate in its energy capacities. It cannot contain the full level of its available soul energy until later. While the fetus is growing, the soul is also going about its work in other realms. It comes regularly to check on the progress of its future body and its future parents. These are the times as pregnant mothers that we sense the soul nearby. Sometimes parents even hear the desired name being whispered in their ears.

**Untimely deaths.** Unexpected deaths are troubling for us. However, what seems to be an untimely death, no matter what the age, may be quite timely from the soul's perspective. For the purpose agreed upon before birth, it was sufficient for the learning chosen. In addition, the learning potential is profound for all those left behind. As families search for answers, they often seize the opportunity to grow through the process of grief and the new understanding that evolves.

**Violent deaths.** The simplest, and often the most accurate explanation for violent deaths is that old friend of ours—karma. That may still seem pat and confusing, so let's explore this a bit more. Just as the other strange and wonderful experiences of life are influenced by karma, so are these seemingly negative departures.

Let me give you an example. My client, Deborah, (PLR in *This Divine Classroom: Earth School and the Psychology of the Soul*, M. Beachy) discovered a very difficult life as a warrior woman named Sonafina. Sonafina told me that I wouldn't understand her ancient culture or dates so gave me little detail except that it was in a time long, long ago. She said she was taken from her family at an early age and trained to be a warrior. It was a most difficult training. In the end, she shut her heart and chose a ruthless rise to power, becoming the dictator of a small kingdom by the sea. The only survival tool Sonafina knew was slaying anyone who threatened her rule. "I have everyone slaughtered who enters my territory without my permission. In this way, I make it clear that there will be no concessions!"

Therefore, when Sonafina died it was quite traumatic and violent. It took several sessions to work through the trauma memories. We also noticed that Deborah's soul chose violent deaths in the ensuing lives. She became the recipient of abuse with very few peaceful departures. In looking at the bigger picture, it appeared that in Deborah's soul memory, there was a belief that she deserved this and she was trying to balance the violence she had perpetrated onto others. Thanks to Deborah and many others, we can better understand how a soul might choose a violent death. It might simply be a quick exit, of course, but it might also be balancing the karmic scales.

Being able to change our views on confusing deaths helps our hearts. Sometimes being able to hold death in the grander scheme helps release us from the clutches of taking it so personally. It frees up departure to be lighter. It takes us deeper to really get what we are about, and to remember that every soul has its own agenda, and with that agenda comes its own departure timing and style.

We've finished a brief foray into the vibrant crossing-over worlds. The portal of PLR sessions has offered us a picturesque story. We have also addressed the soul perspective on difficult departures. Perhaps, some of your questions are answered. Perhaps, this has elicited many more. I hope so. I wish you the blessing of following Aunt Mary's lead—asking questions and continuing to learn—not only now, and while taking your last breath, but long after you have crossed over.

# CHAPTER 16

## The Future of Death

*Down by the river,*
*beneath the sorrow tree,*
*the Universe is calling us to dance...*
—Unknown

IN THE PAST, DEATH WAS GIVEN over to religion, to war, to medicine and to ignorance. Medicine can assist. Religion might bring comfort. But we are doing a remarkable job of bringing death back to the heart where it belongs. To use Zetta's words, "There is just your way to die. Dying is a very individual path...You can't do it anyone else's way." Our ignorance around death may have been the ultimate mind-control program. The negative death archetype has been well-fed over the ages. Thankfully, it is losing its hold. It is our birthright to be as empowered in our departure as we are learning to be in our daily human endeavors. I am convinced of this.

We have touched on teachers who have mastered the quantum physics of life. We have discussed the expanded consciousness necessary for this journey. We have learned some tools for accelerating our frequency and our compassion. Overall, we have opened our minds and hearts. We have looked at death as part of our education for life. We are more informed. Now what? I say, let's dream a new future with death.

It is a good time to dream a new future because things are stirring. The acceleration of time and consciousness presses on us. Humanity is on the move. So is the Earth. So is the galaxy and all of heaven, for that matter. You may feel it somehow or you may just know that life as we have known it is passing.

We may not know the future of death, but I believe we are changing in our orientation to it and therefore death is being transformed. Perhaps there is no particular conclusion we need to reach at this time, except to stay open to the Mystery unfolding through us. Certainly, we can say we are dying more awake because we are living more awake.

So it's important to stay current rather than looking longingly over our shoulders for the past. Staying current also involves handling everything as it rises, including grief. We are learning to keep moving the grief that comes with so many changes in such short order. We are also learning to activate joy, often in the simplest of ways. That way we can board our boat of life that is moving rapidly on the river of consciousness, the river that is gently calling our name.

## FUTURE DEPARTURE OPTIONS

### Future Life Stories

I want to share with you this departure story from my client, Stella. Her intention when she arrived at my office was to have a *past*-life regression session. Instead, she was taken into her *future*, to 3000 AD or about 1,000 years from now. This sometimes happens for people and is always intriguing. The soul, which dwells both in time and beyond time, wants to share something of import—not in the past but in the probable future.

Stella found herself incarnated as a man in a small tribal group living in South America. He described the land as having changed a great deal from our present geography. The beauty of his life was in the simplicity and harmony he felt with his people and their oneness with the Earth. After a fulfilling life, the man and his partner felt their time on Earth coming to a close and disappeared into the forest. Here they found and consumed a plant that aided them in leaving their bodies. They slipped into an altered state and effortlessly departed the planet together. They experienced a deep knowing that their journey was complete and that it was time to go on to the next world. Stella described this decision as "divine intuition and guidance from the soul." No hospitals, no religious dogma, no illness, no social stigma. Instead, they departed in a conscious, soul-guided, painless manner—pure and simple. Because they were tuned-in, they knew when it was time.

Nora, another client, had a somewhat different future-life experience. She found herself in 2200 AD. She had an interesting life as a man associated with a healing center in what was likely Australia. As he died and we began to explore the afterlife experience, Nora suddenly burst into tears. I asked her what was troubling her. She replied, "You think that you want the lives to be over, to not have to do it anymore. But then it's over." Evidently her soul's timeline had been completed. The contract was done and she was sadly saying goodbye. From the higher perspective of the afterlife, Nora's soul-self realized that a grand cycle of incarnations on Earth was finished. The cycle of lives she had agreed to was fulfilled and she would not be returning.

That unexpected grief told her how precious her Earth life experiences were to her, and the importance of living each day fully. It was a poignant moment—a time to pause and sit with the soul's unforeseen sorrow of no more sunrises or heartache or the jungle explorations which she had enjoyed. She was surprised to find grief instead of relief at the completion of her long, arduous education in Earth School.

Stella and Nora model for us some of the projected futures that we carry within us. In one, we are shown the return to simplicity and ease with departure. In the other, we are reminded that each day begs appreciation, for there will come a time when we are done departing this planet. We want to be able to say, "Well, that was grand. I am complete."

## Putting the Body to Use

What if the body could actually be of use after death? What if we have energetic options for this body of ours after our soul takes flight? This possibility is introduced to us by those whose bodies are so filled with light or high frequencies that even after they die, the body remains relatively fresh, still exuding an aura of blessing. We have mentioned this effect with Paramahansa Yogananda's body which, as you recall, remained "undefiled" for 21 days after his departure. Father Pia's body, when exhumed by the Catholic Church after many years, was amazingly whole. We read of others whose soulless bodies seemed miraculously vibrant.

Another example came to me from a PLR client who regressed to a life 11,000-plus years BC. In this life she was a very evolved soul who lived for 2,000 years and remained youthful in appearance. When it came time to depart, her body was placed in a special vault where it continued to radiate higher frequencies for the Earth and the developing species of humans. This seems fantastical to our rather limited take on what our bodies can do at death. However, why not gather up these examples of souls who have imbued the body with so much light and clarity and say, why not? What can it hurt to consider that the future of death is not only about mental/emotional/spiritual evolution? Amazing possibilities stand before us and these possibilities can include giving our bodies back to the Earth as a gift, because we bequeath them in love.

## Re-envisioning our Departures

I see a future where the old karmic patterns have dissipated. The patterns that have dragged us down for eons of lives, like guilt, shame, blame and anger dissolve within the Greater Mind. In this future, our human family has accepted the *Law of Grace*, replacing bitterness with understanding. I see a future Earth free of the gray clouds of souls lost in purgatory. I see a future where we walk side-by-side with our ancestors and guides in the same manner we might stroll with our children. In this future, both those on Earth and those in the higher realms can enjoy each other's company more directly.

Stella, the client mentioned earlier, saw a child of the future swinging back and forth on a swing while her visible angel/guide chatted beside her. She sensed that the heavens of the future would also change, becoming more streamlined and clear. Instead of the burgeoning heavens filled with layers of light, and souls in various levels of learning, she saw a heaven that had opened to the direct light of the Cosmic Creator. Its simplicity and elegance appealed to her. To me, this seems a symbolic description of clearing 3-D and lower 4-D negativity. It seems the result of ascension—that quantum trek into raising our consciousness that we have embarked upon.

Clearing heaven and earth seems pretty grandiose, but it's happening organically in our bodies and lives. I sense that some kind of bright shiny wholeness is pushing through into our inner earth and inner heaven, if we let it. That quiet wholeness is the higher mind that brings heaven's smile. So we learn to bring that heavenly smile to our fears. We smile at the folks who drive us crazy, and smile at the evening news before we turn it off. We smile at the insanity all around us, not as denial, but as an opportune time to choose the higher frequencies of hope and determination. We use distraction and negativity as centering devices. The phone rings and we take a deep breath before answering. That co-worker who insists on saying wounding things becomes a reminder to let anger be a friend, a friend that helps us stay fiercely loyal to the path of wholeness.

Heaven is influenced by the way we die. It has been designed to accommodate our dysfunction and resurrect our light. As we die with more awareness, the spirit realms will shift accordingly. If ascension is the goal of every soul, as some contend, then there will come a time when the afterlife realms will reflect this evolution. As humanity rises out of limitation, access to the higher worlds will be more easily attained.

The way through these days is on the wings of clear light by whatever method gives wind to our sails. When something snags us, we do whatever we need to do to become free, then set sail once again. I like to use the example of driving in traffic. As we drive along, we see a roadblock of some kind ahead. Instead of swearing, we slip into the right turn lane and notice that the side road is clear. With steady intention, we turn onto the side road and are blessed with a completely open street and flowers blooming along the way. We continue to breathe and relax, arriving at our destination in good form. We have turned what could have been a road-rage episode into an opportunity for smooth navigation by changing plans and knowing that there is always another way through. Whatever snags us is usually our ingrained emotional patterning. It is what we are breaking free of, after many lives. Let's be in amazement of our capacity to evolve in the midst of so much uncertainty. Those who don't want to find alternate routes will be allowed to continue at a slower pace within the hard-knock life of 3-D. It's a free-choice world, after all.

Given that we are a culture caught up in being successful, we could add another component for a successful life: A truly remarkable life includes conscious departure as part of the value system for success. Your successful life is defined by you and only you, of course. But I hope that it now includes some of the tools we've shared for departing in style. After all, that point where we take our last breath may very well be the most important moment of our entire life. We don't take that last breath separate from the whole of the life we have lived. The gratitude we bring to our last breath can become that soft, loving whoosh that lifts us up to the clear light of heaven.

In *The Art of Racing in the Rain* by Garth Stein, the main character, Enzo, speaks eloquently about the future of death as he imagines it. His reflections are even more delightful given that Enzo is an old dog who believes that he has advanced his evolution sufficiently to become a human in his next incarnation. I'm with Enzo when he reflects on the "pathetic" nature of getting old. Although it seems this type of limiting exit is our typical option, Enzo sees new possibilities. He says, "...one day a mutant child will be born who refuses to age. Who refuses to acknowledge the limitations of these bodies of ours, who lives in health until he is done with life, not until his body no longer supports him." (p. 311) In Enzo's vision, the genetics of this child's more spacious way of living and dying will be passed on, and more like him will take departure into a welcoming future.

What I want for us all is a gracious crossing into the light and the joy of being welcomed "home" by the highest love. I want us to know when we are "dead." No confusion. Little or no baggage. Traveling light. I want us to KNOW that the human heart is constructed out of love essence. Our hearts are part of the great heart of the Cosmos, the heart of God. We are essentially a kind and considerate species. We weep easily. We want to love and be loved. We are immense in our power to love. We have been misled and have misled others down through time, but we are LOVE. We are being challenged to see the truth of our ever-loving-selves. There are more stop-you-dead-in-your-tracks stories about incredible love now than ever. They won't often be found in the media, but they are showing up in every village and neighborhood.

In the midst of all the confusion and strangeness of life, there is a joy rising that is sweet beyond measure. That joy reminds us that the Universe is calling us to dance beneath the sorrow tree and release the dysfunctional death phantom. In contemplating a more embracing approach toward departure, we might catch the sun. We might notice that our eyes are open and our faces aglow. We might notice love and death are partners. It's not a fairy tale. It's our real love story drifting up through the mist. Our real and future story on the truth of things is smiling over our shoulders like a wise grandmother.

We can trust ourselves on this one.

## Departure Prayer

*All That Is,*
*Beloved Angels,*
*Precious Source of Life,*
*May my departure be magnificent and simple.*
*May this body release itself easily,*
*like a leaf falling into the bosom of the Earth.*
*And may this body, in bones, ashes and energy*
*be as a gift to the land and all her beings.*
*And may the essence of this life,*
*be as a gift to the Spirit of Life and all Beings.*
*May my departure arrive in its own perfect timing.*
*And as the body falls away,*
*May I hear the call of the beauteous Light*
*bequeathed me from the beginning.*
*May the Presence of Love that has sustained me*
*sustain all those I love who remain on this sacred Earth,*
*holding them tenderly throughout their Earthly Sojourn.*
*And when departure beckons, please guide them safely across the bridge and into the*
*Light.*
*Om. Amen.*

# Resources

## Books

Beachy, Marcia, *This Divine Classroom: Earth School and the Psychology of the Soul*, AuthorHouse, Bloomington, IN, 2004.

Blackman, Sushila, *Graceful Exits: How Great Beings Die*, Shambhala Publications, Inc., Boston and London, 2005.

Braden, Gregg, *Walking Between the Worlds: The Science of Compassion*, Radio Bookstore Press, Belleview, WA, 1997.

Cannon, Dolores, *Between Life and Death: Conversations With a Spirit*, Ozark Mountain Publishers, Huntsville, AR, 1993.

_____, *The Convoluted Universe, Vols. I-IV*, Ozark Mountain Publishing, Huntsville, AR, through 2008.

Chopra, Deepak, *Life After Death: The Burden of Proof*, Harmony Books, NY, 2006.

Denning, Helen, Ph.D., *Life Without Guilt*, Llewellyn Publications, St. Paul, MN, 1998.

Govindan, M., *Babaji and the 18 Siddha Kriya Yoga Tradition*, Kriya Yoga Publications, St. Etienne de Bolton, Quebec, 1991.

Greaves, Helen, *Testimony of Light*, Neville Spearman Ltd., Suffolk, England, 1977.

Hart, Roger, *The Phaselock Code: Through Time, Death and Reality, the Metaphysical Adventures of the Man Who Fell Off Everest*, Paraview Pocket Books, New York, 2003.

King, Godfre Ray, *The Magic Presence*, Saint Germain Press, Schaumburg, IL, 1982, Fifth Edition.

_____, *Unveiled Mysteries*, Saint Germain Press, Schaumburg, IL, 2005, recent printing.

Lucas, Winafred, Ph.D., *Regression Therapy: A Handbook for Professionals, Vols. I-II*, Deep Forest Press, Crest Park, CA, 1993.

Moen, Bruce, *Exploring the Afterlife Series, Vol. I-IV*, Hampton Roads Publishing Co., Inc., Charleston, VA, through 2001.

Monroe, Robert, *Journeys Out of Body*, Doubleday, NY, 1971.

_____, *Ultimate Journey*, Broadway Books, NY, 1994.

Newton, Michael, Ph.D., *Journey of Souls: Case Studies of Life Between Lives*, Llewellyn Publications, St. Paul, MN, 1996.

_____, *Destiny of Souls: New Case Studies of Life Between Lives*, Llewellyn Publications, St. Paul, MN, 2000.

Rinpoche, Sogyal, *The Tibetan Book of Living and Dying*, Harper, San Francisco, 1993.

Rinpoche, Lati, & Hopkins, Jeffrey, *Death, Intermediate State and Rebirth in Tibetan Buddhism*, Snow Lion Publications, Ithaca, NY, 1979.

Scallion, Gordon Michael, *Notes From the Cosmos*, Matrix Institute, Inc. West Chesterfield, NH, 1987, 1997.

Stein, Garth, *The Art of Racing in the Rain*, Harper, NY, 2009.

Storm, Howard, *My Descent into Death*, Clairview, London, 2000.

Sugrue, Thomas, *There is a River: The Story of Edgar Cayce*, revised, A.R.E. Press, Virginia Beach, VA, 1997. Originally published in 1942.

Swedenborg, Emanuel, *Heaven and Hell: Drawn From Things Heard and Seen*, Swedenborg Foundation, West Chester, PA, 2000.

Varela, Francisco, Ph. D., ed., *Sleeping, Dreaming, and Dying: An Exploration of Consciousness with the Dalai Lama*, Wisdom Publications, Boston, 1997.

Yogananda, Paramahansa, *Autobiography of a Yogi*, Self-Realization Fellowship, 1946 & The Philosophical Library, NY, 2005 (reprint of original 1946 edition by Crystal Clarity Publishers)

Yukteswar, Sri Swami, *The Holy Science*, Self-Realization Fellowship, 1990.

## Movies and CDs

*Being With Dying: Contemplative Practices and Teachings*. 6-CD set with Roshi Joan Halifax. Sounds True Audio Learning Course, 1997.

*Defending Your Life*, DVD. Movie starring Meryl Streep and Albert Brooks, 1991.

*Departures*. DVD movie, Japanese, 2008.

*Healing the Luminous Body*. DVD interview with Alberto Villoldo, Ph.D., Sacred Mysteries Productions.

*Infinity: Journey Beyond Death*. DVD documentary. Interviews with consciousness researchers, Sacred Mysteries Productions.

*Graceful Passages: A Companion for Living and Dying.* Small book and 2-CD set, by Michael Stillwater & Gary Malkin, Wisdom of the World, 2003.

*Splendors of the Spirit: Swedenborg's Quest for Insight.* DVD on Emanuel Swedenborg by Swedenborg Foundation.

*The Fountain.* DVD movie starring Hugh Jackson, 2006.

*What Dreams May Come.* DVD movie starring Robin Williams, 1998.

*You Can Heal Your Life.* DVD documentary with Louise Hay and friends.

## Other

Denise Chicoine, multidimensional assistance. Soulful Life LLC, Facebook
Suzanne Lie, Ph.D. www.multidimensions.com
Mearah Marqua, multidimensional assistance. www.heartwaves8.com
Christine Peters, multidimensional assistance. www.christineandjulie.com
Jan Tober, "Death Phantom" article. www.kryon.com/jantober

# In Acknowledgement

I want to convey special thanks to:

Gordon Michael Scallion for permission to quote from his book *Notes from the Cosmos* on the story of Private Jamison.

President and Publisher Skip Barrett at Crystal Clarity Publishers for permission to quote from their reprint of the first edition of *Autobiography of a Yogi,* on the story of Sri Yukteswar's resurrection.

Bruce Moen, workshop leader and author (*Exploring the Afterlife, Vols. I-IV*), for taking the time to help me clarify the roles of human and spirit guides in working with confused souls.

Howard Storm for permission to quote from *My Descent into Death* on the initial phases of his near-death experience.

## In Appreciation

I extend armfuls of gratitude to those who have supported this work:

My three beloved daughters, Gwendolyn, Elizabeth and Hannah, and my dear siblings for their familial loyalty and support.

My dear friends Jonia Mariechild, Denise Chicoine, Christine Peters, Jan and Dave Dutton, Gayla Badovich, Teryl Lundquist, Anne Porter and Jim K. Bell for their support of me as an ever-evolving writer. You helped me believe.

My editors and publishing crew; you have been invaluable. To the fine Balboa Press team, thanks so much. Ann Boyden, thanks for the lovely cover design and your formatting smarts. Sister Kathleen Froese, thanks for being willing to give that very rough draft a thumbs up. My courageous friend J., thanks for your great English major critiques that I did, in fact, survive. And Scott Smith, chief editor and hand-holder, your professional expertise and personal support have carried this manuscript into the light of day. I am so, so grateful.

All those clients and friends who offered their stories for the benefit of our greater human family. Your stories become everyone's stories and we are the richer for it.

My teachers over the years: Dolores Cannon, Michael Newton, Roger Wolger and Diane Zimberoff, thanks to each of you for your unique and priceless contribution to raising consciousness through hypnotherapy. The work of the soul is expanding around the world because of your pioneering courage and creativity. I am honored to have worked with you, even though I was often that shy student in the back of the room.

Angel woman Marisha Diez, who heard my guides better than I did, and gave me jolt of incentive in the summer of 2010 and a deadline to finish this project in good time, thank you. I needed to hear more clearly that support from the other side.

CPSIA information can be obtained at www.ICGtesting.com
Printed in the USA
LVOW102147131111

254810LV00004B/53/P